Mother of the Blues

Mother of the Blues: A Study of Ma Rainey

Sandra R. Lieb

1981   *The University of Massachusetts Press*

Copyright © 1981 by
The University of Massachusetts Press
All rights reserved
Printed in the United States of America
Library of Congress Cataloging in Publication Data
Lieb, Sandra R.
Mother of the blues.
Includes bibliography and discography.
1. Rainey, Ma, 1886–1939.   2. Afro-American singers—
Biography.   I. Title.
ML420.R274L5   784.5'3'00924 [B]   81-1168
ISBN 0-87023-334-3   AACR2

Acknowledgment is made to the following publishers and individuals for permission
to reprint previously published material.
Bonanza Books, a division of Crown Publishers, Inc., for material from *American
Negro Songs and Spirituals*, ed. John W. Work, ©1940, 1968 by Crown Publishers, Inc.;
Chicago Defender, for material from national and city editions, 1923–1930;
Corinth Books, for material from Al Young, "A Dance for Ma Rainey," from *Dancing;
poems,* © 1969 by Al Young;
Harper and Row, Publishers, Inc., for "Ma Rainey," ©1932 by Harcourt, Brace &
Jovanovich, Inc., renewed 1960 by Sterling A. Brown (from *The Collected Poems of
Sterling A. Brown,* © 1980 by Sterling A. Brown);
Horizon Press, New York, and Cassell and Co., Ltd., London, for material from Paul
Oliver, *Blues Fell This Morning: The Meaning of the Blues,* © 1960 by Horizon Press, and
Paul Oliver, *Conversation with the Blues,* © 1965 by Horizon Press;
Jazz Journal International, London, for material from Thomas Fulbright, "Ma Rainey
and I" (March 1956), and Norman Turner-Rowles, "The Paramount Wildcat" (March
1954);
Living Blues, for material from Jim and Amy O'Neal, *"Living Blues* Interview: Georgia
Tom Dorsey" (March–April 1975);
Melody Maker, London, for material from Vic Schuler and Claude Lipscombe, "Mys-
tery of the Two Ma Raineys" (October 13, 1951);
Duncan Shiedt, Pittsboro, Indiana, for photograph of Ma Rainey;
Stein and Day Publishers, for material from Derrick Stewart-Baxter, *Ma Rainey and the
Classic Blues Singers,* © 1970 by Derrick Stewart-Baxter; and for material from Chris
Albertson, *Bessie,* © 1972 by Chris Albertson;
John Steiner for lyrics from Big Feeling Blues, Daddy Goodbye Blues, Deep Moaning
Blues, Hear Me Talking to You, Leaving This Morning Blues, Little Low Mama Blues,
Screech Owl Blues, Sissy Blues, Sleep Talking Blues, Sweet Rough Man, Tough Luck
Blues, Trust No Man, Weepin' Woman Blues, © 1956 by John Steiner.
Storyville Publications, Chigwell, Essex, U.K., for material from John Godrich and
Robert M. W. Dixon, *Blues and Gospel Records, 1902–1943* (3rd rev. ed.).

To Chadwick Hansen

Contents

Illustrations

I'm going to cry so sweet

& so low

& so dangerous,

Ma,

that the message is going to reach you

back in 1922

where you shimmer

snaggle-toothed

perfumed &

powdered

in your bauble beads

hair pressed & tied back

throbbing with that sick pain

I know

& hide so well

that pain that blues

jives the world with

aching to be heard. . . .

Al Young, "A Dance for Ma Rainey"[1]

Introduction

$\mathbb{G}$ertrude Pridgett— "Ma Rainey" (1886–1939)—was America's first major woman blues singer, and one of the earliest blues artists whose name has come down to us. She was a great vocalist, minstrel show performer, and comedienne, as well as a fine songwriter, a dancer, and one of the most popular blues recording stars of the 1920s. Properly called "the Mother of the Blues," she performed professionally as early as 1902, was known and respected by veteran jazz people throughout her life, and influenced other singers and musicians from her day to ours. Their feeling for her is characteristically expressed in the blues tribute "Ma Rainey," recorded in 1940, a year after her death, by country blues singer Memphis Minnie. Black writers have always described her with admiration and affection, from Sterling Brown's 1932 poem "Ma Rainey," to Al Young's 1969 "A Dance for Ma Rainey."[2]

She was one of the earliest singers of the "Classic Blues," a black singing style immensely popular in the 1920s. Performed almost exclusively by women, the style was marked by a combination of blues and material from black minstrel shows and vaudeville. Many of its songs were modeled on W. C. Handy's published blues compositions, which mixed folk blues stanzas with popular song forms. During the teens, the Classic Blues were popularized by black stage shows and the recordings and performances of white vaudevillians; they became a nationwide fad in 1920 with the first blues record by a black woman singer. Throughout the twenties, the greatest recording stars were Ma, Bessie Smith, Clara Smith, Mamie Smith, and Trixie Smith (none of them related), Ethel Waters, Alberta Hunter, Bertha "Chippie" Hill, Sippie Wallace, Ida Cox, Lucille Hegamin, Rosa Henderson, and Victoria Spivey.[3]

Whether or not Ma Rainey personally trained Bessie Smith, as legend states, her influence on Bessie is obvious: Ma Rainey was the earliest popular representative of the style which Bessie modified and made internationally famous. Yet today Ma Rainey's name is little known outside of jazz circles, and while most histories of jazz and blues praise her as an important blues singer, they give few details about her life and work. The only book concerning the Classic Blues devotes ten pages to Ma Rainey, noting that her full story has yet to be told.[4]

The reasons for her obscurity lie in the technical quality of her recordings and in the nature of her material. Between 1923 and 1928, Ma Rainey recorded at least ninety-two songs exclusively for the Paramount Record Company, a relatively small, Wisconsin-based operation, with a limited budget as compared to its major rivals—Victor, Okeh, Gennett, Plaza/Perfect, and Columbia. By contrast, Bessie Smith recorded for New York-based Columbia, and an evaluation of the sound quality (as distinct from the vocal quality) of the Rainey and Smith records can only favor Bessie.

In addition, Ma Rainey's records went out of print after Paramount went bankrupt in the 1930s; some were reissued on 78s in the forties and fifties, and a good number of them reappeared on Riverside long-play albums during the fifties, but only since the late sixties has the bulk of her recorded legacy reappeared on the Milestone and Biograph labels. Thus, until quite recently, many of Ma Rainey's records were difficult to acquire, even for those who recognized her greatness.[5]

Perhaps her story remained untold for so long because she voluntarily retired from active performance while still vigorous. Changing times made her style seem temporarily outdated, for the Classic Blues was grounded in both folk blues and a minstrel show tradition—rural, Southern, and black—that stretched back into the nineteenth century. More down-home, less sophisticated than Bessie Smith's, her material and delivery were more directly linked to country blues and black minstrelsy. Although she performed extensively in the North and was well received there, her greatest appeal was always to Southerners of both races. With the Depression and the rise of swing music in the thirties, the Classic Blues went out of fashion, and after the deaths of her mother and sister she retired to her home in Georgia, turning to business pursuits and church affairs.

The last twenty years, however, have seen a resurgence of interest in all early women blues singers. An introduction to the major Classic Blues singers has appeared; Bessie Smith has been the subject of three books and a successful Broadway show; popular white performers like Bonnie Raitt frequently feature Classic Blues songs; and former Classic Blues singer Alberta Hunter has made a spectacular comeback.[6]

Ma Rainey's style is as important as her place in blues history. The popularity and widespread influence of the Classic Blues, part of the larger vogue for all forms of jazz in the twenties, represented one of many breakthroughs by black culture into the American cultural mainstream. One of the first such breakthroughs, and an important influence on the Classic Blues, had been the minstrel show craze of the 1840s, which featured white actors, their faces darkened with burnt cork, performing charades of black songs and of life on the plantation. Although the white minstrel show evolved and changed throughout the nineteenth century, and although blacks later formed their own companies, modifying the stereo-typed presentations to some extent, the minstrel show was still a form dictated by white perceptions, expectations, and fantasies about black people.[7]

To the professional entertainment of minstrelsy, the Classic Blues added songs that had evolved directly from the black folk tradition: the blues. By combining folk blues melodies, themes, and images with tunes and performance techniques from black show business, the Classic Blues offered to whites a glimpse into black culture far less obscured by white expectations, and offered to blacks a more direct affirmation of their cultural identity.

In addition, the immense popularity of Classic Blues recordings opened the way for recording (and thus for preserving) the work of black male folk blues singers (the true roots of blues) and encour-aged the spread of jazz as well as of the blues. And as jazz and the blues in general articulated a uniquely black perspective on life, so the Classic Blues revealed a specifically female awareness, espe-cially about the nature of love. While it is true that many Classic Blues songs were composed by male professional songwriters, they drew on black folk traditions for their attitudes about men, women, and love, and the songs were presented from the female point of view; women singers like Ma Rainey, who wrote at least one-third of the songs she recorded, gave a clearly articulated female perspective in their delivery and performance. The Classic Blues barely outlived the twenties, becoming engulfed in and utterly changed by the Depression and shifts in audience taste, but from 1920 to roughly 1928 Ma Rainey and the other women mentioned above were the greatest artists, enjoying a period of influence, wealth, popularity, and imitation by lesser performers.

The individual styles and abilities of these women varied considerably. While Bessie Smith is clearly the most famous, and Mamie Smith was actually the first black woman to record the blues, Ma Rainey was at least ten years older than her sister singers and had been performing the longest, singing blues-influenced songs professionally as early as 1902. She was, in addition, the least commercialized by non-blues influences, and her material showed a stronger affinity to the folk blues tradition than the work of any other female blues star of equal magnitude. (Bessie Smith's early work reveals her debt to Ma Rainey, and her style grew considerably more diluted with non-blues and popular song forms as her career advanced.)

Ma Rainey was influential and vocally gifted, and her songs reveal both the definitive expression of the Classic Blues and an important insight into the taste and concerns of her black audience during the twenties. Performed by the first representative of a major blues tradition and a highly popular recording, vaudeville, and minstrel artist, her lyrics had widespread appeal and importance, even though she did not personally write them all. Although Ma Rainey sang a variety of songs in addition to the blues, her name will always be linked with the Classic Blues style and with the great blues recordings of the twenties. To explore her life and performance style and to analyze the themes of her recorded song lyrics are the purposes of this book.

Chapter one is the first long biographical discussion of her life ever written; it is not, nor does it intend to be, the final biography of Ma Rainey. In preparing this chapter, I interviewed musicians Clyde Bernhardt, Thomas A. Dorsey (Ma Rainey's pianist and arranger), Sunnyland Slim, Sam Chatmon, and Willie Humphries.

Aside from one article by Charles Edward Smith and brief general treatments in histories of jazz and blues, published materials giving details of Ma Rainey's life have been sparse, obscure, and often out of print; several articles could be found only at the Rutgers Institute of Jazz Studies (Rutgers University, Newark, New Jersey), the John Edwards Memorial Foundation (University of California at Los Angeles), or the Library of Congress (Washington, D.C.).

No files exist for the Paramount Record Company, and the facts of Ma Rainey's recording career and professional appearances were gleaned from four arduous months spent reading the unindexed *Chicago Defender* in microfilm, from 1923 to 1935; the columns "A Note or Two" and "Hits and Bits" were particularly helpful in charting her travels around the country. I also made some use of Charles Edward Smith's unpublished notes on Ma Rainey, on file at Rutgers.

Chapter two examines Ma Rainey's style, analyzing her repertoire and noting the dominance of the blues in her recordings. It also discusses her relationship to her material, the use of copyright information in establishing a valid text of her lyrics, the influences of folk and popular blues on her songs, and the development of her recording style. I took as my basic text for this and the following chapters Ma Rainey's ninety-two extant recordings, which I personally transcribed from available reissues and from tapes of seven original Paramounts.

To establish who wrote the songs and when they were written, I searched through the Library of Congress copyright catalogues month by month for the years 1923 to 1930, and also made occasional searches into earlier catalogues; in all, seventy-four songs were copyrighted. In order to decipher garbled material and check my transcriptions, I sought out and used the songs' lead sheets (typewritten copies of song lyrics), on file at the Library of Congress; the lead sheets are over fifty years old and some are literally crumbling with age, but sixty-eight of them still exist. Lead sheets are often valuable, although they raise several critical issues, discussed in chapter two. Used with caution, however, they helped establish an accurate text of Ma Rainey's song lyrics. (Copyright information for all Rainey recordings cited in this book may be found in appendix C.)

Remaining chapters provide a thematic analysis of Ma Rainey's recorded songs. Chapter three discusses songs of love, noting a range of women's reactions to betrayal and rejection by men, from suicidal depression to murderous rage. Chapter four discusses songs of comedy and cynicism, which touch on broader subjects than love and place the women narrators in more social and communal environments.

While some important thematic studies of the blues in general have been published,[8] mine is the first to focus exclusively on the songs of Ma Rainey and to examine blues expressions of women's attitudes about love. It is my contention that the body of Ma Rainey's recorded songs constitutes a message to women, explaining quite clearly how to deal with reverses in love and how to interpret other areas of life. In striking contrast to the popular concept of the blues as a music of sorrow and despair, the songs of Ma Rainey reveal an astonishing range of emotional reactions to misfortune, from misery to rage and from humor to cynicism. Many songs show women aggressively confronting or attempting to change the circumstances of their lives.

Following the usage of Rudi Blesh and Derrick Stewart-Baxter, I have designated Ma Rainey's style primarily by the phrase "Classic Blues" rather than by "vaudeville" or "city" blues. Although the latter two terms are helpful, in that vaudeville and urban influences are clearly apparent in her material and delivery, readers are probably more familiar with the first term and it describes most fully the character of Ma Rainey's achievement: she was an outstanding representative of the highest class, having recognized worth and lasting significance.[9]

The research for this book was completed in several stages: in 1974 and 1975, as preparation for my 1975 doctoral dissertation at Stanford University; during the summer of 1977; and during a leave of absence from the University of Illinois at Chicago Circle, in 1978 and 1979. The latter two research periods were supported (the first fully and the second in part) by generous grants from the Research Board of the University of Illinois at Chicago Circle; for both grants and leave-time I am most grateful.

One of the great pleasures of writing this book has been the opportunity to work with so many fine people, and I wish to thank sincerely the following musicians, scholars, blues enthusiasts, and friends for their generosity, help, and encouragement. Sunnyland Slim, Thomas Dorsey, Sam Chatmon, and Willie Humphries gave freely of their time and recollections, and Clyde Bernhardt provided a remarkable eye-witness account of Ma Rainey's 1917 minstrel show, as well as assistance on questions of idiom and meaning. Personal help and attention were supplied by Mrs. Ann Allen, Mary Prioli, and Dan Morgenstern of the Rutgers Institute of Jazz Studies; by Richard Allen and Christine Kreyling of the William Ransom Hogan Jazz Archives at Tulane University; and by Jim Murray and Susan Charlin of the Schomburg Collection, New York Public Library. Dr. Albert A. Vollmer first put me in touch with Clyde Bernhardt, and Wayne Shirley at the Music Division, Library of Congress, was indispensable in assisting my research on copyright registrations.

Rossetta Reitz, Chris Albertson, Orrin Keepnews, Franz Hoffman, Frank Driggs, and Karl Gert zur Heide furnished valuable information, contacts, or photographs; Michael Jones aided my transcription of Ma Rainey's more obscure songs. Jim O'Neal, Jerry Valburn, and John Steiner all contributed needed help and tapes of rare Ma Rainey Paramounts, as did Bernard Klatzko, who was in addition an invaluable help on chapter two, supplying useful information and explanation about women country blues singers. I am especially in debt to Robert Dixon, John Godrich, and Laurie Wright, who graciously allowed me to see proofs of the Ma Rainey section in their forthcoming third edition of *Blues and Gospel Records, 1902–1943*, and to Howard Rye, who typeset and proofread that passage out-of-sequence to help me meet my press deadline.

Bill Herman and David Evans read and commented sensitively on the manuscript during its early stages of revision, and my parents, Dr. and Mrs. Bernard Lieb, freely spent many days photocopying materials, checking my copyright documentation, and helping me proofread the manuscript. My colleague at the University of Illinois at Chicago Circle, Professor Chadwick Hansen, has seen the manuscript in every stage of its development; it is with gratitude for his supportive and constructive criticism that I wish to dedicate this book to him.

Chicago, December 1980

1 The Paramount Wildcat: An
Introduction to the Life and Times of Ma Rainey

She jes' catch hold of us, somekindaway.

Sterling Brown, "Ma Rainey" (1932)

Ma Rainey died in 1939, just before the editors of the magazine *Jazz Information* attempted to contact her.[1] In its issue of September 6, 1940, *Jazz Information* published the first known biography of Ma Rainey: a letter written by her brother, Thomas Pridgett, Jr. Because the letter's statements, both accurate and inaccurate, were to be repeated until quite recently, it is quoted here in full:

> Gertrude Rainey, better known to the theatrical world as "Ma" Rainey, was born in Columbus, Ga. April 26, 1886. Her parents, Ella and Thomas Pridgett, were Georgians by birth also, therefore Georgia claims "Ma" Rainey as her songbird of the South.
>
> At a very early age her talent as a singer was very noticeable. Her first appearance on the stage was at the Springer Opera House, Columbus, Ga., with the "Bunch of Blackberries," a small show that was gotten up among the local talent of Columbus. Shortly after this appearance, Will Rainey, better known as "Pa" Rainey, wooed and married her, after which they traveled with a road show called "Rabbit Foot Minstrels."
>
> "Ma" Rainey operated two theaters in Rome, Ga., viz., "The Lyric" and "The Airdrome." Her career as a recording artist did not interfere with her stage work. All her recordings were made in Chicago. Her first recording was "Moonshine Blues."

She was in the theatrical business for a little better than thirty-five years. The death of her sister and mother called her back to Columbus, Ga. in 1933.

During her years of labour she did not forget her family. She purchased a beautiful home in Columbus for them. She and her brother, Thomas Pridgett, Jr., lived in this home until she passed into the Great Beyond, December 22, 1939.[2]

As we shall see, her parents were from Alabama, not Georgia, she recorded and performed in New York as well as Chicago, and her mother and sister died in 1935, not 1933.

Ma Rainey's full story encompasses such diverse topics as the relationship between black and white minstrelsy, the great northward migration of rural black people in the early twentieth century, the development of jazz, the history of the blues, and the birth and growth of the recording industry. Her life is not only complex, but often obscure as well: as noted previously, Ma Rainey has been eclipsed by Bessie Smith, whose more accessible material and sophisticated style commended her to early jazz writers like Carl Van Vechten during her life, and to white audiences and critics alike after her death.

Even to those who knew her name, Ma Rainey was often only a legend. A host of misconceptions grew up about her life: it was said that she kidnapped young Bessie, taking her on the tent show circuit and teaching her own art to her pupil; that she never or rarely performed in the North; and that there were two Ma Raineys, one who recorded for Paramount and another who sang in Harlem cellars and never made records. Part of the process of understanding her life involves identifying and separating legend from fact.[3]

On April 26, 1886, Gertrude Pridgett was born in Columbus, Georgia, the second of five children, including two brothers (Thomas, Jr., and Essie), a younger sister (Malissa), and another child whose name has not been identified.[4] Gertrude has sometimes been confused with her sister Malissa, who married Frank Nix and lived in Chicago, resulting in several accounts which incorrectly claim that Ma Rainey's full name was Gertrude Malissa (or Melissa) Nix Pridgett Rainey.[5] Her parents, Thomas and Ella (Allen) Pridgett, were Alabamians, and although her father's occupation is not known, Charles Edward Smith has established that after his death in 1896 her mother worked for the Central Railway of Georgia. A grandmother, described as "a very stately lady," was supposed to have been on the stage after Emancipation.

At an early age, Gertrude was baptized into the First African Baptist Church,[6] and around 1900, when she was fourteen, she made her first public appearance in the Bunch of Blackberries revue, as her brother's letter indicates. She began to perform widely in tent shows after this time, adding what she called "blues" to her repertoire as early as 1902. In the late 1930s she explained the circumstances to musicologist and Fisk University Professor John Wesley Work, Jr., who interviewed her in Nashville after watching her performance.

> "Ma" Rainey heard them [the blues] in 1902 in a small town in Missouri where she was appearing with a show under a tent. She tells of a girl from the town who came to the tent one morning and began to sing about the "man" who had left her. The song was so strange and poignant that it attracted much attention. "Ma" Rainey became so interested that she learned the song from the visitor, and used it soon afterwards in her "act" as an encore.
>
> The song elicited such response from the audience that it won a special place in her act. Many times she was asked what kind of song it was, and one day she replied, in a moment of inspiration, "It's the *Blues.*"
>
> That is what "Ma" Rainey said when she allowed me to interview her in the Douglass Hotel in Nashville where her company was playing. She added that a fire destroyed some newspaper clippings which mentioned her singing of these strange songs in 1905. She added, however, that after she began to sing the blues, although they were not so named then, she frequently heard similar songs in the course of her travels.[7]

This appealing story is most likely a distortion, because "the blues" (short for "blue devils") as a description of depression or despondency first appeared in Anglo-American speech in the late eighteenth century. In addition, the blues were developing into a distinct song form in various areas of the deep South around the turn of the century, and thus any individual's claim to naming them must be highly suspect.[8]

Evolving gradually out of antebellum work songs, street cries, hollers, ballads, and various West African musical traditions, the earliest blues were probably irregular, improvised, and unaccompanied, more like musical speech than song. After 1890 there is evidence of twelve-bar, blues-like vocal tunes, based on the pentatonic scale, with stanzas of three lines, and accompanied by guitar. Blues melodies also began to appear in contemporary piano playing, and by the turn of the century the word "blues" was mentioned in titles and lyrics to songs.[9]

Although the structure of folk blues varied widely, a standard form emerged during the first ten years of the twentieth century, finding its fullest expression in the East Texas and Mississippi Delta regions.[10] This most prevalent form was a twelve-bar melody with a three-line stanza, whose first line was generally repeated in the second line and whose third line rhymed with the first (AAB). Thus although Ma Rainey surely did not name the blues, she probably did hear and learn them in the manner she described.

On February 2, 1904, at the age of eighteen, she married William "Pa" Rainey, a dancer, comedian, and singer some years older, whom she may have met when he came through her town with a traveling show.[11] The pair became a song-and-dance team, with Pa continuing to do comedy as well. They worked extensively in the black tent shows, and Gertrude served her artistic apprenticeship as part of a great tradition of black minstrelsy.

White minstrel shows had burst upon the country during the 1840s, creating a sensation with their "authentic" portrayal (using burnt cork and grotesque physical exaggeration) of slave life on the plantation. By 1855, companies of black minstrels had appeared as well, becoming firmly established in show business by the 1870s, with the successful promotion methods of showmen Charles Callender and J. H. Haverly. During the 1860s blacks owned and ran several black minstrel companies, but by the following decade they were forced out by richer and more influential white entrepreneurs, who took over the most successful troupes.

The content of black and of white minstrelsy had been similar until the 1870s. But the success of black minstrel companies and their authenticity as "real Negroes" (in contrast to white actors in blackface) helped turn white shows away from portrayals of black life and toward more lavish productions, national subject matter, and social commentary. Black minstrel shows after this time emphasized plantation scenes and black culture, making use of authentic spirituals, comic marching units, "refined" singers and dancers, joking comedians, and caricatured specialty acts.[12]

Despite their stereotyped characterizations, inherited from white minstrelsy, black minstrel shows proliferated, providing steady employment to such fine black performers as Billy Kersands, the great wide-mouth comic and dancer, who probably invented the buck-and-wing step. Major shows included Richard and Pringle's Georgia Minstrels, Tolliver's Circus and Musical Extravaganza, Hicks and Sawyer's Minstrels, the King and Bush Wide-Mouth Minstrels, the Georgia Smart Set, and its follower and rival, the Smarter Set, and Pete Werle's Cotton Blossoms Show. Most famous of all were Silas Green's from New Orleans, and the Rabbit Foot Minstrels.[13]

In the early teens, Ma Rainey appeared with Pa in many of these companies; as her fame spread, she eventually headed shows of her own. Billed as "Madame Gertrude Rainey," she performed with many troupes, including the Smarter Set, the Florida Cotton Blossoms, Shufflin' Sam from Alabam', and the Rabbit Foot Minstrels, and she worked with managers such as C. W. Parks, Al Gaines, and Silas Green. From 1914 to 1916 she and Will toured with Tolliver's Circus and Musical Extravaganza, billed as "Rainey and Rainey, Assassinators of the Blues" (figure 1). When working with the circuses, the Raineys most likely appeared in something called "the After Show," a musical entertainment accompanied by the band and presented after the circus performance, for an extra charge.[14]

Her increasing fame coincided with the growing popularity of the blues: by 1912, four blues songs (including W. C. Handy's "Memphis Blues") had been published, and Handy aggressively popularized the form with more written compositions.[15] In the country the blues were well received by tent show audiences, white as well as black, while in the cities they spread through published sheet music and the performances of white vaudevillians.

The minstrel shows that Ma Rainey appeared with usually followed the harvests all over the South, often concluding their tours and spending the winter in New Orleans, where she met such jazz luminaries as King Joe Oliver, Louis Armstrong, Sidney Bechet, and Pops Foster. In New Orleans she sometimes appeared with

Figure 1. Rainey and Rainey, Assassinators of the Blues. (*The Indiana Freeman*, 25 December 1915, p. 13.)

local jazz bands in tent performances and may have spent a season with Kid Ory's pioneering jazz band. Sometimes her New Orleans comedy was unintentional, as drummer Zutty Singleton recalled: around 1914, while appearing at a tent show at Louisiana Avenue and Howard in New Orleans, she sang a well-known blues which included the line, "If you don't b'lieve I'm sinkin', look what a hole I'm in." At the line, "look what a hole I'm in," the stage collapsed.[16]

By far her most famous show was the Rabbit Foot Minstrels. Rivaled only by Silas Green's from New Orleans, the "Foots" was organized by F. S. Wolcott from his home in Port Gibson, Mississippi. Centrally situated on the Mississippi, the troupe employed blues singers, and featured jungle scenes, novelty acts, comedians, jugglers, and vaudeville teams as well. The show traveled by railroad car, playing one-night stands all over the South in a portable 80 by 110 foot canvas tent. Whenever the Foots came to town, a brass band would march around to advertise and drum up business for the show. Wooden boards on a folding frame served as the stage; the footlights were Coleman lanterns. In this era before the invention of microphones, singers developed strong vocal projection, and weaker-voiced women who relied on megaphones were scorned.[17] The Rabbit Foot Minstrels was strictly a Southern phenomenon: they never got out of the canebrakes, and never went north of Virginia.[18]

Ma Rainey's band included drums, violin, bass, and trumpet, and the show featured comedy and circus acts as well: "We had another man was outstandin' by the name of John Pamplin, he did that Devil Act, that Faust; rattled that big iron ball and did a lot of juggling . . . Delamon Miles, a contortionist who could turn himself around completely . . . he was able to move around and walk backwards with his feet turned in opposite directions . . . acrobats from down in New Orleans called the Watts Brothers, and also the Miles [Brothers] who had an aerial act."[19]

Sometimes the Rabbit Foot Minstrels followed the cotton harvest through Mississippi in the fall, spent the winter in Florida, and went back through the Carolinas in the spring; they traveled as far as the Georgia Sea Islands, Texas, Oklahoma, and even Mexico, but we cannot be certain that Ma Rainey appeared with them in all these places, although she reportedly spent a brief retirement in Mexico around 1921.[20]

She was the most renowned big-time entertainer who worked with the Foots:

> I guess Ma Rainey was the most famous. Because Ma Rainey was quite a character or legend in America here, in that she had such an outstanding voice for the blues, and she sang songs like the "Florida Blues" and the "Kansas City Blues" and the "Jelly Roll Blues." She sang songs then that would sound as up-to-date as if it were played right now. During that time people didn't dress like they do now. In that people then used to have more clothes on and she used to have those real long dresses sometimes with a high neck, well like you would call it—like the Gay Nineties. But she had one of those voices you never forget—particularly for singing the blues.[21]

Besides blues, she performed comedy, dancing, novelty, and topical songs, as well as the latest paper "ballits"—song sheets from the city—and was accompanied by a small jug band, a pianist such as Long Boy, or a small jazz combo.[22]

Photographs and accounts by her contemporaries reveal that Madame Rainey was a short, heavy, dark-skinned woman with luminous eyes, wild, wiry hair, and a large mouth filled with gold teeth (figure 2). She often wore a famous necklace and earrings made of gold pieces, or diamond-studded tiaras, rings, and bracelets. Conforming to the prejudice against dark skin (shared at that time by many blacks as well as whites), she lightened her face with heavy greasepaint, powder, and rouge, so that she looked almost gold-colored under the amber stage lights. Her gowns were elaborate creations of maroon, blue, or gold beaded satin, and her personality outshone her homely face, as trombone player Clyde Bernhardt recalls: "Yes, she was ugly. But I'll tell you one thing about it: she had such a lovely disposition, you know, and personality, you forget all about it. She commence to lookin' good to you."[23]

Although she was still officially billed as "Madame Gertrude" in the tent shows, people began to call her "Ma," a nickname rich in implication. She was about ten years older than most of the other performers; even in 1915, when only twenty-nine, she seemed like a mother to young Artiebelle McGinty of the Smarter Set company.[24] She performed as part of a team with "Pa" Rainey, and is remembered by contemporaries as having a compassionate, maternal

Figure 2. Madame Gertrude Rainey. (Courtesy Frank Driggs collection.)

nature. Years later, as a Paramount recording star, Ma Rainey would be touted as the Mother of the Blues, a title no doubt dreamed up by a press agent, but generally true in historical terms.

But by far the major significance of her name was as shorthand for "mama"—a lover, a voluptuous and desirable woman. Her comedy frequently depended on good-natured self-mockery about her looks, and on the contrast between her uninhibited, provocative movements and the discomfort of more straight-laced characters (see chapter four). White culture after World War I glorified slenderness and considered fat women ugly, and many black female vaudeville performers were thin and light-skinned, but black folk culture has always admired a "heavy-hipped mama" with "great big legs." Whatever Ma Rainey's shortcomings by conventional standards of beauty, when she became a recording star many advertisements for her records would depict a very fleshy but sensual woman (figure 3). Onstage, Madame Gertrude became a big mama, at once a comic and literal sex symbol.

In 1917, Ma Rainey and Her Georgia Smart Set appeared in the small town of Badin, North Carolina, and was seen by Clyde Bernhardt, whose remarkable memory provides us with a detailed description of the show.[25] In some ways Badin typified the new, more industrialized South of the teens—a town practically created by an ALCOA plant which employed some five thousand people, many of them "hungry for entertainment." At that time, Ma Rainey's show traveled by train. Although Southern railroads were strictly segregated, the smaller lines could spare only half a car for black people to travel in, and thus any black minstrel show with more than twenty-five people kept its own, separate baggage and coach cars which would link up with the smaller railroad lines. In the jim-crow South, black performers were not allowed in the dining car; they bought their own food wherever they could and were housed with families along the way.

The group performed in a large tent, bigger than a medium-sized theater, and blacks and whites attended the same performance, buying their tickets from the same vendor, although the whites sat on the right side of the tent, while the blacks sat on the left. Mr. Bernhardt recalls that Ma Rainey was very popular among white audiences in North Carolina, although she preferred performing for her own people. (Guitarist Sam Chatmon of the Mississippi

Figure 3. Big Mama. "Dead Drunk Blues." (*Chicago Defender*, 13 August 1927, Part I, p. 7.)

Sheiks recalls that most of Ma Rainey's tent show performances in
Jackson, Mississippi, were for white people, who brought in more
money. Sometimes she would provide background music for white
parties: "They just had her for entertainment. Like they'd have a
sociable, you know, and they wasn't gonna dance . . . they'd always be sittin' around, drinkin' and eatin' and listenin'." But when
the show was over, she would go to a dance at the local black cafe
behind a gas station, to entertain and socialize with her own
people.)[26]

Her show included a variety of acts and usually lasted about
two hours. Mr. Bernhardt recalls a band consisting of violin, piano,
guitar, bass, and drums, but instrumentation probably varied. After
the band played an opening instrumental, the lights flashed, the
curtain rose, and a chorus of young men and women performed
dances like "Strut Miss Lizzie," "The Cut-Out," or "Pickin'
Peaches." The women wore flashy costumes, with skirts a little
below the knee, and laced-up, high-heeled shoes, and Mr. Bernhardt recalls that although the entire chorus was quite attractive, the
men were light-skinned, while the women were very dark, because
Ma Rainey did not want them to look lighter than she did! This was a
departure from the usual minstrel show chorus, with its "sepia
lovelies."

Next, the comedians performed a skit, which could include
ethnic humor; one man imitated a Japanese character, complete
with Oriental makeup.[27] Broad comedy was provided by a
chicken-stealing episode:

> . . . they had live chickens on the stage, and a chicken coop,
> and a scene where one of these old guys would try to steal [the]
> farmer's chicken. They had a scene where . . . [the] curtain . . .
> looked like a farmhouse. And at night . . . this old guy, he's
> creepin' around, you know. . . . And then, one guy . . . he'd
> have heavy powder on his face, made up so he looked like a
> white man; he'd come out there and have a old long beard and a
> shotgun. And he'd shoot the guy that was stealing the chick-
> ens. And when he'd shoot, you know, this guy would run, and
> old chickens would fly all over the stage, but they never come
> out there where the people were. . . . I think they were trained.

Then a young woman singer (the "soubrette") sang a fast dance tune like "Ballin' the Jack," and the chorus reappeared to dance it with her. Next the comedians returned for another skit, and finally Ma Rainey herself made her entrance, telling jokes about her craving for young men, and then singing.

> Oh yeah, she would tell jokes to the audience. . . . You know, back in those days, they used to call young men, you know, "pig meat." And, like, if they was around eighteen or nineteen, they called them "bird liver." . . . So she used to come out there and crack—"Yeah, I like my pig meat men. I like 'em young and tender . . . I ain't got nothin' for an old man to do. I like mine young and tender. . . . If they be nice, I take care of 'em." . . . And she'd get up there and say, "I'm gonna tell you about my man." And then probably she'd start to singin' "A Good Man Is Hard to Find."

She sang "Memphis Blues," "Jelly Roll Blues," "I Ain't Got Nobody," among others, and "Walking the Dog," which she also danced. Usually she ended with the famous "See, See Rider," knowing she would receive an encore. Clearly the song was a showstopper; she was to record it years later, in a magnificent collaboration with Louis Armstrong. After her performance, the entire cast assembled on the stage to sing and dance the finale.

By all accounts, she electrified her audience, creating immediate rapport as she articulated their joys and sorrows. In his moving poem "Ma Rainey," Sterling Brown captured the marvelous power of her performance.

I

When Ma Rainey
Comes to town,
Folks from anyplace
Miles aroun',
From Cape Girardeau,
Poplar Bluff,
Flocks in to hear
Ma do her stuff;

Comes flivverin' in,
Or ridin' mules,
Or packed in trains,
Picknickin' fools. . . .
That's what it's like,
Fo' miles on down,
To the New Orleans delta
An' Mobile town,
When Ma hits
Anywheres aroun'.

II

Dey comes to hear Ma Rainey from de little river settlements,
From blackbottom cornrows and from lumber camps;
Dey stumble in de hall, jes' a-laughin' an' a-cacklin',
Cheerin' lak roarin' water, lak wind in river swamps.

An' some jokers keeps deir laughs a-goin' in de crowded aisles,
An' some folks sits dere waitin' wid deir aches an' miseries,
Till Ma comes out before dem, a-smilin' gold-toofed smiles,
An' Long Boy ripples minors on de black an' yellow keys.

III

O Ma Rainey,
Sing yo' song;
Now you's back
Whah you belong,
Git way inside us,
Keep us strong. . . .
O Ma Rainey,
Li'l an' low;
Sing us 'bout de hard luck
'Roun' our do';
Sing us 'bout de lonesome road
We mus' go. . . .

IV

I talked to a fellow, an' the fellow say,
"She jes' catch hold of us, somekindaway.

She sang Backwater Blues one day:

'It rained fo' days an' de skies was dark as night,
Trouble taken place in de lowlands at night.

'Thundered an' lightened an' the storm began to roll
Thousan's of people ain't got no place to go.

'Den I went an' stood upon some high ol' lonesome hill,
An' looked down on the place where I used to live.'

An' den de folks, dey natchally bowed dey heads an' cried,
Bowed dey heavy heads, shet dey moufs up tight an' cried,
An' Ma lef' de stage, an' followed some de folks outside.''

Dere wasn't much more de fellow say;
She jes' gits hold of us dataway.[28]

At the same time Ma Rainey was becoming a major, established minstrel star, a young woman from Tennessee was beginning a career destined to eclipse Ma's. The full details of the relationship between Ma Rainey and Bessie Smith may never be known, but they have been and will be debated for years. According to the legend, Ma Rainey was the leader of the Rabbit Foot Minstrels when she discovered the talented young Bessie in Chattanooga, kidnapped her, took her along with the show, and taught her to sing the blues. But Maud Smith, Bessie's sister-in-law, denies the kidnapping story: "I remember one time when we were in Augusta, Georgia. . . . Bessie and Ma Rainey sat down and had a good laugh about how people was making up stories of Ma taking Bessie from her home, and Ma's mother used to get the biggest laugh out of the kidnapping story whenever we visited her in Macon. Actually, Ma and Bessie got along fine, but Ma never taught Bessie how to sing. She was more like a mother to her."[29]

Although Ma Rainey never kidnapped anybody, the two women did work together in at least two traveling shows, but possibly not in the Rabbit Foot Minstrels. Charles Edward Smith believes that they met in Tolliver's Circus and Musical Extravaganza, sometime between 1914 and 1916, while Albertson implies that the date was 1912, when Bessie had her first professional job as a dancer with Moses Stokes' traveling show, whose cast included both Raineys; that same year she appeared in another show with them.[30] Without romanticizing, it is safe to say that Bessie, as a young chorus girl, must have been tremendously impressed by the older Ma Rainey's voice, authority, and performance, and certainly absorbed elements of her art without needing any conscious teaching.

Apparently Bessie got her big break independently from Ma Rainey and became a star on her own by 1914, when she performed at the 81 Theater in Atlanta; it is said that Ma Rainey never claimed to have helped her. Bessie herself asserted that her inspiration was Cora Fisher, an obscure singer from Chattanooga, but the statement is dubious. Despite her great success, Bessie Smith had a vulnerable ego and felt extremely competitive with other women blues stars, especially during the recording era, when she often "carved" them by deliberately recording their material in her own superior style.[31] Although she was a close friend of Ma Rainey, she probably would not have cared to attribute her art to another reigning blues queen.

Thomas Dorsey, later to be Ma Rainey's pianist, arranger, and band director, had worked as a boy at the 81 Theater, and insists to this day that Ma directly guided Bessie: "When I worked at that theater in Atlanta, Ma taught Bessie Smith. Ma was comin' to this theater singin', she and Pa Rainey, when I was a boy in Atlanta, workin' there at that theater. . . . And she was a natural drawing card, and she's the ma of all of 'em. She taught Bessie Smith, Butterbeans & Susie [a famous black comedy team], a lot of those black actors who came along in that day. That's why they called her Ma."[32] The vaudeville-flavored minstrel tradition that shaped Bessie had both molded Ma Rainey and been molded by her at least a decade earlier, and Bessie's material—her choice of songs, her comedy and dancing—must have shown affinities to that of the Mother of the Blues.

While Bessie had a reputation for fiery temper, hard drinking, and abusive language, Ma Rainey was generally outgoing, sweet-tempered, warm, clean-spoken, and at least publicly temperate.[33] She apparently forbade drinking on her shows and did not share Bessie's enthusiasm for physical fights:

> Ma Rainey wasn't that type of a person. She didn't approve of
> nothin' like that. I don't say she was the type to let nobody walk

over her, but she knew how to avoid things like that. Ma Rainey acted more like a real religious person, that's the way she'd appear to you when you'd be talkin' to her. I never heard her use no bad language, or curse, or nothin' like that. . . . She didn't put on no airs, or nothin' like that; she never did use no bad language. But Bessie Smith, she'd get mad at you, she'd curse you out and fight you too. But Bessie was a nice person if nobody didn't cross her.[34]

Those who had seen both blues singers agreed that Bessie had the better voice, but Ma was the greater performer, as Sterling Brown recalled: "Ma Rainey was a tremendous figure. She wouldn't have to sing any words; she would moan, and the audience would moan with her. She had them in the palm of her hand. I heard Bessie Smith also, but Ma Rainey was the greatest mistress of an audience. Bessie was the greater blues singer, but Ma really *knew* these people; she was a person of the folk; she was very simple and direct."[35]

Although Bessie would deny it at certain times in her career, the two women were close friends who frequently spent time together when their shows stopped in the same city. They may have been more than friends; there is strong evidence to indicate that Ma Rainey, like Bessie Smith, was bisexual. There is no doubt that both were interested in women: Bessie had several affairs with her chorus girls, and Ma Rainey was arrested in 1925 for an indiscretion involving her chorines:

It seemed that Ma had found herself in an embarrassing tangle with the Chicago police. She and a group of young ladies had been drinking and were making so much noise that a neighbor summoned the police. Unfortunately for Ma and her girls, the law arrived just as the impromptu party got intimate. There was pandemonium as everyone madly scrambled for her clothes and ran out the back door. Ma, clutching someone else's dress, was the last to exit, but a nasty fall down a staircase foiled her escape. Accusing her of running an indecent party, the police threw her in jail, and Bessie bailed her out the following morning.[36]

Later in her career, Ma Rainey wrote and recorded an explicitly lesbian song, "Prove It on Me Blues."[37]

Finally, Sam Chatmon, who played guitar for Ma Rainey's tent show in Jackson, Mississippi, believes that she and Bessie were lovers:

> I believe she was courtin' Bessie . . . the way they'd talk. . . . I
> believe there was somethin' goin' on wrong. . . . She [Bessie]
> said, "Me and Ma Rainey had plenty of big times together." I'd
> talk to her [Ma] and she'd say, her and Bessie had big times . . .
> she was actin' so funny, I believe one or the other of them was
> the man, the other one was the girl. . . . I believe Ma Rainey
> was the one, was cuttin' up like the man. . . . If Bessie'd be
> 'round, if she'd get to talkin' to another man, she'd [Ma] run up.
> She didn't want no man to talk with her.[38]

Lacking more conclusive evidence, we may only suggest that a relationship between them was possible.

If Ma Rainey's sexual interest in women was covert, her taste for the company and attentions of young men was obvious, as she admitted in her stage patter. Sterling Brown, who accompanied John Work to the interview cited earlier in this chapter, recalled Ma Rainey's unprovoked advances to them both: "That night when we saw her, she was having boy trouble. You see, she liked these young musicians, and in comes John Work and I—we were young to her. We were something sent down, and she didn't know which one to choose. Each of us knew we were not choosing her! We just wanted to talk, but she was interested in other things. She was that direct. She was tops for my money."[39]

Her relationship with Pa Rainey becomes very shadowy after their early collaboration as assassinators of the blues. At some point they adopted a son, Danny, who worked as a dancer in the show, billed as "the world's greatest juvenile stepper." Ma Rainey's contemporaries imply that only adoption could give them a son, and get hysterical at the idea of Ma Rainey as a natural mother to a child.[40] Apparently in the late teens the Raineys separated and Pa died; Ma was later remarried to a younger man not connected with show business, who sometimes accompanied her on tour when he could spare the time.[41]

Ma Rainey's influence may have extended to other performers besides Bessie Smith. Thomas Dorsey claims that Ma taught entertainer Susie Edwards (of the popular vaudeville team Butterbeans and Susie) to sing, and Clyde Bernhardt believes that Classic Blues singer Clara Smith (no relation to Bessie) imitated Ma Rainey's voice, mannerisms, and performance.[42]

Ma continued to tour with tent shows into the late teens, and may have retired briefly to Mexico around 1921.[43] Soon she was active again, working for a few years with pianist Troy Snapp. But 1923 saw the beginning of her leap from Southern minstrel star to national recording artist: that year she won a contract with Paramount Record Company and went to Chicago to make her first recordings. Although she had been the fountainhead of the Classic Blues, she was only now acknowledged in a blues mania that had begun three years earlier with Mamie Smith, the first woman blues singer to record. A brief survey of the emergence of black artists on record will provide the context for Mamie's achievement and its impact on Ma Rainey's career.

Black entertainers had appeared occasionally on records from the earliest days of the invention. George W. Johnson recorded a "Laughing Song" on an Edison phonocylinder as far back as 1895, comedian Bert Williams made some recordings for Victor Records in 1901, and around 1914 James Reese Europe's Society Orchestra was the first black instrumental group to record. In general, early black recordings were restricted to comic monologues, "plantation airs," choral arrangements of religious music, and "coon songs." These last were defined by Victor Records as "up-to-date comic songs in negro dialect"; they tended to be aimed at white audiences and to reinforce racist stereotypes inherited from minstrelsy.[44]

In the teens, white entertainers began to perform and record material that was labeled, with some accuracy, blues. Sophie Tucker, among others, sought out and used blues songs in her vaudeville performances, introducing her white audiences to the blues and helping create a greater demand for it. By 1919, blues songs were included in the repertoire of many white vaudevillians and cabaret performers, and white vocalists and jazz bands had recorded blues.[45]

In 1916, the *Chicago Defender* began an aggressive campaign to persuade phonograph companies to record black classical perform-ers. The first "jazz" record was issued in 1917 by a white group, the Original Dixieland Jass Band. By being in the right place at the right time, the group enjoyed spectacular sales; their recordings both represented and helped promote an interest in black music of all kinds. To the success of W. C. Handy's published blues compositions were added the increasing appearances of blues songs on piano rolls. Henry C. Speir, a white man who later became an important talent scout and agent for many black recording artists, tried in 1919 to interest companies in recording more black music. It was becoming obvious that America had a vast and largely untapped market for recorded black music: a population of fourteen million black people, thousands of Southern whites who had enjoyed minstrelsy for years, and urban audiences of both races who liked vaudeville and cabaret.[46]

None of these developments were lost on Perry "Mule" Bradford, a black composer, bandleader, and singer. With aggressive and almost unbelievable determination, Bradford went from company to company until he convinced Fred Hagar, a white manager of the General Phonograph Company, to record Mamie Smith on the Okeh label. A native of Cincinnati, Mamie had years of experience in the Smart Set minstrel show, and her vaudeville-style singing had already made her popular with Harlem audiences.[47]

On February 14, 1920, Mamie Smith made history, recording two Bradford compositions originally slated for Sophie Tucker: "That Thing Called Love" and "You Can't Keep a Good Man Down." Although the tunes were neither authentic blues nor memorable performances, Mamie was the first black woman to record, and the black press and public responded enthusiastically, with reported sales of ten thousand copies, predominantly in the South, during the release month of August.[48]

This encouragement led Hagar to record Mamie again. Her previous accompanists had been called the Rega Orchestra, but now the group, with some personnel changes, was labeled Her Jazz Hounds. This time she sang a true blues, again written by Bradford, which he had originally called "Harlem Blues," but whose title was changed to "Crazy Blues." Within a month of its issue, "Crazy Blues" sold seventy-five thousand copies, equivalent today to a gold record.

Such phenomenal success induced other record companies to record blues singers throughout the twenties, usually inviting them to studios in the North, but also sending mobile recording units to the South. As the blues boom progressed, companies such as

Paramount, Columbia, Vocalion, Perfect, Brunswick, and Victor, as well as Okeh, all established separate numerical listings for their "race" catalogues; at that time, "race" was a term of pride in the black community. Although race records included spirituals, instrumentals, comedy, sermons, and even occasional classical arias, the biggest money was in the blues: Columbia recorded Bessie Smith, "Empress of the Blues," Okeh had Mamie Smith and Victoria Spivey, and Paramount Records signed Ma Rainey, who recorded her first eight songs in Chicago in December 1923, at the age of thirty-seven.

Throughout the twenties, the demand for black music was so widespread and profitable that several black-owned companies appeared, achieving varying degrees of success. Entertainer Winston Holmes' Meritt Records issued seven titles from 1925 to 1928, and Mayo Williams' Black Patti label was active in 1927, but the most important black-owned record company was Black Swan. Operated by Harry Pace and W. C. Handy, Black Swan was formed in 1921 and hired bandleader Fletcher Henderson as musical director and recording manager.[49] With justifiable pride, the company boasted: "Only bonafide Racial Company making talking machine records. All stockholders are Colored, all artists are Colored, all employees are Colored. Only company using Racial Artists in recording *high class* song records. This company made the only Grand Opera Records ever made by Negroes. All others confine this end of their work to blues, rags, comedy numbers, etc."[50] Despite this appeal to high culture, Black Swan also recorded Trixie Smith and Ethel Waters, "Queen of the Blues." Unfortunately, the company proved no match for its larger and stronger competitors, and in 1924 it was merged with the growing Paramount Record Company.

Paramount Records began as the New York Recording Laboratories, a subsidiary of the Wisconsin Chair Company of Port Washington, Wisconsin, which originally manufactured home furniture and phonograph cabinets. The Paramount label had first appeared in 1917, and by 1922 the company reserved its 12000 series for race records. From 1923 to 1926, along with Okeh and Columbia, Paramount dominated the race market, and it continued to be one of the most important companies recording black music until 1930.[51] Like many other companies, Paramount hired a black talent scout and recording director; he was J. Mayo Williams, nicknamed "Ink" for his readiness to sign up promising performers. His forceful recruiting helped develop Paramount into a major company by acquiring Blind Lemon Jefferson, Ida Cox, Lovie Austin, and Blind Blake, among others.[52]

Although Paramount offered an impressive array of talent, including such stars as Alberta Hunter as well as Ma Rainey, its operation was limited compared to that of Columbia Records and its recordings suffered accordingly. Unfortunately for posterity, Ma Rainey recorded only on the Paramount label and many of her sides were produced acoustically (a crude process in which she sang into an enormous horn), making the final product primitive by today's standards. Paramount eventually switched to some kind of electrical process around 1925, as did Columbia, but cynics joked that Paramount did nothing more than put an electric light bulb in the recording studio.

The Chicago that witnessed Ma Rainey's arrival in 1923 had become a magnet in the great northward migration of Southern blacks, including many blues singers, guitarists, and instrumentalists. Between 1910 and 1920, the black population of Chicago increased from roughly forty thousand to more than a hundred thousand: from two to four percent of the total. This enormous influx of people included many future great blues musicians: Big Bill Broonzy, Georgia Tom Dorsey and Tampa Red (both destined to work closely with Ma Rainey), Blind Lemon Jefferson, and many others. They worked in theaters and taverns, and at house parties when they could, often supplementing their low tips with odd jobs as shoeshine boys, janitors, or delivery men.[53]

By drawing so many diverse people, the city also served to amalgamate a number of varied blues and jazz styles brought from all over the South and Midwest. Although Ma Rainey recorded, worked, and kept an apartment there, the city never became her home. Like Ida Cox, Alberta Hunter, and many other blues singers, she used the city as a base to start her tours; Bessie had the same relationship to New York.[54]

Ma Rainey's recordings in 1923 were both a solid artistic achievement and a significant new voice of the rural South. Mamie Smith, who started the blues craze, was a Northerner with a sophisticated style, and most early blues records emphasized the slick, refined manner of singers like Lucille Hegamin, Edith Wilson, and their imitators. But Ma Rainey's (and to a lesser extent, Bessie Smith's) recordings of 1923 brought a rougher, more down-home feeling, with country blues, folk-influenced composed blues, songs from the minstrel shows, and popular tunes sung in a blues style.[55]

Long-time fans of Ma Rainey must have laughed when they saw her "discovery" in a 1924 *Chicago Defender* advertisement:

> Discovered at Last —"Ma" Rainey, Mother of the Blues!
>
> "Moonshine Blues"—the first record by Madame "Ma" Rainey, the wonderful gold neck woman who starred for five years in three theaters in Pensacola, Atlanta, and Jacksonville! If it's Blues you want, here they are. "Ma" sings "Moonshine Blues" like she meant 'em ("I Ain't Never Goin' to Drink No More!")—it's the last word in Blues. "Ma" Rainey is the only Blues singer in the world elevated to the heights of "Madame." Now she sings *exclusively* for Paramount. . . .[56]

The ad included a drawing of this new discovery, bedecked in a necklace and earrings made of gold pieces (figure 4).

"Bad Luck Blues" was actually Ma Rainey's first recording, but "Moonshine Blues" was the first to be released and promoted. Although Paramount records were available in stores throughout major cities, most of the company's business came from mail orders, seventy-five cents COD. Ma Rainey's popularity increased tremendously through recordings like "Bo-Weevil Blues" and "Moonshine Blues," which brought her to the attention of Northern blacks, but her fame still remained strongest among black and white Southerners.

While Southern whites, whose taste for black music had been stimulated by live performances of black tent shows, became part of the race record-buying public, it was possible for some Northern whites to live through the twenties ignorant of black records. For although some black minstrel troupes did perform in theaters in the North, their audiences were predominantly black, in contrast to the mixed audiences for Southern tent shows. Moreover, in the North, race records were advertised only in the black press and distributed only to record outlets in black areas.[57] Since Ma Rainey was based in Chicago rather than New York, and performed in a rougher, more down-home style, she most likely escaped the notice of Carl Van

Figure 4. "Discovered at Last—'Ma' Rainey, Mother of the Blues!" (First newspaper advertisement for Ma Rainey's recordings, *Chicago Defender*, 2 February 1924, Part II, p. 10.)

Vechten, the white novelist, critic, and self-styled interpreter of black culture, who idolized Bessie Smith. This lack of a Northern white audience and significant promotion by a white critic no doubt contributed to Ma Rainey's relative obscurity to this day.

In the black press, however, she was publicized aggressively and extensively by Paramount, billed as "the Mother of the Blues," "the Songbird of the South," "the Gold-Neck Woman of the Blues" (in reference to her necklace), and "the Paramount Wildcat." In order to compete with other record companies, which gave away free pictures of their stars, Paramount organized several publicity stunts concerning Ma. The "mystery record contest" was announced in a full-page ad in the *Defender,* inviting fans to compete in naming "a special super-Blues hit—sung by Madame Rainey upon request of thousands of her admirers! This record is so good—so unusual—that we couldn't think of a name good enough for it. Then 'Ma' suggested we let the public name it."[58] Prizes, valued at fourteen thousand dollars, included lavish console phonograph cabinets, selections of records from the Paramount-Black Swan catalogue, and pictures of Ma Rainey; the judges were Harry Pace and Mayo Williams. Although the response was apparently quite good, "Ma Rainey's Mystery Record" is neither original nor outstanding in comparison with "Moonshine Blues" or her later work with Louis Armstrong, and the winning title was nothing more than the first line of the song: "Lawd, I'm Down Wid de Blues."[59]

Paramount's next promotional attempt was the "souvenir record," featuring a picture of Ma Rainey on the label. "The famous Mother of the Blues doesn't want you to ever forget her—that's how much she loves her friends! So we put her picture on her latest record, 'Dream Blues.' On the other side is 'Lost Wandering Blues' by 'Ma.' Accompaniments by Pruitt Twins on those guitars that made Kansas City famous. . . . This is the first time, to our knowledge, that any artist's picture has ever appeared on a record. Paramount is always first with the features."[60] This time, the result is more satisfying: although the acoustic recording technique makes the Pruitt Twins' guitar playing sound crude, Ma Rainey herself is in fine voice.

She continued to record in Chicago and spent time with other musicians—some of them old friends from her minstrel days—at

parties given by Richard Morgan, a friend of Bessie's and a successful South Side bootlegger.

> . . . night rarely turned to day without Morgan's having a party
> in one of his many houses on the South Side. The music, always
> in ample supply, was provided by guests from just about every
> bandstand and stage in town. It was . . . not unusual to find Ma
> Rainey there, singing to the accompaniment of pianist Jelly Roll
> Morton, or Louis Armstrong cutting through the smoke-filled
> air in royal musical battle with violinist Eddie South, while the
> rest of Jimmy Wade's Syncopators—who were almost nightly
> guests—joined in.[61]

Morgan's nephew, Lionel Hampton, recalled the scene:

> Yeah, my uncle was a real cool dude, and he used to take me
> everyplace with him—he furnished whiskey and bathtub gin
> for almost all the dives on the South Side. He was crazy about
> piano players, but all the musicians used to love to come to his
> place because they could meet all the chicks there, and my uncle
> would give them all the whiskey they could drink, and all the
> chitterlins they could eat. I used to dream of joining Ma
> Rainey's band because she treated her musicians so wonder-
> fully, and she always bought them an instrument. . . .[62]

In 1924 Ma Rainey recorded eighteen songs for Paramount,
including two memorable sessions with Fletcher Henderson's
group in New York. On three songs, "Jelly Bean Blues," "Countin'
the Blues," and "See, See Rider," Louis Armstrong is one of the
accompanists, and the results are magnificent. Ma was the first
singer to record "See, See Rider," a traditional, well-known blues,
and it is surprising in view of the song's universal appeal and
popularity that Paramount's subsequent ad in the *Defender* stressed
instead the flip side, "Jealous Hearted Blues."[63]

By now, her popularity was so great that Paramount booked
her on a tour of the Theater Owners' Booking Agency (T.O.B.A.),
a circuit of the theaters located in major Southern and Midwestern cities, geared to black vaudeville entertainment, and managed by an interracial and not overly scrupulous group of theater
owners. The T.O.B.A. had been around as early as 1907, and
starting in 1909, several theaters were opened and successfully

operated on Beale Street in Memphis. Although the nightly shows were aimed at black audiences, Thursday nights had separate performances for whites. A standard feature of T.O.B.A. theaters throughout the South was the "Midnight Ramble"—a late show which featured the blues. Although some performers said the initials stood for "tough on black artists" because of the grueling work schedules, low pay, and often inadequate dressing rooms and stages, the circuit's theaters offered regular employment in one-week engagements to hundreds of blues singers and assorted entertainers. In 1921 the circuit was taken over by Milton Starr and Charles Turpin, who ran it with increasing efficiency. Locations of "Toby-time" theaters ranged from Jacksonville, Florida, to Little Rock, Arkansas, from Kansas City, Missouri, to Bessemer, Alabama, and while there was no official T.O.B.A. theater in New York, black artists performed at the Seventh Avenue Lafayette Theatre and at the Alhambra. According to the *Defender*, by 1925 the circuit had more than fifty theaters, employing over 25 revues and 106 singles, teams, and trios, and attracting audiences of 4,500 people daily.[64]

Despite hard schedules and often inadequate theaters and salaries, the entertainers seemed to enjoy it anyway. In the words of blues singer Lonnie Johnson, "At that time on T.O.B.A. you *work*—you do five, six shows a day; you got little money, but everybody was happy."[65]

Like the minstrel shows, the T.O.B.A. included a wide variety of entertainment—comedy, circus acts, dramatic scenes, and pure vaudeville hokum as well as singing and dancing. An advertisement for the Standard Theater in June 1924 gives the flavor of many T.O.B.A. performances:

Philadelphia, Pennsylvania—A great bill is presented here this week and the attendance is right up to the standard, despite the heat. The acts are Five Sensational Balasis, an [sic] European novelty, carrying a wide angle of work; Doc, Dinks, and Davis, in a knockout singing, talking, and dancing feature; Mason and Henderson, a comedy singing and talking pair with a great rep; Bailey and Tears in a fast working turn, giving a world of satisfaction; Eddie Green, properly billed "The One Man Show"; Johnson and MacIntosh, upside down dancers and pianists, and the Sandy Burns company in the screaming comedy tab, "I Wonder Who's [sic] Affair It Is?"[66]

In order to tour this circuit, Ma Rainey needed a piano player and a touring band, and thus Mayo Williams introduced her to Thomas A. Dorsey, a young musician from Villa Rica, Georgia, who had seen her perform at the 81 Theater in Atlanta, back in her minstrel days. A skilled pianist who could read music, Dorsey had arrived in Chicago around 1916 and made his living by working odd jobs and by playing piano in the wine rooms behind saloons. When he first met Ma Rainey in Chicago, she was keeping an apartment in the Angelus Building at the corner of 35th and Wabash, although her home was still in Georgia.

Dorsey, who found her "grand, gracious, and easy to talk with," auditioned some tunes for Ma Rainey and rehearsed some blues she wanted to use on the road. Impressed with his performance, Ma hired him as her accompanist and band director. Dorsey then assembled the Wildcats Jazz Band, including himself on piano (billed as "Georgia Tom"), David Nelson on trumpet, Eddie Pollack on saxophone and clarinet, Albert Wynn on trombone, and Gabriel Washington on drums (figure 5).[67]

The group made its debut in April 1924 at the Grand Theater in Chicago, and the *Defender* was approving, if not exactly gushing with praise: "Strickly [sic] first-class vaudeville for this week. The feature attraction of the program was Madam [sic] 'Ma Rainey,' a Paramount star. This is her first Chicago appearance and she was well received. She clearly proved that she was far superior to any of her predecessors. The curtain goes up and finds her concealed in a Victrola box. While her Jazz Wild Cats played she sang her first number. Her gowns were wonderful creations of the dressmaker's art."[68]

Dorsey remembers the occasion far more vividly:

Ma Rainey's act came on as a last number or at the end of the show. I shall never forget the excited feeling when the orchestra in the pit struck up her opening theme, music which I had written especially for the show. The curtain rose slowly and those soft lights on the band as we picked up the introduction to Ma's first song. We looked and felt like a million. Ma was hidden in a big box-like affair built like an old Victrola of long

Figure 5. Ma Rainey and her Wildcats Jazz Band, 1923. *Left to right:* Gabriel
Washington, drums; Albert Wynn, trombone; David Nelson, trumpet; Ma
Rainey, vocals; Eddie Pollack, saxophone; Thomas Dorsey, piano. (Cour-
tesy Duncan Schiedt.)

ago. This stood on the other side of the stage. A girl would come
out and put a big record on it. Then the band picked up the
Moonshine Blues. Ma would sing a few bars inside the Victrola.
Then she would open the door and step out into the spotlight
with her glittering gown that weighed twenty pounds and
wearing a necklace of five, ten and twenty dollar gold-pieces.
The house went wild. It was as if the show had started all over
again. Ma had the audience in the palm of her hand. Her
diamonds flashed like sparks of fire falling from her fingers.
The gold-piece necklace lay like a golden armor covering her
chest. They called her the lady with the golden throat. . . .
When Ma had sung her last number and the grand finale, we
took seven [curtain] calls. [69]

Fresh from their Chicago success, the group began a T.O.B.A.
tour of the South and the Midwest. Dorsey wrote songs for Ma
Rainey, autographed pictures for her fans, and served as her musical arranger and leader of her band, while his young wife came
along as Ma Rainey's wardrobe mistress. Although the personnel
varied from time to time, as the show picked up some supporting
acts and dropped others, the various performers were well treated:
"Jack Wiggins, he was the world's greatest tap dancer then. . . .
And Dick & Dick was a great act at that time . . . sing, dance and
joke. And Stovepipe Johnson, he used to be on. . . . We always kept
a good show, bunch of actors, because everybody wanted to work
for Ma, for she paid off, see. And some of the heads of the shows
didn't pay the folk—they'd leave 'em stranded in the town."[70]
Despite Ma Rainey's generosity to her performers, she still maintained ultimate authority as the star of the show: "Oh, she did most
of the blues singing. She'd have these prima donnas, yeah, but they
didn't sing blues on her shows, see, they'd sing something else.
Like hot pop. . . . Naturally you wouldn't put another blues singer
on your show, may outsing you."[71]

Her trombone player, Al Wynn, also recalled the tour with
great fondness, despite crowded working conditions for the
musicians:

> In most of the places the theatres had large bands in the pit who
> played the overtures before the curtain would go up, and we
> being the main attraction, we would be crowded on the stage

with along about four pieces. But when she would come out to sing she would prove herself to be the real star of the whole evening. Her entrance was—she would come out of a large victrola—it was made just like an old-style phonograph and she would walk out of that singing the "Moonshine Blues" which was her big hit at that time:

I was drinkin' all night, babe, and the night before,
When I get sober, ain't gonna drink no more,
Because my friend is standin' in my door. . . . [72]

Ma Rainey's fondness for jewelry has been noted by everyone who knew her. Once she was arrested for innocently buying some stolen jewelry:

Once she bought some jewelry from some fellows down in Nashville, Tennessee. . . . And she didn't know it was hot. We left, we went on across the circuit, and when we were closin' in Cleveland one Sunday night, the officer come up there and took her off the stage, you know, arrested her. Gonna take her back to Nashville after she did the last show. But the rough part about it, we were supposed to open down in Pennsylvania that Monday night. But we had no Ma. But I took the show on down there. . . . And we kinda concocted a scheme there. We still had Ma's trunk full of clothes, and we had another big girl on there, and she was about Ma's size. She had a heavy voice but she couldn't sing like Ma. We decided to open up and put some of Ma's clothes on this girl. . . . And so Ma's act come on, where she stepped out of this big Victrola thing. And this girl, she sang inside the box, but when she stepped out there, somebody hollered way up in the balcony, "That ain't none o' Ma Rainey! That ain't none o' Ma Rainey!" And the show closed right then. They fired us there and we stayed in the town.

The authorities detained Ma for only a week in Nashville, where she was forced to give back the jewelry. Returning to Chicago, she was reunited with the band, her spirit somewhat dimmed by the incident. [73]

Although it has often been stated that Ma Rainey seldom appeared professionally outside the South, and never in New York, she in fact played many successful engagements in Chicago, and

performed in Cleveland, Cincinnati, and other Ohio cities, Pittsburgh, Detroit, Indianapolis, Philadelphia, and Newark as well.
Because she lived in Chicago, she was not a regular Harlem performer, but did appear at the Lincoln Theater in 1923 and in March
1926; most likely she gave other local performances when she recorded in New York in 1924 and 1925.[74]

Around 1927 the New York Recording Laboratories published
The Paramount Book of Blues, which featured photographs of
Paramount recording stars and sheet music to some of their most
popular songs (figure 6). The caption to Ma Rainey's picture praises
her as "the true mother of the blues"—a pioneer who faced skeptical
New York audiences early in her career (figure 7): "She took up the
stage, as a profession . . .—not for a moment losing sight of her life
ambition—to bring to the North, the beautiful melodies of the
South—and a better understanding of the sorrow-filled hearts of its
people. After many years of appearing in theaters of the South, Ma
Rainey went to New York—astounding and bewildering the North-
erners with what they called 'queer music.' She left, and still they
did not understand. . . ."[75]

This is a sentimental distortion of the truth. As we shall see, Ma
Rainey was a fine comedienne who sang about many other emotions besides sorrow, and we have noted that she preferred Southern audiences, who gave her the most enthusiastic response. Thus it
seems doubtful that she had any burning desire, much less any
missionary zeal, to carry the message of the blues to the North. It
was true, however, that the New York black audience tended to
have more urbane, sophisticated taste than its counterpart in the
South or among new migrants to Midwestern cities. The blues were
never as popular in New York as they were in Chicago and else-
where, and indeed the blues boom was declining in New York by
1924.[76] In contrast to the *Chicago Defender's* enthusiasm for blues,
Romeo Dougherty, sports and entertainment editor of the black
New York Amsterdam News, constantly praised legitimate black musical comedies such as "Shuffle Along," while deprecating both
"those rotten and suggestive blues" and the entire tent show
circuit.[77] Thus it is quite possible that Ma Rainey's down-home
performance was not a complete success in New York, at least in
1923.

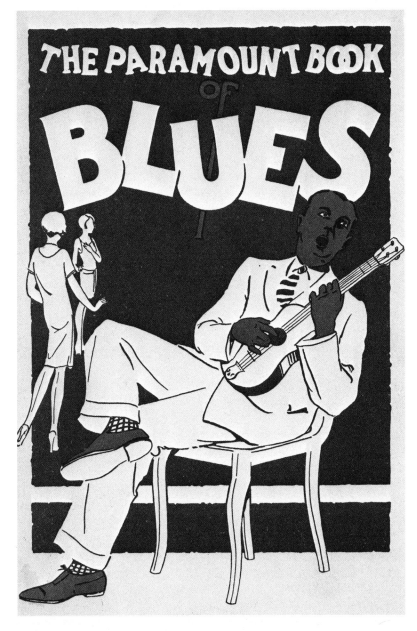

Figure 6. Cover, *The Paramount Book of Blues*. (Port Washington, Wisconsin: The New York Recording Laboratories, n.d. Courtesy John Steiner.)

Figure 7. The Gold Neck Mama of Stageland. (*The Paramount Book of Blues*, p. 9. Courtesy John Steiner.)

Largely because many people thought that she never appeared in New York, "the mystery of the two Ma Raineys" developed. Although Ma Rainey died in 1939, bluesman Big Bill Broonzy claimed to have seen her in 1945 in Atlanta, Georgia, and speculation grew that there had been two Ma Raineys, the first or "ghost" possessing the greater voice, although never recorded. In 1951, writing about the controversy for *Melody Maker* magazine, record collector Claude Lipscombe drew attention to Wilder Hobson's claim of a second Ma Rainey: "Wilder Hobson, in his book *American Jazz Music*, mentions Malissa Nix 'Ma' Rainey who sang in a Harlem cellar in the early and middle 'twenties, and who made a number of records accompanied by Fletcher Henderson and members of his band."[78] Obviously this is our Ma Rainey, again confused with her sister, Malissa; the recordings are her 1924 and 1925 sessions with Henderson's group.

To this day, a Memphis woman, Lillie Mae Glover, calls herself Ma Rainey No. 2. Now in her seventies, she recorded for the Sun label in 1953 as Big Memphis Ma Rainey, and still performs in the Memphis area, singing modern blues songs and rhythm-and-blues hits like "What'd I Say." Although her style and repertoire differ greatly from those of the first Ma Rainey, she recalls working with her namesake in Memphis during the twenties. She is most likely the woman Big Bill Broonzy described.[79]

From 1924 through 1928 the first Ma Rainey alternated T.O.B.A. and independent engagements of one and two weeks with Chicago recording dates and performances. In 1925 she was almost constantly on the road, with only two recording sessions for Paramount. At the beginning of the year she returned from her first and highly successful five-month T.O.B.A. tour to give sold-out performances in Chicago's Monogram Theater; then she was back on a Midwestern swing through Kentucky, Ohio, Detroit, St. Louis, and Kansas City. While *Variety* speculated that she was sixty, and the *Defender* guessed as high as seventy-five, she danced a vigorous Charleston with partner Broadway Fred Walker, befitting her actual age of thirty-nine. Her touring band, called variously the Five Harmony Boys, the Jazz Hounds, and the Jazz Babies, was supplemented by Cedric Odum on drums and George Hooks Tilford on saxophone; the *Defender* had high praise for her woman cornetist, Doll Jones.[80]

After another week's performance in Chicago during August, she finished the year playing the deep South, and crossed paths with Bessie Smith, whose fame had outshone her own. In September 1925, when both blues stars were appearing in Birmingham, Alabama, Bessie and her young niece Ruby Walker went to see Ma's show at the Frolic Theater.

As the ovation died down and Ma Rainey's five-piece Georgia Jazz Band began assembling in the pit, the restless audience fell silent. Suddenly someone in the balcony shouted, "The Phaaantuhm," and a growing chorus of voices from all parts of the theatre joined in.

Lon Chaney's silent movie *The Phantom of the Opera* had recently received widespread publicity. . . . When the Georgia Jazz Band started playing, the shouts grew louder as the curtain rose to reveal a giant replica of a Victrola, bathed in a bluish hue on the otherwise darkened stage.

From inside this huge cabinet there rose a familiar, gravelly voice, its delivery of a mournful song undeterred by the commotion out front. When the enormous doors of the cabinet swung open, the audience chatter stopped. . . .

Looking closer to fifty than to her real age of thirty-nine, Ma Rainey was no beauty by anyone's standards, but neither did she deserve the reputation for having—as black performers like to put it—"the ugliest face in show business." . . . With her thick straightened hair sticking out in all directions, gold caps on her huge teeth, a fan of ostrich plumes in her hand, and a long triple necklace of shiny gold coins reflecting the blue spotlight that danced on her sequined black dress, Ma was a sight to behold.

Her audience had been rude to her, but she took it with good humor; it was obvious that they loved her as much as they loved Bessie. In fact, Southern audiences sometimes preferred Ma's more earthy delivery, material, and accompaniment to Bessie's. . . .[81]

After another recording session with Fletcher Henderson's group in New York, around December 1925, Ma began the new year at Chicago's Grand Theater, where audiences lined up from the box office to the streetcar tracks. In late February 1926 Thomas Dorsey was hospitalized with what proved to be a nervous breakdown. Unable to continue directing Ma's band, he turned the piano over to Lillian Hardaway Henderson, whose husband, Ma's cornetist Fuller "Kid" Henderson, now became the bandleader. Dorsey was ill for about two years, and was not to work with Ma Rainey again until their Paramount recording sessions in 1928.[82]

Ma's all-star vaudeville revue also included her adopted son Danny, "the world's greatest juvenile stepper," who sang, danced, and did female impersonations and other comedy routines. After a tour of the Midwest that included SRO performances in Louisville, the show played the Lincoln Theater in New York. Spring found Ma Rainey appearing in Baltimore (figure 8), with a new seven-person limousine for road travel.[83] Reviewing a Detroit performance, the *Defender* praised the show's chorus girls, dramatic scenes, comedy sketches, and main attractions:

> The jazz band of five pieces appears on the stage in several select numbers that are full of harmony and glee. Hoofing by Mr. Stewart assisted by band was really good. . . . "Everything is Hotsy Totsy Now," a strut . . . by Mr. [Broadway Fred] Walker and girls is a feature that's hard to beat. Ma Rainey, famed record artist, in several of her own classy blues, was well received by the entire audience.
>
> Master Rainey delivers a real K.O. punch with his "Mama, You Done Put That Thing on Me" and created a riot. This lad is good and a bright future is in front of him as a comedian. Ma Rainey and the entire company in "Nobody's Business," a real out and out number, with each and every member doing a Charleston closes the show. The house shakes with laughter when the madam displays her Charleston dancing. . . .[84]

The year included five recording sessions for Paramount, and ended with performances in the deep South.

Around 1927, a combination of events began to bring about the decline and ultimate death of vaudeville, the T.O.B.A., and the Classic Blues style. All forms of live vaudeville had been affected by competition from radio and records, and in the cities, increasingly sophisticated and demanding black audiences found the T.O.B.A. a dated, countrified, and crude throwback to earlier minstrelsy. This response was reflected in diminished business for the circuit and

Figure 8. "With Chorus of Swift, Snappy, Soothing Songsters": Ma Rainey in Baltimore. (*Baltimore Afro-American*, 3 April 1926, p. 5.)

most other black theaters, which had their worst box office year on record in 1927. While urban black vaudeville was in a decline, the rural tent shows were still doing good business, but clearly the same acts that charmed little towns in Georgia would no longer satisfy audiences in Cleveland, Detroit, or Chicago.[85]

At first Ma Rainey was not harmed by these developments; in 1927 she made nineteen more recordings for Paramount, including new versions of her two biggest hits, "Bo-Weevil Blues" and "Moonshine Blues," both originally recorded in 1923. She again toured the South, giving both T.O.B.A. and tent show performances, and business was good enough for her to buy a thirteen thousand dollar Mack bus, emblazoned with her name. In June she went into partnership with showman Dad James, co-starring with him in the Louisiana Blackbirds revue. The troupe traveled in her bus, which carried a Kohler electric plant to light the tent show performances. But by August the brief partnership had ended amicably. Dad James then continued with the Louisiana Blackbirds, while Ma's company left the tent circuit and headed for Pittsburgh, Detroit, and Indianapolis.[86]

As if presaging the future, Paramount's 1927 Christmas advertisement in the *Defender* relegated Ma to a more peripheral position. Under a caption reading, "These famous Paramount Record stars wish you all a Merry Christmas," the ad shows a Christmas tree decked with stars that enclose photographs of Paramount's leading artists. Ma Rainey's small star is at the top, but the center of the tree is dominated by a larger picture of Ida Cox.[87]

While the competition of radio and records and the change in audience taste had subtly begun to affect the vaudeville livelihood of Ma Rainey and her contemporaries, more obvious threats were the introduction of sound to motion pictures and the increasingly monopolistic and centralized control of the entertainment business. In the early days of film, silent pictures had played on the same bill with live vaudeville acts, but with the arrival of talking pictures in 1927, live entertainment of all kinds was gradually forced out of the theaters. At the same time, as show business grew to encompass radio and motion pictures as well as records, it became more centralized and was increasingly controlled by larger corporations, whose more mainstream and Puritanical taste brought the entire entertainment industry closer to traditional white middle-class values. Those who owned and managed the entertainment business now wished to sell the music to as many people as possible by exploiting simultaneously every aspect of entertainment. Thus they encouraged the same music "product" for radio and films, which attracted a general, nationwide audience, as for dance halls, the stage, and phonograph records, which had all formerly attracted minority, specialized, or risqué tastes.[88]

Predominantly white or manipulated by white East Coast businessmen, this national audience had little or no interest in jelly rolls, mistreating men, and little low mamas, and it thought of jazz as the saccharine orchestrations of Paul Whiteman rather than the sound of Louis Armstrong. Such a public, which had probably never heard of Ma Rainey, now dominated the entertainment field. Ironically, the widespread popularity of jazz on radio and records finally appealed to the lowest common denominator of public taste and helped destroy improvised jazz as a livelihood. Brilliant musicians like Armstrong were forced to dilute their material and style in order to make a living, since well-paid jobs playing live music were more and more limited to "refined" jazz "orchestras."[89] Even within the diminishing sphere of black recording, Classic Blues singers faced new threats. Record companies now began to phase them out in favor of male country blues singers, who were promoted extensively while being paid far lower salaries than the former blues queens.[90]

Ironically, 1928 was one of Ma Rainey's finest years, both artistically and commercially, but her success was not to be sustained. She recorded twenty titles for Paramount throughout the year, once again working with Thomas Dorsey, who had recovered from his illness and found a full-time job arranging music for the Chicago Music Publishing Company (the publishing arm of Paramount). With a hit song, "It's Tight Like That," Dorsey had also begun a successful recording partnership with bottleneck guitar player Tampa Red. Except for two songs accompanied by solo piano, all of Ma's 1928 material sounds down-home and countrified, perhaps in an attempt to emulate the recent success of recordings by male country blues singers. Her various accompanists (a jug band, Dorsey and Tampa Red, Papa Charlie Jackson on banjo) contrast strikingly with the more sophisticated jazz bands on her earlier recordings.[91]

Produced by showman and tuba player Charles M. Russell, who now directed Ma Rainey's band, Ma and her Paramount Flappers began 1928 with Chicago performances and once again took their bus through the Midwest and South. The *Defender*'s Kansas City critic raved about the show's clean, hilarious comedy, Fred Walker's "hoofing" and William McKelvie's "eccentric dancing," "little Emma Smith, the girl with the diamond tooth," as well as Ma Rainey's joyous singing, "umpteen costume changes," and execution of the "Paramount Black Bottom." ("Ma Rainey's Black Bottom" was released in February of that year.)[92]

By mid-year, Ma's long-time dancing partner Fred Walker left the show to work with Ringling Brothers' circus, and trumpet player Dan Perkins replaced Russell as band director. In July, Ma and Dan Perkins paid a social call on the *Defender*'s theatrical critic, who reported, "Both look the picture of health and predicted a great season for show business." The year ended with a triumphant, month-long engagement at Chicago's Monogram Theater, where the Paramount Flappers broke attendance records with block-long lines every night, and were the biggest hit of the Monogram's season.[93]

Perhaps a more realistic sign of the times was the closing of the Chicago T.O.B.A. office, agreed on unanimously by all Midwestern and many Southern theater managers; bookings were now transferred to the main office in Chattanooga. Toby time was drawing to a close, and in one of Ma's most successful years, her recording contract was terminated. Questioned by Charles Edward Smith in the 1950s, a former Paramount executive explained that "her down-home material had gone out of fashion."[94]

Ma Rainey had perfected the Classic Blues style and showed an increasingly down-home influence during her five-year recording career, remaining faithful to a country, deep South tradition of minstrelsy, blues, and vaudeville that was fast becoming outdated. Bessie Smith, on the other hand, was far more malleable and her style tended to be more topical, more susceptible to changes in public taste.

Bessie began with a style similar to Ma Rainey's, and in 1924 she even recorded Ma's two biggest hits, "Bo-Weevil Blues" and "Moonshine Blues." Usually whenever Bessie "covered" another singer's material, she vocally demolished the original performance, but in this case, her excellent recordings do not surpass their models and some differences in interpretation are apparent.

On both tunes Ma is backed by Lovie Austin and Her Blues Serenaders, including Tommy Ladnier on cornet. This group enlivens Ma's recordings with blues feeling, while Bessie's pianist Irving Johns contributes a plodding 4/4 beat that makes his accompaniments more pop than blues. Vocally, Bessie follows Ma quite closely for most of "Bo-Weevil Blues," although she changes its coda, varying the phrasing and repeating the final line. In "Moonshine Blues," Ma sings the melody up-tempo and without embellishment, while Bessie sings variations on the melody and again changes the phrasing, emphasizing different words, syncopating the tune, and using melisma (shifts of pitch on a single syllable) at the end of almost every line.

Bessie was known as a great blues singer, and she used blues-styled musicians like Joe Smith on horn and master-of-hokum Charlie Green on trombone, but compared to Ma Rainey's repertoire, a greater percentage of Bessie's songs was non-blues, and she sang more topical and Tin Pan Alley material, like "There'll Be a Hot Time in the Old Town Tonight." She recorded more songs than did Ma Rainey—160 to 92—and her recording career spanned a longer period—from 1923 to 1933, although the peak years of her fame were identical to Ma's: 1923 to 1928. In addition, the lyrics of her songs reveal an influence of current events and trends not found in Ma Rainey's work. Perhaps Ma Rainey's only topical reference was "Titanic Man Blues," which used the Titanic as a metaphor for a lover's misfortune, and never directly mentioned the sea disaster. By contrast, Bessie recorded songs directly associated with historical occurrences: "Florida Bound Blues" with the feverish land speculation in Florida; "Back Water Blues" with the terrible misery and destruction of the 1927 Mississippi flood; "Nobody Knows You When You're Down and Out" with the Depression. Even a song like "Yes Indeed He Do!" (1928), while not concerned with current events, is definitely not a blues, and has references to "sheiks and shebas."

It is clear from listening to Bessie's final 1933 Columbia session, backed by a swing accompaniment, that she might have made the transition to swing music had she lived, but the same cannot be said of Ma Rainey. Never at ease with urban sophistication, she would have been lost in the new music, which substituted larger bands for small, hot combos, complex written musical arrangements for free improvisation, and lively, up-tempo vocals for "slow-drivin' moans."

After 1928, Ma Rainey's recording career was over and Paramount placed only one more major ad for her work in the *Defender*. But her records would be released into 1930, and she continued to tour on the ailing T.O.B.A. circuit and the tent show trail. In January 1929 producer Chick De Lotch staged a new show for her with a cast of thirty-five; the revamped Paramount Flappers then toured T.O.B.A. houses in Louisiana, Texas, Alabama, and Tennessee. In April they gave a midnight ramble benefit at Nashville's Bijou theater; proceeds went to flood victims in Alabama.[95]

Despite this apparent activity, business was becoming progressively worse for all black performers, as Salem Tutt Whitney lamented in the *Defender*:

> Except in a few places, the bottom seems suddenly to have fallen out of Colored show business. . . . From all reports, the southern route of the T.O.B.A. is shot to pieces. . . . Too many managers have been . . . satisfied to have the companies and the company managers take all the risks.
>
> . . . If the business of a house was doubtful, the company was booked on a percentage basis, with the house always getting the best of the percentage contract.
>
> If the house was doing "good" business, the company was forced to take a guarantee, with the house figuring on the big end of the contract.
>
> In other words, the road companies must share the adversities of the managers, but they were not allowed to share their prosperity. . . .[96]

By April the Flappers were no longer operating independently and now traveled with the C. A. Wortham circus, playing Arkansas, Missouri, and Kansas. In May, Ma Rainey's producer and seven other cast members quit the show because they had not been paid; considering Ma's well-known generosity to her performers, her situation must have been desperate.[97]

The rest of the year brought increasing instability and financial problems. She toured Michigan with the Wortham circus in the summer, but by November she was with the Sugarfoot Green tent show. December brought another attempt at collaboration, this time with minstrel man William Jordan, in a musical comedy, "The Arkansas Swift Foot." The forty-person cast included a fifteen-piece orchestra, chorus girls, two comedians, a novelty dancing team, a soubrette, a leading man, and Ma. After stopping in Arkansas to have the bus overhauled, the show opened in Memphis in early December. Despite reported record turnouts in Alabama and in her home town of Columbus, Georgia, the show ultimately collapsed on the road in 1930; Ma was forced to join up with Boisey de Legge's Bandanna Babies, an established show that was also meeting with hard times.[98]

Even Ma Rainey's personal talent finally fell victim to the economic and cultural changes of the early thirties. The Classic Blues style and the T.O.B.A. circuit had been severely damaged by increasing urban sophistication in audiences, the competition of talking pictures and radio, the monopolistic control of the entertainment business, the decline of vaudeville, and the development of swing music. They were given the death blow by the Depression.

Surveying the Northern end of the circuit in January 1930, T.O.B.A. manager Sam E. Reevin blamed the lack of money for poor audience attendance, but limited funds and hard times had led to a loss of morale and to increasingly substandard offerings on Toby time. Even as the theaters presented talking pictures on the same bill with live performances, producers assembled mediocre touring companies, whose slipshod performances were greeted with boos, hisses, and walkouts. "Hundreds of Performers Seek Bookings in Vain," reported the *Defender*, describing the general slump in theatrical employment, as independent bookings, night clubs, and white vaudeville were all forced to retrench.[99]

Despite several reorganizations, the T.O.B.A. was clearly foundering, and in June 1930 Reevin announced that "managers over the circuit have definitely decided that it is high time to close the doors of their theaters and give the public a rest for the summer and in the meantime allow the managers and producers of shows and vaudeville to pull themselves together, think out new ideas and build bigger and better shows for the coming fall season."[100] There was no fall season; the theaters did not reopen.

The blues boom was finally over, as Thomas Dorsey recalls:

. . . the blues ran out. It collapsed, seemingly, or the blues singers, they had nothing to do. I don't know what happened to the blues, they seemed to drop it all at once, it just went *down* and Mayo Williams and . . . all the big wigs there . . . couldn't see what was happening, and the artists were falling out because they couldn't get work. Well, there was just a slump on the record business after two or three years. And I just did get out before it happened. It just seemed like the whole thing changed around, and wasn't no work for anybody and they began to lose contact with each other. The record companies, they started publicizing some other types of music. . . .[101]

Another victim of the Depression was Paramount Records, which reduced its blues and gospel recordings from over a hundred in 1930 to about three dozen in 1931, and recorded its final race session in 1932.[102]

The impact and significance of these changes were unmistakable: in the early thirties an entire style of music (New Orleans "classic" jazz as well as the Classic Blues) died as a means of professional employment. Most artists who survived either worked on a diminished scale, and strictly for a race audience (the male country blues singers), or maintained popularity among mixed audiences through the commercialization of their style and the sheer triumph of personality (Louis Armstrong). The swing era was to belong to jazz singers like Billie Holiday and to large orchestras like Goodman's and Ellington's. Splendid and popular as they were, swing artists were performing something vastly different from what came before. More than just the close of a profession, the thirties signaled a change in the influence of black music on the mainstream of American culture. For a brief period in the twenties, the authentic black sound of New Orleans jazz and the Classic Blues swept the country, black and white alike. But by the thirties, swing became the most popular product—a style diluted with commercial influences and no longer purely black—and most remaining blues people returned to the race market.

Faced with the collapse of the blues style and motivated by sincere religious feeling, Thomas Dorsey began to write and publish gospel songs, a position he maintains to this day. (Now over eighty, he is still vigorous as head of the National Gospel Singers Convention. He has composed some four hundred religious songs, including "Precious Lord, Take My Hand," runs the Dorsey Gospel Music Publishing Company, and serves as choir director of the Pilgrim Baptist Church in Chicago.)

With the race record industry in shambles and the T.O.B.A. defunct, Ma Rainey fell back on the minstrelsy that started her career. The early thirties found her troupe in East Texas oilfield towns, booked with the Donald MacGregor Carnival. MacGregor, a native Scotsman, had once appeared as the Scottish Giant in Ringling Brothers' circus; now he served as barker for his carnival. Dressed in a kilt, he would stand outside Ma Rainey's tent, hyperbolically describing the show within; then he would introduce Ma to the audience, calling her "the Black Nightingale" and comparing her to other renowned singers.[103]

The Mother of the Blues no longer had her famous necklace of gold coins; now she wore one of imitation pearls. Vanished, as well, was her opulent touring bus; now she traveled in a house trailer built by her fellow performers: an old car chassis with a floor and sides of rough timber and a roof of waterproof canvas. She cooked her meals on a small gasoline camp stove and even canned her own vegetables. If she was still married at this time, her second husband was not with her, and her constant companion was Yellow, a concessionaire for the carnival.

But if her standard of living was diminished, her performance was as fine as ever. She sang a lovely, moving version of the old folk song "Careless Love" (which she never recorded; the tune was made famous by Bessie Smith). Her favorite blues at that time was "Traveling Blues," which she acted out in performance: "Baby, I come out on that stage, dressed down! I had on a hat and a coat and was carrying a suitcase. I put the suitcase down, real easy like, then stand there like I was thinkin'—just to let 'em see what I was about. Then I sing. You could jes' see them Jiggs wantin' to go some place else."

Her showstopper was a production number featuring the entire company onstage, singing and dancing "It's Tight Like That." Each person in the company would sing a chorus and then do a fast time-step. Ma Rainey sang the last chorus:

See that spider crawling up the wall;
He's going up there to get his ashes hauled;
Oh it's tight like that,
Be De Um Bumm,
I say it's tight like that.

Then she would pull up her skirt and dance, to the cheers and applause of the crowd.

While continuing to perform in tent shows, Ma slowly faded into obscurity in the early thirties. Pianist Sunnyland Slim remembers working with her in the autumn of 1931, touring Missouri and Arkansas. Slim quit after only a week because she paid him a dollar a day (short wages even for the Depression) and pocketed the tips herself; he had to sleep in a tent and woke up shivering.[104] Perhaps the hard times had soured her temper as well: in 1933 she appeared at the Fat Stock Show in Fort Worth, sharing the bill with Bessie Smith, and accompanied by young guitarist Aaron "T-Bone" Walker, whose memory of her differs from most accounts: "She was a heavy set dark lady and mean as hell, but she sang nice blues and never cursed *me* out."[105]

By contrast, those of her contemporaries who had made the transition to more popular music were not forgotten. Ida Cox toured the South in a successful show, "Raisin' Cain," Alberta Hunter and Edith Wilson performed in Europe, Mamie Smith's films attracted black audiences, Bessie Smith played New York's Apollo Theater, and Clara Smith's death merited a large headlined obituary in the *Defender*'s theatrical pages.[106]

In 1935, Ma Rainey's sister Malissa died. Ma then retired from performing and returned to Columbus, Georgia, to live in the home she had built for her family with her earnings; that same year her mother died. Despite economic setbacks, Ma Rainey was a good businesswoman who managed to acquire two theaters in Rome, Georgia—the Lyric and the Airdrome—which she continued to operate although she no longer performed. Like Thomas Dorsey and many former blues singers, she turned to religion in later life, joining the congregation of the Friendship Baptist Church, where her brother Thomas Pridgett, Jr., was a deacon.

In 1937, Bessie Smith was killed in a tragic automobile accident. On December 22, 1939, at the age of fifty-three, the Mother of the

Blues succumbed to heart disease and was buried in the family plot at Porterdale Cemetery in Columbus. Her death certificate lists her usual occupation as "housekeeping," an ironic end for one of the earliest and greatest women blues singers. [107]

Ma Rainey had been one of the last great minstrel artists and one of the first professional women blues singers. She had worked for Paramount, a leading race record company; she was its most-recorded female star, and along with Blind Lemon Jefferson, its most popular artist. In a brief span of five years, she made at least ninety-two records and left an indelible mark on recorded blues. More than those of her rivals and contemporaries, her records reveal and preserve for posterity the Classic Blues—that synthesis of folk blues melodies, themes, and images, and a style of black minstrelsy and Toby-time vaudeville—which was to vanish from live performance by the thirties.

In crystallizing this style, she also left memorable recordings: "Bo-Weevil Blues," "Moonshine Blues," and the blues standard "See, See Rider," to name only a few. Her style remained impervious to ephemeral changes in public taste, and she sang the blues with a sincerity and a depth of feeling seldom matched by her contemporaries. She could invest a popular tune with blues spirit through her phrasing and delivery, and she never drifted too far from her background to ignore country instruments—fiddle, banjo, kazoo, jug band, even a slide whistle and musical saw. And her rough contralto could moan in anguish as easily as it could belt out a song or cut loose with hokum humor. Her acting, dancing, and comedy cannot be fully reconstructed, but the legacy of her recordings remains, and it is to these that we now turn.

2 "Blame It on the Blues":
Ma Rainey's Style

If anybody asks you who wrote this lonesome song, (2)
Tell 'em you don't know the writer, but Ma Rainey put it on.
"Last Minute Blues" (1923)

Now that we have a basic understanding of the Paramount Wildcat—Ma Rainey—and the world in which she lived and worked, we may begin to examine what she sang, how she sang it, and what her songs meant. I propose to analyze her recorded songs as a poetic unity, discussing themes and imagery. Thematically, her recordings divide into two general categories: chapter three discusses songs directly concerned with love, which reveal a variety of responses to a love gone wrong, while chapter four deals with songs about broader issues, which comment on life humorously or cynically. But before any thematic analysis may take place, we must clarify Ma Rainey's style, the critical problems of establishing a valid text for blues lyrics, and the nature of the blues themselves. The present chapter also analyzes the structure of Ma Rainey's songs, discusses her debt to folk blues, popular blues, and black professional entertainment, and examines the development of her recordings from 1923 to 1928.

My aim is to discuss the songs as if they were a single body of poetry. Since Ma Rainey was a major but not the only composer of her recorded songs, it may be argued that no such unity exists, but this objection misconstrues the character of the blues and their relationship to the particular blues singer. In contrast to white popular songs of the twenties, usually written by individual composers who occasionally used traditional melodies, most of Ma

Rainey's recordings draw to some extent from the black folk traditions of country blues, either in the structure of the songs themselves or in her manner of performance. With roots in a common
body of folk material, many of her songs show striking similarities
in form, melody, diction, theme, and imagery, regardless of
composer.

Structurally, Ma Rainey's recordings cover a wide range of
material, but her vocal style and three-quarters of her songs were
directly influenced by the blues: over half her recordings are
twelve-bar blues, and almost a quarter more are mixtures of
twelve-bar blues and popular song forms (table 1).[1] Of this large
group of blues-influenced songs, the overwhelming majority are
popular (composed) blues. This term includes the mixtures of blues
and pop stanzas, as well as certain twelve-bar blues whose lyrics are
either completely composed or contain combinations of composed
and traditional (folk) blues verses.

Table 1. Analysis of Ma Rainey's recordings, 1923–1928[a]

Year	Blues[b]	Mixtures of blues & pop	Other	Non-blues	Total
1923	5	2	2[c]	1	10
1924	9	4	0	5	18
1925	7	1	0	2	10
1926	8	3	3[d]	7	21
1927	6	4	3[e]	4	17
1928	18	0	0	2	20
Total	53	14	8	21	96[f]

[a] Discographical information from John Godrich and Robert M. W. Dixon, *Blues and
Gospel Records, 1902–1942,* 2nd ed. (London: Storyville Publications, 1969).
[b] All are twelve-bar blues, except for "Shave 'Em Dry Blues" (1924) and "Daddy,
Goodbye Blues" (1928), which are both eight-bar blues.
[c] Two untraced recordings, probably by Ma Rainey.
[d] "Stack O' Lee Blues" is a ballad. There are also two untraced recordings.
[e] "Blues the World Forgot" Parts I and II are comedy, featuring Ma Rainey speaking with an unidentified man, and accompanied by instrumental blues. Ma also
sings two twelve-bar blues verses on Part II. "Georgia Cake Walk" is comedy,
with dialogue between Ma and a man, accompanied by a sixteen-bar non-blues
instrumental.
[f] This figure includes four untraced recordings; the total of Ma Rainey's extant recordings is 92.

Table 2. Analysis of Ma Rainey's recorded eight- and twelve-bar blues

Year	Traditional blues	Composed blues	Total blues
1923	1	4	5
1924	0	9	9
1925	1	6	7
1926	2	6	8
1927	5	1	6
1928	3	15	18
Total	12	41	53

While most of Ma Rainey's twelve-bar blues are composed, twelve are completely traditional (table 2), and folk blues stanzas, themes, and melodies appear frequently in the composed blues as well. Unlike the more urbanized and commercialized Bessie Smith, who recorded such Tin Pan Alley material as "Alexander's Ragtime Band," Ma Rainey rarely recorded purely "popular" songs: less than a quarter of her recordings show few discernible blues elements in chord structure or melody.[2] (Songs under each category are itemized in appendix A.)

The standard blues discography (John Godrich and Robert M. W. Dixon, *Blues and Gospel Records, 1902–1942,* second edition [London: Storyville Publications, 1969]) definitely attributes to Ma Rainey ninety-two titled recordings; it suggests that four additional recordings are probably hers. No doubt other unissued recordings have existed. At the Copyright Division of the Library of Congress, Washington, D. C., I have discovered copyright entries to seventy-four of Ma Rainey's songs, and lead sheets (typed copies of song lyrics) to sixty-eight. In addition, I have found "notices of use" for five other songs; these list only the publisher (Chicago Music Publishing Company) and date, and do not guarantee rights to the songs. I have also discovered information about two additional songs not listed in Godrich and Dixon: a copyright entry and the lead sheet for "Goodbye Mama Forever Blues" (written by Ma Rainey), and a notice of use for "Ma Rainey Blues" (Chicago Music Publishing Company, 1926). It seems quite possible that these are two of the missing recordings mentioned by Godrich and Dixon (see explanation in appendix B).

Most of Ma Rainey's recorded songs were originally copyrighted by the Chicago Music Publishing Company. In the following
discussion, "untraced" recordings will mean those for which no
copyright registrations or notices of use could be found. (See appendix C for copyright information and Paramount issue numbers
for all Ma Rainey recordings cited by title or quoted in this book, and
for the issue numbers of pertinent songs by other blues artists
mentioned in the text.)

Although Ma Rainey did not write all the songs she recorded,
copyright entries show her responsible for thirty-eight: sole composer of twenty-two and joint composer of sixteen. Having written
at least forty percent of her extant recorded songs (thirty-eight out of
ninety-two), she was responsible for more of them than anyone else
who contributed to her recorded repertoire.

Sixteen songs were copyrighted jointly. Four were written with
"Selma Davis," a pseudonym for Althea Dickerson, secretary to
Paramount's race records manager, J. Mayo Williams; another four
were written with J. Sammy Randall, and two with Bessie Smith.
Ma Rainey shared composer credits on one song each with William
Jackson, Lovie Austin, Hooks Tilford, Thomas Dorsey, Billie
McOwens, and J. Mayo Williams.

Thirty-three songs were composed by other people. Ten were
by Thomas Dorsey, four by Lovie Austin, and three by J. Guy
Suddoth. Remaining composers were Tom Delaney (two songs),
Lena Arrant (two), and H. Strathdene "Tiny" Parham (two), and
the following, with one song apiece: Katie Winters, C. J. Parker,
Everett Murphy, Paul Carter, Jasper Taylor, Glasco and Glasco,
Leatha McAllister, Sid Harris, Lillian Hardaway Henderson, and
George W. Thomas. Most of these people were musicians or vau-
deville performers themselves: Austin, Parham, Henderson, and
Dorsey all recorded with Ma Rainey.[3]

Popular (composed) blues dominate the songs Ma Rainey
wrote herself, just as they dominate her entire repertoire. By far the
largest number of her own compositions are twelve-bar blues, and
she always wrote more blues-influenced songs than non-blues
songs, and more twelve-bar blues than songs mixing blues with
other types of stanzas.[4] For the years 1923 to 1927, she wrote an
average of one-third of the songs she recorded, but in 1928 she

wrote almost two-thirds of them, and every song she wrote that year, save one, was blues (see table 3).

Although twelve of Ma Rainey's total recordings are traditional, the rest have at least some composed verses, and while she wrote at least one-third of her songs, at least another third was written by others; yet all are united by their blues influence. It is obvious in her vocal style, no matter what she sings, and three-quarters of her songs—regardless of composer—draw to some extent from folk blues in melody, chord progression, imagery, stanza structure, and accompaniment.

Ma Rainey reflected the folk tradition, but she was a professional entertainer as well, and we should be wary of identifying her personal views too closely with the themes of her music. Sometimes she sang about an issue which directly touched her own life—for example, the lesbianism in "Prove It on Me"—but at other times she obviously adopted a professional persona, as for example, the multiple murderess of "Rough and Tumble Blues," who contrasts so strikingly with Ma Rainey's own good-natured personality. It is more useful to assume that the female protagonist who recurs in Ma Rainey's songs represents black women and their general experience, than to draw too many direct biographical or psychological inferences about Ma Rainey; in this respect the singer is sometimes more a vehicle for the songs than someone revealing personal information.

Table 3. Analysis of Ma Rainey's sole and joint compositions (based on copyright information)

Year	Eight-bar blues	Twelve-bar blues	Blues + pop	Non-blues	Total by Ma	Total all songs
1923	0	2	2	0	4	10
1924	1	1	1	1	4	18
1925	0	4	0	1	5	10
1926	0	4	2	1	7	21
1927	0	1	2	2	5	17
1928	1	11	0	1	13	20
Total	2	23	7	6	38	96

Beyond the specific issues of Ma Rainey as composer and performer lie more general problems common to all blues scholarship: the distortion of the material and the condition of the "text." Regardless of their roots in the folk tradition, race records of the twenties were produced to make money and this commercial intent often led to changes in the original material. Songs were sometimes sensationalized to promote wider sales, as Thomas Dorsey, who composed many Rainey selections, recalls: "I wrote suggestive blues, well, you had to have something suggestive, or they wouldn't hit, in some places, the folks wouldn't want 'em."[5]

Since our only tangible evidence of Ma Rainey's art is her ninety-two extant recordings, we are dealing with only part of her work, for she was a comedienne, actress, and dancer as well as a singer. Although much of her recorded material was blues, she used other song forms in performance and did not record everything she performed. To give only two of many examples: in his poem "Ma Rainey," Sterling Brown mentions her singing "Back Water Blues," and Clyde Bernhardt recalls her singing "A Good Man Is Hard to Find," "Memphis Blues," and "Royal Garden Blues," among others which she never recorded.[6] In addition, a commerical 78 rpm recording was generally shorter than three minutes, and there is no doubt that many songs were longer in performance than in the recording studio; we have no way of knowing what verses may have been omitted, what shades of meaning lost.

By listening to a recording, we also lose the song's context; the singer's live performance might have suggested a very different interpretation. Ma Rainey apparently featured some songs within a comic vaudeville sketch which was usually too long to record. We do find one recorded example in "Gone Daddy Blues" (untraced) which chops the song down to two stanzas in order to leave room for a comic introduction, featuring Ma Rainey as an unfaithful wife who vainly tries to win back her husband after she becomes dissatisfied with her lover.

> *(Knocking on a door is heard.)*
> *Man:* Who's that knockin' on that door?
> *Ma Rainey:* It's me, baby!
> *Man:* Me who?

Rainey: Don't you know I'm your wife?
Man: Your—wife?
Rainey: Yeah!
Man: Ain't that awful? I don't let no one quit me but one time.
Rainey: But I just quit one li'l old time, just one time!
Man: You left me with that other man, why didn't you stay?
Rainey: Well, I'll tell you why I didn't stay, baby—I got home
and I had to come on back home to you!
Man: Well, I'm leavin' here today, what have *you* got to say?
Rainey: Well, all right, I'll tell you, baby.
Man: O.K. [?]

At this point Ma breaks into a mournful song, but the humorous context tempers our sympathy for the fickle wife. We may only guess how many other recorded and apparently sad songs were actually performed in a comic setting.

Distortion and editing for time considerations may have been unavoidable, but both performers and record companies engaged in more conscious censorship. Paul Oliver has noted that black blues singers often refused to repeat bawdy or controversial songs to the white folksong-hunters who first notated and published their music, and that record companies often refused to release directly obscene material. But sexually suggestive, double-entendre songs like Bessie Smith's famous "Empty Bed Blues" were issued in the late 1920s, apparently to reverse declining record sales.[7] Although none of Ma Rainey's songs is pornographic, her later recordings do explore more controversial topics: homosexuality in "Sissy Blues," recorded in 1926; and prostitution in "Hustlin' Blues," lesbianism in "Prove It on Me Blues," and sado-masochism in "Sweet Rough Man," all recorded in 1928 (see chapter three).

While Ma Rainey's recordings may be studied as one aspect of her art, an aspect which does not claim to represent her total performance, the nature of the "text" we examine poses more complex problems. Unlike published fiction, poetry, or even broadside ballads, recorded blues are heard rather than read, and their written lyrics are in part created by the critic who transcribes recordings; such transcriptions are inevitably subject to human error. Even the finest reissues are ultimately copied from fifty-year-old records, and Ma Rainey's broad Georgia accent, her lisp, and the recording techniques of Paramount Records all make the words open to several interpretations. One is tempted to take what the ear hears for truth, neglecting idiomatic black constructions or pronunciations which a critic may mishear or confuse.

My personal transcriptions of Ma Rainey's recordings have been checked against the lead sheets on file at the Copyright Division of the Library of Congress. The lead sheet is a typewritten copy of the lyrics, attached to the sheet music for a song; together these two items are called a copyright deposit. Unfortunately, the lead sheets do not always yield a pure text, because they show a bewildering range of accuracy, sometimes agreeing with my own transcriptions word for word, at other times including stanzas not on the record or omitting stanzas found on the record, and at still other times changing the meaning of a song.

During the 1920s, the only way to protect a recording of a new song was to copyright its words and music and to sue anyone who made an unauthorized copy. The record itself could not be sent to the copyright office; instead, both words and music had to be transcribed and mailed in. In general, copyright deposits were not detailed musical transcriptions used for performance; they were rather the minimum of melody and accompaniment needed to protect a song, and different record companies prepared them in different ways.[8]

The Chicago Music Publishing Company (a division of Paramount Records) copyrighted most of Ma Rainey's recorded songs, but as far as we know, it seldom published her sheet music, except for the brief booklet, *The Paramount Book of Blues*, which includes words and music to several Ma Rainey songs but is not always accurate (see figures 9, 10, 12, and 20). This practice of not publishing the sheet music to its blues songs definitely hurt both Paramount Records and its artists. In general, however, sheet music was quite rare for vocal blues recorded by black artists of the twenties.

Both lead sheets and sheet music for Ma Rainey's records were generally transcribed from the recordings; of the sixty-eight lead sheets I have discovered, only six show copyright dates earlier than their recording sessions. Although we do not know precisely how all copyright deposits were prepared, Thomas Dorsey transcribed the words and music from many of Ma's early records and probably from her 1928 sessions as well; Lovie Austin may also have done some transcribing. Dorsey worked with Ma Rainey from 1923 to 1926, and became a music arranger for the Chicago Music Publishing Company in 1928; some of the early Rainey copyright deposits show his sophisticated piano transcriptions. After a song was transcribed, the handwritten copy was given to Mayo Williams' secretary, Althea Dickerson, who then typed the lyrics on Chicago Music Publishing Company stationery and sent both lyrics and music to the Copyright Division.[9]

Ma Rainey probably did not personally prepare any transcriptions of lyrics, even for songs she wrote herself, because their lead sheets still vary from the records. For example, in the recording "Titanic Man Blues," by Ma and J. Mayo Williams, she clearly sings "Titanic," while the lead sheet insists on "Titantic" throughout. Ma may have helped the transcribers, however, which would explain why some verses not found on a recording appear in certain lead sheets: she might have included a few extra verses used in performance in order to protect them by copyright.

Songs not originally recorded by Ma Rainey present further complications: in such cases, copyright deposits were often made for the first performer; thus variations between these lead sheets and the Rainey records could occur because she misheard or mislearned a word or line, or because she decided to omit, add, or revise some lyrics in making her own recording. We cannot be absolutely sure for which songs Ma Rainey was the first performer, but we may safely assume it for all songs copyrighted in her name and for those copyrighted in Thomas Dorsey's name, since he was her pianist, arranger, and songwriter during much of her recording career. Since at least thirty-four of the ninety-two songs I have analyzed are by either Rainey or Dorsey, the lead sheets agree substantially with the recordings for at least one-third of the songs.

If a lead sheet conflicted with my transcription, I trusted my own hearing, except when the lead sheet printed entire stanzas not found on the recording. When a particular line of a recording was unintelligible, I transcribed a recording of the same song by another blues singer of that period, if such a song existed; otherwise, I trusted the lead sheet if it had been accurate for the rest of the song, and left the line blank if the lead sheet had been inaccurate for the rest of the song.

Transcribed in most cases directly from the records, lead sheets have the advantage of having been prepared when the recordings were new, without the noise and distortion found on even the best reissues. While lead sheets are clearly imperfect, they agree with my own transcriptions often enough to be a valid check for the song lyrics. Having thus established a working text of the song lyrics, we may begin to discuss how the music was performed.

Although no one has ever satisfactorily defined the blues— attempts range from "a good man feeling bad" to technical musical explanations—we may say something about the common features of Ma Rainey's style, the so-called Classic Blues, which emerged partly from black minstrelsy and vaudeville and partly from the work of anonymous male folk blues singers whose songs appeared most prolifically in the East Texas and Mississippi Delta regions after 1890. In the following discussion, I will use interchangeably the terms folk blues, traditional blues, and country blues.[10]

To the best of our knowledge, the very earliest folk blues singers were men; confined to one place by domestic jobs and the responsibilities of childcare, most women lacked the mobility of male itinerant laborers, and probably did not begin to sing blues professionally until around the turn of the century, when they appeared in traveling shows, as Ma did. Solitary, wandering men originally sang a crude, *a capella* blues, which evolved after 1890 into a twelve-bar song; they accompanied themselves on guitar and harmonica, punctuating their singing with falsetto, hollers, whoops, and shouts. Reflecting their experience, their imagery was generally rural, and most of the men were farmers or traveling laborers who performed for Saturday night parties and dances, amid dancing, loud conversation, and even fights in the audience.

Surviving folk blues singers today describe the blues as a worried feeling; traditional blues songs were generally lyric, rather than narrative, told in a highly emotional manner and from a first person point of view. The mood of folk blues often fluctuates widely from intense self-pity to exaggerated fantasy, sometimes alternating from stanza to stanza. The most common but by no means the only form of folk blues is a twelve-bar composition, built on a I IV V chord structure, and having three-line stanzas, whose first line is repeated and rhymes with the third (AAB). A characteristic melodic device in blues is the appearance of "blue notes," which are generally found in the third and seventh tones of the scale, pitched somewhere between the major and minor.[11]

"Lost Wandering Blues" (untraced) contains an example of a folk blues stanza recorded by Ma Rainey; the Roman numerals represent typical chord changes, with I as the tonic:

I   IV   I

I'm leavin' this mornin' with my clothes in my hand,

IV   IV   I

I'm leavin' this mornin' with my clothes in my hand,

V   IV   I

I won't stop movin' 'til I find my man.

David Evans has shown that the early folk blues were generally traditional, with uncomposed, conventional verses which singers recombined in various ways, adding improvised verses to form new compositions. The lyrics of these blues were generally "nonthematic": they failed to continue a single theme, scene, or story, and often presented conflicting or even contradictory images from stanza to stanza. Although many folk blues seem illogical because of these abrupt shifts in subject, image, and mood, some use a principle of contrast to convey the meaning, while others, less contradictory in nature, link stanzas through the association of related ideas. While some traditional blues were performed differently each time, others contained a "core" (a vocal melody, an instrumental part, and a single stanza or line of text containing a particularly vivid image or figure of speech), to which various floating stanzas were added.[12]

Ma Rainey's songs clearly reflect this country blues influence: twelve of her songs are traditional, and similar melodies, images, and stock phrases recur from song to song, appearing in her composed blues as well. For example, Blind Lemon Jefferson, one of the greatest and most recorded country blues singers, recorded his famous "Match-Box Blues" in 1927; the song contains the following conventional lines (the parenthetical 2 indicates that the line is repeated):

Sittin' here wonderin', will a match-box hold my clo's? (2)
I ain't got so many matches but I got so far to go.

Ma Rainey used the same image four years earlier in "Lost Wandering Blues"; she may have learned the matchbox image from Blind
Lemon Jefferson, or perhaps both discovered it independently by
listening to other singers.[13] Ma substitutes for Jefferson's final line:

I got a trunk too big to be botherin' with on the road,

which is also traditional.

The blues influence is also evident in Ma Rainey's antiphonal
accompaniments. In many of her twelve-bar blues, she sings a line
and then the instrumentalist repeats or improvises a variation on the
melody. Thus the line actually has two parts: vocal melody and
instrumental answer. It is generally believed that this arrangement
derives from the call-and-response pattern common to West African
music, in which a leader sings out a line and the chorus repeats it.

In contrast to the improvised and traditional nature of early
country blues, the Classic Blues (also called "vaudeville" or "city"
blues) were a highly sophisticated form of paid entertainment, sung
by professional women performers who had years of experience in
the tent shows and who could act, dance, and do comedy as well as
sing. Instead of being drifters or neighbors who sang for local parties
on Saturday night, the blues "queens" were self-conscious stars;
they wore makeup, elaborate gowns, and jewelry, and they appeared in traveling revues complete with a stage and footlights.
While country blues singers sang in a raspy, even noisy timbre,
slurring their consonants, some Classic Blues singers like Ethel
Waters trilled their r's, aimed for a sweet vocal timbre, and enun-
ciated their words precisely. Unlike folk blues singers, Classic Blues
singers did not accompany themselves, and their accompanists
were usually solo pianists or jazz bands composed of music hall
professionals, rather than harmonica players and guitarists.[14]

Although they were called blues singers and although most of
their songs were called blues, these women were actually much
more flexible, and Ma Rainey was representative in featuring a wide
range of material: some traditional blues, many popular (composed)
blues, an occasional ballad like "Stack O' Lee" (titled "Stack O' Lee
Blues" when she recorded it), and popular non-blues songs. She

probably sang a larger percentage of blues than any of her sister singers, with the exception of Ida Cox.

Most blues recorded by vaudeville blues singers were popular rather than folk, and were generally composed by black professional songwriters (or sometimes, as in Ma's case, by the singers themselves). Structurally, they were either twelve-bar blues, songs derived from blues, or songs mixing blues stanzas with other song forms. Popular twelve-bar blues constituted the bulk of *all* commercially recorded blues, and they were generally thematic, maintaining a clearly defined subject and a consistent point of view.[15] Those recorded by Classic Blues singers were often more narrative than lyric. Images of urban life, themes of travel to the North or of longing to return to the South, and more topical references are all found in popular blues.

Such songs could include combinations of composed and traditional lyrics. Ma's popular twelve-bar blues range from unified narratives using completely composed lyrics, like "Hustlin' Blues," to songs with traditional verses and a composed chorus, like "Jealous Hearted Blues"; in a few songs, like "Ma Rainey's Mystery Record," only a single verse is composed and the others are traditional. Since some songs are so evenly divided between composed and traditional elements, I have arbitrarily called "composed" any song showing at least one stanza of non-traditional lyrics. Under this classification, forty-one out of the fifty-three eight- and twelve-bar blues Ma recorded are composed (see appendix A).

The popular blues sung by Ma and her contemporaries also emphasize the public expression of private pain. Many of Ma's recordings begin with or contain the idea of "spreading the news" or instructions to "tell everybody, Mama's got the blues," or even to telegraph the story:

> I'm going to the Western Union, type the news all down the
> line, (2)
> 'Cause Mama's on the warpath this mornin' and I don't mind
> dyin'.
>
> "Rough and Tumble Blues"

Another common feature is to mention the song title in the final line of the last verse:

When day starts to breaking, it seems to bring good news, (2)
But it finds me broken hearted, trying to overcome these night
   time blues.

"Night Time Blues" (see figure 9)

Four of Ma Rainey's popular blues, all written by Dorsey,
contain a blues coda which substitutes an additional sung half-line
for the antiphonal instrumental ("Slave to the Blues," "Black Cat,
Hoot Owl Blues," "Victim of the Blues," and "Blame It on the
Blues"). The apparent effect is to double the line without actually
changing it or lengthening it. The words are sung at a more rapid
rate (because there are twice as many) and thus the tempo seems to
double as well. The double lines are tied together by internal rhyme,
while line endings do not rhyme. (In the following example, / /
represents the place where the vocal line would end in an antiphonal arrangement.)

Can't blame my mother, can't blame my dad, / /
   can't blame my brother for the trouble I had,
Can't blame my lover, that held my hand, / / can't blame
   my husband, can't blame my man,
Can't blame nobody, guess I'll have to blame it on the blues.

"Blame It on the Blues"

Other composed twelve-bar blues have a four-line stanza, consisting of two lines of verse and two lines of chorus, with the chorus
repeated every stanza. In this case, the first line is never repeated,
antiphonal accompaniments are usually confined to the chorus, and
all four lines are distinct, as opposed to the traditional, three-line,
AAB blues stanza. The rhyme scheme may be *aabb* (/ / indicates an
antiphonal instrumental):

I been lookin' for a man I can call my own,
Been married many times but they left my home;
Chorus:
Ah—big feelin' blues, worst I ever had, / /
I got the big feelin' blues, I mean I've got 'em bad. / /

"Big Feeling Blues"

Or else it may be *aabc:*

Figure 9. "Night Time Blues" sheet music. (*The Paramount Book of Blues*, p. 13. Courtesy John Steiner.)

See me reelin' and rockin', drunk as I can be,
Man I love tryin' to make a fool of me,
I'm leavin' this mornin', / / I'm leavin' this mornin', / /
I'm leavin', trying to find a man of my own. / /

"Leaving This Morning Blues"

Some of the more commercialized Classic Blues songs offer a non-blues introduction (usually in rhymed couplets or quatrains) explaining why the singer is blue, followed by a series of twelve-bar blues stanzas, often traditional. This mixture of blues stanzas with popular song forms was first introduced by W. C. Handy in his published blues compositions of 1912 and 1914.[16]

"See, See Rider Blues" is an example of such a mixture recorded by Ma Rainey:

I'm so unhappy, I feel so blue,
I always feel so sad;

I made a mistake, right from the start,
'Though it seems so hard to part;

Oh but this letter, that I will write,
I hope he will remember, when he receives it:

See, see rider, see what you done done, Lord, Lord, Lord,
Made me love you, now your gal done come,
You made me love you, now your gal done come.

I'm going away, baby, won't be back till fall, Lord, Lord, Lord,
Goin' away baby, won't be back till fall,
If I find me a good man, then I won't be back at all.

I'm gonna buy me a pistol, just as long as I am tall, Lord, Lord, Lord,
Gonna kill my man and catch the Cannonball,
If he don't have me, he won't have no gal at all.

"See, See Rider" is an old, traditional blues, and while the copyright calls Lena Arrant the composer, she is responsible for only the three rhymed couplets at the beginning of the song.[17] In other cases, a song begins with blues stanzas, followed by a bridge or coda consisting of non-blues quatrains or more irregular forms. (See, for example, "Cell Bound Blues," discussed in the next chapter.)

Distinct from traditional and popular blues are Ma Rainey's non-blues songs, which contain no blues elements in melody, chord progression, or stanza structure. They are generally eight- or sixteen-bar compositions derived from the ragtime tradition, and their lyrics may usually be written as quatrains:

Honey, where you been so long?
Honey, where you been so long?
Ever since the day, the day you went away,
I'm been cryin', felt like dyin', I'm not ashamed to say:

Never thought you'd treat me wrong,
Look how you have dragged me down;
I have been almost insane, but I'm so glad to see you home
again,
Honey, where you been so long?

"Honey, Where You Been So Long?"

In dealing with more irregular non-blues stanzas, I have transcribed them as closely as possible to the way the songs were sung, generally using the musical phrase of four measures as the basis of the written line: the lengths of the verse lines may differ, but in most cases each one occupies the same number of musical measures. For example, Glasco and Glasco's "Jealousy Blues" actually has a tango rhythm and is not a blues at all. (Tango rhythms were used by W. C. Handy in his "St. Louis Blues" [1914]; they appear as well in Ma Rainey's popular blues song, "Goodbye Daddy Blues.")

All the days have passed and gone, still my blues, they linger
on,
Used-to-be daddy, used-to-be daddy, your used-to-be baby's
blue, for you.

Jealousy, jealousy, that's who stole my daddy,
My lovin' sweet daddy, from me.

Jealousy, oh me, oh my, poor me,
I've got the cruel, jealousy blues.

In many ways Ma Rainey stands midway between the most commercialized Classic Blues singers and the earliest male folk blues singers. Most of her recorded songs were composed and thematic rather than traditional and non-thematic, her accompanists were often jazz bands, rather than lone guitarists, and she did not accompany herself on record. On the other hand, she wrote at least a third of her recorded songs, as opposed to such Classic Blues singers as Clara Smith and Ethel Waters, who composed almost none of their songs. Over half her repertoire was twelve-bar blues, in contrast to Bessie Smith, who recorded a much higher percentage of non-blues and popular material. In addition, traditional stanzas, images, themes, and melodies appear in many of Ma's popular blues, regardless of composer; her diction is slurred and her tone often rough, and on many songs she is accompanied by countrified instruments like jug bands or bottleneck guitar. Having discussed folk blues, popular blues, and non-blues songs in Ma Rainey's repertoire, we now turn to an examination of her recorded style.

Listeners accustomed to the lively, up-tempo rhythms of New Orleans classic jazz, which preceded the Classic Blues, and swing, which supplanted them, notice immediately how slow are the Classic Blues, and how much they subordinate the accompaniment to the vocal performance. Although a distinguishing feature of Classic Blues is their use of non-blues material from minstrelsy and vaudeville, all Ma Rainey's recordings reveal to some degree the influence of the blues in her vocal delivery.

Compared to the most commercialized Classic Blues singers, Ma Rainey has a rough, unsophisticated voice. Her heavy contralto shows little or no vibrato; it is not sweet, is often forced, and sometimes cracks. Her tone is not bright or smooth, and her diction is sometimes unclear. In addition to having a heavy Georgia accent, she lisped, and Lucien Brown, who recorded with her, claims that she used to put a dime under her tongue to keep from stuttering when she sang.[18] But her voice has enormous energy and conviction: even when she moans, she is full of life, and although her tempo is seldom fast, she is never depressing or maudlin.

Her vocal style reveals direct links to the blues. She often sings blue notes, and her characteristic technique is the moan, which evolved in blues from Southern field hollers. Ma often moans when she holds a single note, and she moans for entire lines or stanzas in several songs: on an "oh" or "oo" in "Ma Rainey's Mystery Record," "Levee Camp Moan," "Ma and Pa Poorhouse Blues"; on a hum in "Deep Moaning Blues." She moans on a single word for a whole stanza in "Slow Driving Moan" (see figure 10):

Ah Lord; Lordy, Lordy, Lord,
Ah Lord; Lordy, Lordy, Lord,
Ah Lord; Lord, Lord, Lord, Lord.

Similar stanzas appear in "Little Low Mama Blues" and "Damper Down Blues."

Her slurs and glissandos recall the earliest formation of the blues as sung speech, sweeping in between notes, eliminating the classical sense of pitch or absolute distinction between one note and the next by touching on quarter-tones and smaller microtones between notes. For example, in "Daddy Goodbye Blues" she slurs down an octave in a single syllable "-bye," and in her second recording of the popular "Bo-Weevil Blues," she divides one word into three parts, dropping a minor third in pitch and then rising a half tone: "I don't want no ma-a-an, to put no sugar in my tea." This melisma is common in blues singing, and continues to appear in the work of later singers like Billie Holiday.

Ma Rainey frequently lends variety to blues singing through her phrasing. The blues line divides naturally with a caesura in the middle, which she sometimes obviously marks with a pause for breath. (In the following example, # marks the caesura.)

I can't blame my daddy, # he treats me nice and kind,
I can't blame my daddy, # he treats me nice and kind,
Shall I blame it on my nephew, # blame it on that trouble of
  mine?

"Blame It on the Blues"

Other times the caesura is only implied, and she sings through the line without a pause:

Goin' to New Orleans to find that lucky rock,
Goin' to New Orleans to find that lucky rock,
Tryin' to rid myself of this bad luck I've got.

"Lucky Rock Blues"

But in addition to the blues, her voice reflects the years of show business experience in the traveling minstrel shows. A dramatically

Figure 10. "Slow Driving Moan" sheet music. (*The Paramount Book of Blues*, p. 14. Courtesy John Steiner.)

wide range of emotions, a sense of immediacy and empathy, and a quality of acting all distinguish Ma Rainey as a great artist, regardless of the technical estimate of her voice. She can be tragic, her voice breaking with a sob in "Oh Papa Blues" and "Morning Hour Blues." She can be disdainfully haughty, insulting her unfaithful man in "Titanic Man Blues," or broadly comic, complaining about her aching feet in "Those Dogs of Mine." She can be arch and cynical, amused at her own naiveté in "Trust No Man," or tough and aggressive, talking frankly about lesbianism in "Prove It on Me Blues," or distrusting all appearances in "Shave 'Em Dry Blues." She leers and insinuates in the racy "Hear Me Talking to You," and she coyly accepts Papa Charlie Jackson's proposition in their comic duet, "Big Feeling Blues." Sometimes her songs seem like soliloquies, intense, tragic, and deeply personal, while at other times they are clearly performances, more distanced from the material.

Like all great jazz musicians, she excels in performing good songs and triumphs over trite ones. An illuminating contrast between popular blues style and real blues feeling may be seen by considering Ethel Waters' 1921 recording of "Oh Daddy" and Ma Rainey's "Oh Papa Blues," recorded six years later.

Ethel Waters recorded "Oh Daddy," a non-blues song, in 1921; it was her second recording, and her first to appear on the Black Swan label. She was accompanied by the Cordy Williams Jazz Masters: Edgar Campbell, clarinet; Cordy Williams, violin; Fletcher Henderson, piano; probably Chink Johnson, tuba; probably Henry Brashear, trombone; and an unknown trumpet player. Her lyrics are sung in alternating twelve- and sixteen-bar stanzas:

> Just like a flower I am fading away,
> The doctor calls to see me 'most every day,
> But he don't do me no good, why?
> Because I'm longing for you,
> And if you care for me,
> You will listen to my plea:
>
> Oh daddy, look what you're doing, look what you're doing,
> Oh daddy, you with your fooling, think what you're losing,
> All my little money that I gave to you,
> It's going to make you feel awfully blue,

When you miss me, and long to kiss me,
You'll regret the day that you ever quit me;

Oh daddy, think when you're all alone:
Now you want me, just wait and see,
That there'll be someone else making love to me,
Then daddy, daddy, you won't have no mama at all.

(*Instrumental break*)

Oh daddy, look what you're doing, look what you're doing,
Oh daddy, you with your fooling, think what you're losing,
All the little money that I gave to you,
Is going to make you feel awfully blue,
When you miss me and long to kiss me,
You'll regret the day that you ever quit me;

Oh daddy, think when you're all alone:
Why do you want me, just wait and see,
That there'll be someone else making love to me,
Then daddy, daddy, you won't have no mama at all.

"Oh Daddy, You Won't Have No Mama at All"

Ethel Waters' diction is precise: she stresses her consonants,
enunciates the *d*'s in "Daddy," and even trills her *r*'s. The song is
pitched rather high (D major) and her tone quality is quite pure,
lacking any blue notes: only in the lower register does she show she
is capable of real blues singing. Cordy Williams' Jazz Masters are
hardly that, despite the presence of Fletcher Henderson at the
session: their tempo is leaden and the beat is lifeless and draggy. On
their instrumental break, the group plays a few enervated jazz riffs,
but their strongest influence seems to be popular ragtime, as revealed in syncopation played against a steady 4/4 beat, precise
articulation of eighth notes, and use of arpeggios. In all fairness, the
acoustic recording technique distorts the band's tone quality, and
Ethel Waters, who went on to make some fine blues records, was at
the start of her recording career; her clear voice still lends charm to
this recording.

The popularity of this song led to several versions in 1923 by
other women singers: Edna Hicks, Mattie Hite, and Eva Taylor and
Bessie Smith, who both recorded it as "Oh Daddy Blues." Bessie's

version is more relaxed and bluesy than Ethel's. Although every word is characteristically distinct, Bessie substitutes some dialect for Ethel's prissy circumlocutions, and simplifies the lyrics somewhat, even adding a new final verse about "baking jelly roll." Her tone, while not as pure as Ethel's, is quite sweet and open, almost yawny. Clarence Williams' piano is equally at ease and pleasant, but his beat is still squarely 4/4.

Ma Rainey recorded the song in 1927, as "Oh Papa Blues," backed by Shirley Clay, cornet; Kid Ory, trombone; Claude Hopkins, piano; and a tuba player and banjo player who have not been identified. Paramount gave Ma the composer credit on the record label; while she obviously did not write the lyrics, she transformed them through her phrasing and delivery:

> Just like a rainbow I have faded away,
> My daddy leaves me 'most every day,
> But he don't mean me no good; why?
> Because I only wish he would;
> I'm almost goin' insane,
> I'm forever tryin' to call his name:
>
> Oh papa—look what you doin', look what you doin',
> Oh papa—you caused me ruinin' [?], you caused me ruinin' [?],
> All my money, I give you,
> You treat me mean and made me awfully blue,
> Then you'll miss me, you're going to kiss me,
> You'll 'gret the day that you ever quit me;
>
> Oh papa—think when you away from home:
> I'll give you money, don't want me nohow,
> But you will love me someday, not now,
> Papa, papa, now you don't have no mama at all.
>
> Oh papa—look what you doin', look what you doin',
> Oh papa—you caused me ruinin' [?], you caused me ruinin' [?],
> All my money, I give you,
> You treat me mean and made me feel so blue,
> You're going to miss me, you'll long to kiss me,
> You'll 'gret the day that you ever quit me;
>
> Oh papa—think when you away from home,
> You just don't want me now, wait and see,

You'll find some other man makin' love to me, now,
Papa, papa, you ain't got no mama now.

Ma's diction, as always, is imprecise, and her tone is rough. She sings the melody in a lower key (B major) than does Ethel, and she forces the note on "Oh," in "Oh, papa," letting her voice break dramatically.

In her revision of the text, Ma transforms a rather trite pop song into a bluesy lyric. The hackneyed "fading flower" of the first line becomes a rainbow—a striking image; the doctor who attends the singer becomes the lover who leaves her. Ma's dialect makes her drop and slur final consonants of words, and she constantly substitutes simple vernacular expressions for the original text's phrasing. The stilted "And if you care for me / You will listen to my plea," (which Bessie retained) becomes the equally conventional but far more forceful "I'm almost goin' insane / I'm forever tryin' to call his name"; Ethel's "All my little money that I gave to you" becomes the more succinct "All my money, I give you"; and "Daddy, daddy, you won't have no mama at all" becomes in Ma's final line "Papa, papa, you ain't got no mama now." By editing and condensing the lyrics, Ma reduces the number of syllables and thus the number of eighth notes required to sing them: she simplifies both the text and the melodic line, eliminating Ethel's embellishments. In this simplification she shows some influence of Bessie Smith's earlier recording, but her energy and accompaniment both surpass Bessie's.

Both her phrasing and the band emphasize the off-beats, providing a lively tempo; the line swings with a feeling of cut time rather than plodding along in 4/4. And while Ethel's accompanists were unimaginative, with the tuba player simply marking the first and third beats of a measure, Ma's Kid Ory on trombone, Shirley Clay on trumpet, and the tuba player all complement the vocal melody with harmonic, blues-flavored riffs. Ory's trombone weeps on Ma's "Oh," and the tuba player's "dirty" tone mirrors the roughness in Ma's voice. On the chorus, the band spotlights the vocalist, building a phrase and then letting Ma sing *a capella*, "You'll 'gret the day that you ever quit me." The recording certainly lacks polish, and everyone, vocalist included, misses a note at times, but the energy, good humor, and emotion turn a popular song into a memorable performance.

Like her voice, Ma Rainey's accompanists show the influence of both blues and minstrelsy; they reveal in addition a tension between down-home and popular styles. Although her first eight recordings were with a jazz band, Lovie Austin's Blues Serenaders, country instruments appear occasionally in subsequent years and dominate the accompaniments by the end of her recording career.

Both vocally and instrumentally, Ma had strong links to Southern blues; part of the reason is geographical. Ma kept an apartment in Chicago and recorded in that city exclusively, except for two sessions with Fletcher Henderson in New York. She thus responded to an audience and drew from a pool of musicians who had migrated North directly from the deep South: New Orleans and the rest of the Mississippi Delta region. Ma used New Orleans musicians in both her touring and recording bands, including (at various times) Louis Armstrong and Tommy Ladnier on cornet, Dave Nelson on trumpet, Johnny Dodds and possibly Barney Bigard on clarinet, Al Wynn and Kid Ory on trombone, Happy Bolton on drums, and Lil Hardaway (Henderson) on piano.

On the other hand, blues singers based in New York faced an audience which had migrated from the eastern seaboard and southeastern states—the Carolinas, Washington, D.C., the Georgia coast. Chicago black music has always been "bluesier" and more indebted to the deep South than its counterpart in New York. While the Chicago-based Paramount roster included such important blues artists as Blind Blake, Ida Cox, Blind Lemon Jefferson, and Alberta Hunter (in the early part of her career) as well as Ma Rainey, the New York-based blues singers included Mamie Smith, Lucille Hegamin, Edith Wilson, and Bessie, who all sang a good deal of popular material as well as blues, and whose styles were far more sophisticated.

Although Classic Blues singers did not personally decide who would accompany them on record, whoever chose musicians for Paramount and Columbia, respectively, thought blues-styled musicians, kazoos, and jug bands appropriate to Ma Rainey, and more sophisticated instrumentalists suitable for Bessie Smith. Given these preferences, Ma's musicians are usually more down-home, are not always as consistent or technically accomplished, and show a far greater range in ability, quality, and technique.[19]

Ma's accompanists on her first Paramount session (1923) and on eight recordings of 1924 were Lovie Austin and Her Blues Serenaders, which included Austin on piano, Tommy Ladnier on cornet, and Jimmy O'Bryant on clarinet. Tennessee-born Austin had studied piano in college, and traveled the country on the T.O.B.A. circuit as the piano-playing half of the vaudeville team, Austin and Delaney. She was the house pianist for Chicago's Monogram Theater for over twenty years and an accomplished studio musician for Paramount and Vocalion. As a member of the Blues Serenaders, along with O'Bryant and Ladnier, she accompanied many of the great Classic Blues singers, including Ida Cox, Alberta Hunter, Ethel Waters, and Ma.[20] The renowned Tommy Ladnier was considered by many to be one of the greatest jazz trumpet men in the Armstrong-Oliver tradition. On cornet, he often approached Louis at his greatest, and his blues presence inspires Ma's recordings of "Bo-Weevil Blues," "Moonshine Blues," "Southern Blues," and "Lucky Rock Blues."

Except for a few solo accompanists and country duos, described later in this chapter, Ma was accompanied from 1924 to 1927 by the Georgia Band, a name applied to several different groups of varying ability, from Fletcher Henderson's musicians to unidentified instrumentalists. Ma recorded two New York sessions with Fletcher Henderson's group, in 1924 and late 1925. The earlier session produced six songs, of which three included Charlie Green on trombone, Buster Bailey on clarinet, Henderson on piano, and Louis Armstrong on cornet, among other musicians. All the songs from this session are fine, but the three including Armstrong—"See, See Rider Blues," "Jelly Bean Blues," and "Countin' the Blues"—are undisputed masterpieces. Armstrong's brilliance as a soloist has been formidable enough to obscure his sensitive work as an accompanist, strongly in evidence here. The later session, minus Armstrong, resulted in eight more sides, including some excellent work on "Yonder Come the Blues," "Titanic Man Blues," and "Stack O' Lee Blues," but the selections with Armstrong surpass the others.

Although Ma Rainey used excellent musicians on cornet, clarinet, and trombone, and although Dorsey, Fletcher Henderson,

Jimmy Blythe, Lovie Austin, and Lil Henderson often provided good ensemble piano, she rarely used solo piano, in contrast to other Classic Blues singers. This is unfortunate, since her six songs accompanied by piano are both relaxed and rhythmically interesting: "Trust No Man" with Lil Henderson, "Don't Fish in My Sea" and "Mountain Jack Blues" with Jimmy Blythe, "Dead Drunk Blues" with Claude Hopkins, and "Screech Owl Blues" and "Black Dust Blues" possibly with Eddie Miller.

If Ma Rainey's musicians show her preference for the blues, they also reveal the influence of minstrelsy and vaudeville. Two common devices from black professional entertainment are accompaniments which literally imitate the lyrics, and "hokum." In contrast to the deep feeling of the blues, hokum is lighthearted, funny, and unemotional; it includes a good deal of nonsense and humorous sexual innuendo, and its instrumentals often use clichéd phrases from popular or classical music and novelty sound effects. This sense of imitating and satirizing serious or pretentious things passed into black minstrelsy from nineteenth-century white minstrel shows, which often featured a comic blackface marching band and frequently parodied popular plays like the dramatization of *Uncle Tom's Cabin* or Gilbert and Sullivan's *The Mikado*.[21]

Sometimes Ma Rainey's musicians directly mimic the lyrics: in "Jelly Bean Blues," the clarinet laughs after Ma sings "he'll make you laugh," and weeps after "he'll make you cry." (Almost the exact same pattern appears in the middle of Bessie Smith's "Rocking Chair Blues," recorded only six months earlier.) Other times the band creates a mood suggested by the lyrics. In "Hustlin' Blues," as Ma Rainey sings about a prostitute who confronts and rebels against her abusive pimp, the band plays "villain music" from the melodrama tradition. When Ma Rainey describes a terrible storm in "Stormy Sea Blues" the band plays fragments from *Die Valkyrie.*

The band may also provide humorous sound effects. "Black Cat Hoot Owl Blues" is prefaced by a meowing cat; the band imitates the whine of a train engine in "Bessemer Bound Blues" and provides a wailing wind and crashes of thunder in "Stormy Sea Blues." Besides making direct sound effects, the accompanists sometimes play for laughs by counterpointing or even contradicting vocal lines. In "Blues, Oh Blues," a flatulent, growling slide trombone makes hash of the mournful lyrics; the bass jug is leering and bawdy in the racy "Hear Me Talking to You," and the musical saw, shrill and off-key, is slyly insinuating in "Sissy Blues," a song about a triangle between a woman, her man, and a homosexual.

Although many of Ma's recordings are accompanied by jazz bands, country instruments appear sporadically from 1924 to 1927. Down-home instrumentals may be heard on four recordings of 1924 (two by the Pruitt Twins on guitar and banjo, and two possibly by Milas Pruitt on guitar plus a second, unidentified guitarist). Ma's 1925 songs are backed by jazz bands but one tune features a slide whistle or kazoo. The 1926 sessions include a musical saw on three songs, and a country-styled guitar and violin accompaniment by Blind Blake and possibly Leroy Pickett on two; Blind Blake also appears, with piano, on one recording in 1927. In addition, during 1927 Ma recorded five traditional blues, a larger percentage of her total blues than ever before.

In 1928 the picture changes dramatically. Of the twenty songs Ma recorded that year, seventeen are twelve-bar blues, one is an eight-bar blues, and only two are non-blues songs. Although only three of the blues are traditional, the accompaniments—with the exception of solo piano on two songs—are the most countrified she ever used, and contrast strikingly with her earlier jazz bands. Her eight tunes with the Tub Jug Washboard Band have hokum accompaniment: kazoo, banjo, jug, and Dorsey's piano; another eight selections feature Dorsey on piano, with Tampa Red playing Delta-style bottleneck guitar. Her final two recordings—vocal duets with Papa Charlie Jackson—are accompanied by his strummed banjo; their comedy might have graced a minstrel stage before World War I.

The recordings with Dorsey and Tampa Red are some of her most expressive songs. Hudson Whittaker (Tampa Red) was a native of Georgia who migrated to Chicago, where he and Dorsey began a prolific joint recording career in 1928. Their first duet, the bawdy "It's Tight Like That," was an enormous popular success, and Tampa Red recorded almost ninety songs with Dorsey; he was in great demand as a studio musician and continued performing and recording well into the thirties. The liquid tone and down-home harmonics of his National steel guitar bring out the country blues aspect of Ma Rainey's voice, particularly on "Daddy Goodbye Blues" and "Runaway Blues."[22]

While Ma's vocal style had changed little in her five-year recording career, the shift in her instrumentation followed a trend shared by other women singers. In response to the popular recording success of male country blues singers like Blind Lemon Jefferson in the late twenties, some Classic Blues singers shifted to a more down-home style, and a new generation of women country blues singers began to record. For example, Lottie Beaman recorded vaudeville blues with jazz band accompaniments until 1928, when she began recording under her married name, Lottie Kimbrough, using guitar accompaniment and a more countrified singing style. Lucille Bogan recorded vaudeville blues in the mid-twenties, but began recording more down-home material in 1928 under the name of Bessie Jackson. Memphis Minnie, perhaps the greatest female country blues singer, made her recording debut in 1929, and more obscure women country singers like Mae Glover, Rosie Mae Moore, and Elvie Thomas appeared on records in 1928 and 1929.[23]

In conclusion, Ma Rainey's style shows a dynamic interaction between black professional entertainment and folk blues: the balance of components shifted during her career, first favoring one side, then the other. Bewigged and elegantly gowned, masked by greasepaint and glittering jewelry as she performed professionally on the footlit stage of a traveling show, she seems at first a far cry from the country bluesmen who preceded her.

There is no doubt she felt the influence of black minstrelsy and vaudeville in her performance and her music. Appearing on the same bill with jugglers, comedians, dancers, and variety acts, and aided by makeup, costumes, and props, she assumed a strong presence onstage, and her range of emotions was dramatically broad. In contrast to the work of country blues artists, her songs were often rigidly structured and frequently showed composed lyrics, greater narrative unity, and some infusion of popular ragtime stanzas and tunes. Some of her saddest blues were sung within comic skits, and she danced and joked as well as sang, accompanied by musicians whose style was often imitative or hokum.

But the relationship between the blues performer and her material is unique; it had no parallel in white commercial music of her day. In a stronger sense than for any mainstream white performer, the woman (or man) who sang the blues *created* the material she sang, and communicated feelings shared with her community. This quality places Ma Rainey further from the professional entertainers and actually closer to the country blues singers, whom she resembles in several ways.

As a songwriter with a strong hand in composing at least one-third of her recorded material, she was intimately involved in shaping her own lyrics and exercised a measure of control over what she sang. Like the folk blues singers, she frequently used a core of traditional lyrics, to which she added new material, and by performing her own compositions she retained at least the appearance of speaking from her own experience. Structurally, her recorded material reveals an overwhelming dominance of the blues—composed blues, to be sure, but with a great number of twelve-bar blues and a close relationship to the folk heritage. That folk blues survived and flourished in her work may be seen in the twelve-bar blues form, with its conventional chords, three-line stanzas, and rural imagery; in her rough, unsophisticated voice with its imperfect diction, blue notes, moans, and slurs; in her recording base in Chicago, a center for migration directly from the deep South; in the call-and-response technique of her accompanists; and in the final dominance of country instruments and arrangements on her recordings.

Ma Rainey's great accomplishment was to perfect a synthesis of these two modes, folk blues and black show business, in such a manner that her material in performance became the blues, regardless of its technical definition. If Ethel Waters' "Oh Daddy" began as an appealing pop sentiment, in Ma Rainey's version the song is transformed into a blues in spirit, if not in fact. Much of Ma Rainey's recorded material *was* blues in terms of structure, and in performing the rest, her rough voice and the style of her accompanists served to recast her material in the manner of the blues.

At her recording debut in 1923, she may have sounded uncouth compared to Ethel Waters, but she was more sophisticated than the early folk bluesmen: accompanied by jazz bands, she sang material that was mostly written by other people, and featured blues, mixtures of blues and pop, and non-blues songs. But by 1928 she recorded twelve-bar blues almost exclusively, wrote most of them herself or helped others write them, and was accompanied by a jug band, by bottleneck guitar, and by banjo. In five brief years, both her songs and her instrumentation moved backward historically toward their roots in the folk tradition in the deep South.

For her audience, whether listening to her records in a small Mississippi town or watching her perform in Chicago, she was a reminder, a witness, an affirmation of Southern black culture as positive, resilient, and life-affirming, even as great numbers of people were being uprooted and displaced from that culture by migration to the North. Short, heavy, and dark-skinned, she was a defiant contradiction to white standards of beauty, and her singing almost purposely rejected the lyrical polish and refined phrasing of an Ethel Waters. In a sense, the exact identity of specific song composers or the structural definition of her recordings both become irrelevant: in performing her repertoire Ma Rainey both made it hers and made it blues, uniting its most disparate components by her powerful presence and delivery.

 **"Blues About a Man**

the Worst I've Ever Had": The Themes

of Ma Rainey's Love Songs

People have different blues and think they're mighty sad,

But blues about a man the worst I've ever had,

I get disgusted and all confused,

Everytime I look around, yonder come the blues.

"Yonder Come the Blues"

(1926, possibly written by Ma Rainey)[1]

Despite some varia-
tions in structure, melody, chord progression, versification, and
rhyme scheme among Ma Rainey's traditional blues, popular blues,
and non-blues forms, all are united by common themes, which tend
to cut across categories. Thematically, the songs Ma Rainey composed herself show no striking differences from the rest of her
recorded material: blues sentiments often appear in non-blues
songs, songs which are structurally and harmonically blues sometimes deal with comic subjects, and all her songs show certain
thematic affinities to the folk blues tradition.

In *Living Country Blues*, Harry Oster collected and transcribed
two hundred and thirty examples of country blues which he had
recorded between 1955 and 1961 from live performances in Louisiana.[2] While styles and themes would naturally vary somewhat
from place to place, and while the tradition we are interested in
antedates Oster's work by fifty years, we may still accept his
findings as fairly representative of country blues subjects. Oster

divides the songs into many thematic categories: black sharecrop-
pers and the cotton crop; the relationship between plowmen and
their mules; the joys and pains of drinking; reactions to sickness and
death; poverty and economic depression; compulsive gambling; a
singer's abandonment by his woman, who takes a train to leave him;
wandering men and the trains they ride; the call of the road, especially when used to reach the big city; voodoo and magic; natural
disasters: fire, flood, and hurricane; sub-castes according to skin
color within black culture; dancing; prison and prisoners; the rebel-
lion of a young man against his parents; sexual metaphors: fruit,
baked goods, animals, insects, automobiles, and trains; reactions to
love, ranging from tenderness to murderous anger; the importance
of going to school in the modern world.[3] Apart from the references
to the city, automobiles, and school (all obviously more contemporary), these subjects have a long history in the folk blues tradition.

   Ma Rainey's songs clearly owe a debt to the country blues,
especially in songs of love, where the women's lyrics are sometimes
quite similar to the men's, and where patterns of loss, grief,
defiance, or hostility expressed toward the departed lover are frequently the same. But the Classic Blues describe a considerably
narrower range of human experience than do folk blues, although
we cannot be sure this occurs because women's activities were
actually more physically and geographically limited than men's, or
because the public and the record companies demanded from
female singers more songs about love than about other subjects. For
example, Ma Rainey has few songs about hopping freight trains (a
common theme in country blues), although she does at times express a wish to buy a ticket or ride a train, either to find a lost lover or
to escape from an unhappy affair. Whatever the motivations, the
country blues singers described many topics, while the Classic Blues
singers concentrated on love.[4]

   What do Ma Rainey's songs say about women's lives? Curi-
ously, she seems to ignore many major events: birth and mother-
hood, childhood and children, adolescence, family relations, old
age (except for an occasional mocking reference), and formal religion or church affairs. Such omissions, although more pronounced
and obvious in blues by and about women, occur in men's blues as
well, and despite the variety of subject matter observed by Oster,

the blues still concentrate on certain aspects of human experience at the expense of others.

For the most part, Ma Rainey's songs omit direct mention of race discrimination or white oppression, and they ignore lynchings and riots—at the very time when the Ku Klux Klan was at its greatest strength since Reconstruction, and when the pages of the *Chicago Defender* were filled with stories of Southern atrocities against black people. While both social and racial protest do appear in blues recorded during the thirties and afterward, most blues records of the twenties (with some notable exceptions) tend not to discuss national affairs, politics, and racial protest.[5]

Clearly, Ma Rainey's blues communicate not historical details but some essential truth about the black experience in this country: poverty, suffering, heartbreak, and pain, as well as humor, fortitude, strength, and endurance. Her great theme is the intense sexual love between men and women, and her secondary themes concern the sensual, earthy, and often rough side of life: music and dancing, drunkenness and superstition, lesbianism and homosexuality, women in prison, jealousy and murder. Most strikingly, she sings of mature, highly sexual women, in contrast to the ingénues of most white popular music of the same period. Only in traditional white ballads does the characterization of women approach the violence and sexuality of women in the blues.

In that violence lies one key to interpreting the love songs. It is by now a common assumption of the women's liberation movement that female depression is actually a state of anger turned against the self. Blues about love performed and written by black women in the twenties contain a similar sense of fury toward black men, a fury that is internalized as depression in the most passive songs, but becomes murderous rage in the most active songs.[6]

Like those of her sister Classic Blues singers, Ma Rainey's recorded songs deal with several themes, dividing generally into two categories: songs about love gone wrong, and songs which do not concern love at all, or in which love has a clearly subordinate role. Because the love songs are the most numerous, conform most sharply to the popular conception of the blues, articulate in a variety of ways the complicated relations between the sexes, and illustrate most directly a strong sense of anger, we turn to them first.[7]

Popular opinion and some blues songs themselves would have us believe that while a man is active in grief, a woman cries passively when her lover leaves:

When a woman gets the blues, she hangs her head and cries, (2)
But when a man gets the blues, he flags a freight train and rides.

"C. and A. Blues," recorded by Peetie Wheatstraw[8]

This assumption is roundly disproved by examining the ninety-two extant Ma Rainey recordings: her blues are not always blue. Only thirteen of her songs describe a woman in abject sorrow, lying in bed and weeping for her absent man, while the others cover many subjects: some are not about love at all, others discuss love and sex in highly comic and cynical terms, still others give a range of responses to a broken love affair. In addition, the songs about love allow the woman a variety of emotional stances: active, passive, depressed, or murderous, to name only a few. Finally, Ma Rainey's flair was decidedly comic, and I have already observed that many of her sad songs were undoubtedly performed within comic scenes.[9]

Perhaps the best way to understand the love songs is to see them as reactions to the central fact of women's blues: men mistreat the women who love them. Mistreating a woman may mean ignoring her, exploiting her sexually, taking her money, beating her, being unfaithful, or abandoning her for no good reason or (worst of all) for another woman. The woman's response to such mistreatment forms Ma Rainey's great theme: a black, sensual song cycle about depression, and about a woman's anger which is directed both against herself and against others. The songs reveal a range of responses, from utter misery and suicidal depression, to attempts to shake off the depression by taking action, to imagined or real revenge (including murder), to indifference toward men. They yield as well various expressions of female hostility: the woman may hate herself in the most depressed songs, or express her rage externally (killing her lover in the most violent songs), or move beyond anger to a cynical understanding of men.

In the most passive songs, the woman's fury is turned against herself, her depression is almost catatonic, and she yearns for death. The action is generally confined to the bedroom, and the image of a lone woman lying on the bed and weeping all night for her absent lover powerfully unites eros and loneliness, sleep and death, sex and misery. Many songs are almost deliberately vague about anything except the man's departure:

> Hey, people, listen while I spread my news, (2)
> I wanta tell you people all about my bad luck blues.
>
> Did you ever wake up, just at the break of day?
> Did you ever break up, just at the wake of day?
> With your arms around the pillow where your daddy used to lay.
>
> Lord—look where the sun done gone, (2)
> Hey, Lord, there's something going on wrong.
>
> What's the use of living if you can't get the man you love? (2)
> You might as well go die and give your soul to the Maker above.
>
> "Bad Luck Blues"

Although most of these lyrics are traditional, the language is strong and the images are affecting: the inversion of meaning and the image of the woman hugging an empty pillow in the second stanza, and the metaphor of the lost lover as the sun in the third.

A woman sobs all night long for a week in "Those All Night Long Blues," and Ma Rainey's composition "Daddy Goodbye Blues" combines night-time sorrow with the fear of and wish for death:

> Left my man this mornin', standin' in my door,
> When I got back he said, "I don't want you no more";
> *Chorus:* Goodbye, goodbye, Daddy, goodbye.
>
> Can always tell when you ain't treated right,
> Your man go out from you, stay out all day and night;
> *Chorus.*
>
> My daddy wrote me a letter, said, "Mama please come home,"
> When I got home last night, I found my man had gone;
> *Chorus.*
>
> Ain't got nobody to tell my troubles to,

Laid down in my bed, cried all night 'bout you;
Chorus.

Goodbye, daddy, daddy please tell me goodbye,[10]
If you don't want me daddy, Mama'll sure lay down and die;
Chorus.

"Daddy Goodbye Blues"

At other times the singer explicitly wishes for death by drowning:

I'd rather be in the river, driftin' like a log, (2)
Than to be in this town, treated like a dog.

"Weepin' Woman Blues"

or by hanging:

I'm gonna build me a scaffold, I'm gonna hang myself, (2)
Can't get the man I love, don't want nobody else.

"Little Low Mama Blues"

The woman's passivity is further emphasized by songs which describe her as a slave or a victim. Thomas Dorsey's "Slave to the Blues" shows the singer pleading with her blues and bewailing her emotional bondage to them (figure 11).

Blues, please tell me, do I have to die a slave? (2)
Do you hear me pleadin', you gonna take me to my grave.

If I could break these chains, and let my worried heart go
free, (2)
But it's too late now, the blues has made a slave of me.

Of course the slave image has a cruel historical antecedent; hopelessly trite in a white song, it evokes in a blues the most painful, bitter responses and memories of literal chains.

In "Victim of the Blues," the helpless singer is attacked by depression and conflicting feelings:

My man left this mornin', just about half past four, (2)
He left a note on his pillow, says he couldn't use me no more.

Then I grabbed my pillow, turned over in my bed, (2)
I cried about my daddy, till my cheeks were cherry red.

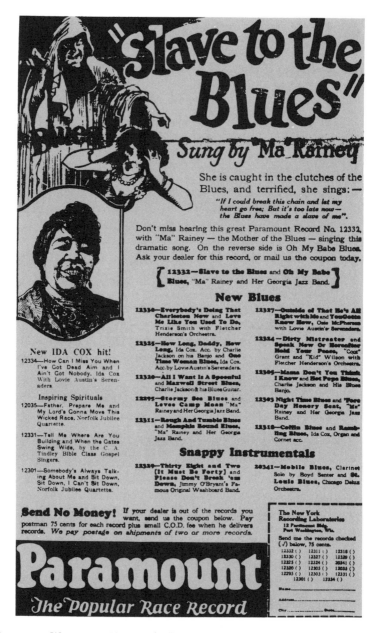

Figure 11. Woman as Victim. ("Slave to the Blues," *Chicago Defender*, 30 January 1926, Part I, p. 7.)

It's awful hard to take it, it's such a bitter pill, (2)
If the blues don't kill me, that man and mean treatment will.

Too sad to worry, too mean to cry,
  too slow to hurry, too good to lie;
That man who left me, never said goodbye,
  too worried to stay here, too sick to die;
Folks, they think I'm crazy, I'm just a victim to the blues.

"Victim of the Blues"

And in "Deep Moaning Blues," depression makes the woman sink
to the floor, unable to move:

My bell rang this mornin', didn't know which-a-way to go, (2)
I had the blues so bad, I sit right down on my flo'.

"Deep Moaning Blues"

Ma Rainey's own composition "Bo-Weevil Blues" stands apart
from these songs, combining shifting images of power and weakness, action and depression, independence and dependence, and
using a powerful symbol from black folklore to depict a proud,
lonely woman:

Hey, hey, bo-weevil, don't sing them blues no more, (2)
Bo-weevil here, bo-weevils everywhere you go.

I'm a lone bo-weevil, been out a great long time, (2)
I'm gonna sing these blues to ease a bo-weevil lonesome mind.

I don't want no man to put no sugar in my tea, (2)
Some of them's so evil, I'm afraid they might poison me.

I went downtown and bought me a hat,
I brought it back home, I laid it on the shelf,
And looked at my bed,
I'm getting tired of sleeping by myself.

"Bo-Weevil Blues"[11]

In traditional boll weevil songs, black people identify with the little,
apparently defenseless black bug who always defeats the farmer by
eating his cotton crop, despite the farmer's attempts to exterminate
him. Although the song carries this connotation, and although Ma

Rainey apparently sang some traditional verses in live performance, the weevil here is female, a symbol of proud loneliness, apart from its mate, with no mention of the farmer or the cotton.

Stanza one may be a suggestion not to grieve, because there are plenty of men around ("bo-weevil here, bo-weevil everywhere you go"), but the second stanza states the singer's intention to "sing these blues": as a solitary woman, manless and alone ("been out a great long time"), she has every right to ease her isolation with song. The traditional third stanza is used here to mean that the singer is avoiding men. "Putting sugar in my tea" was commonly understood double-entendre for sexual penetration, although Ma Rainey rarely used such double meanings and was usually more direct about sex. Here she asserts that some men are so bad-natured she fears they will betray, hurt, or even kill her. Finally, the simple but moving coda undercuts all her assertions about wanting to leave men alone. To ease her misery, the woman buys a new hat, but when she brings it home she puts it away instead of trying it on and glancing at herself in the mirror: the purchase means nothing, and has not cheered her. Instead she looks at her empty bed, and is swept by a wave of loneliness; she is tired of sleeping alone.

The beauty and power of this song arise from its conflicting images of the woman, conveying her ambivalence and shifting states of feeling: the tough, lone boll weevil, who has "been out a great long time"; the experience-wise woman who fears the complications of a new lover; the lonely, vulnerable woman whose new hat brings her no pleasure, with no one to show it to. Although this final image seems the strongest by being placed last, the lead sheet (which places the coda at the beginning of the song) indicates that the order of verses is arbitrary. Thus we are left with several pictures of weakness and strength; such differing and often contradictory images were common in the folk blues tradition.

In contrast to the songs of passive misery are another group in which the woman tries to change her depressed state by thinking, getting drunk, or having a violent tantrum. In Ma Rainey's own composition "Countin' the Blues," the woman analytically lists her sorrows by mentioning the names of blues songs; Ma Rainey recorded some of them and probably sang most of the others in live performance.

Layin' in my bed with my face turned to the wall, (2)
Tryin' to count these blues, so I could sing them all.

Memphis, Rampart, Beale Street set them free, (2)
Graveyard, 'Bama Bound, Lord, Lord, come from Stingaree.

Lord, sittin' on the Southern, gonna ride all night long, (2)
Downhearted, Gulf Coast, they was all good songs.

Lord, 'rested at midnight, jailhouse made me lose my mind, (2)
Bad Luck and Bo-weevil made me think of old Moonshine.

Lord, going to sleep now, just now I got bad news, (2)
To try to dream away my troubles, countin' these blues. [12]

"Countin' the Blues"

Turning her face to the wall—an image of despair, the turning inward instead of outward—the singer counts the blues; although she does not mention her man, he dominates the song. It is important not to take the misery too literally, since it is prefaced by Ma droning in mock-piousness, "Lord, I got the blues this mornin', I want everybody to go down in prayer—Lord, Lord."

Ma's list of songs sounds like the hit parade of 1923. Memphis, Rampart Street, and Beale Street all echo titles of compositions by W. C. Handy, self-proclaimed "father of the blues." "Memphis Blues" was one of the first blues ever published (1912), while "set them free" refers to the myth of Memphis as the supposed birthplace of the blues. "Graveyard Dream Blues," " 'Bama Bound Blues," and "Stingaree Blues" had all been popularized by recent recordings of women singers, including Bessie Smith, Ida Cox, and Alberta Hunter.

The third stanza refers both to the Southern railroad line, often invoked in blues, and to Ma Rainey's own 1923 recording of the traditional "Southern Blues" (analyzed in chapter four). "Downhearted Blues" (written and first recorded by Alberta Hunter) and "Gulf Coast Blues" (first recorded by Monette Moore), often paired, were two of the most popular blues of the year, and were recorded by many women singers, including Lucille Hegamin, Bessie Smith, Eva Taylor, and Viola McCoy, as well as by instrumental groups like W. C. Handy's Orchestra, and Fletcher Henderson and his

Orchestra. Both "Midnight Blues" and "Jailhouse Blues" were widely recorded in 1923; the most famous versions were by Bessie Smith. "Bad Luck Blues" was Ma Rainey's first recording, and "Bo-Weevil Blues" and "Moonshine Blues" were among her most popular songs.

But "Countin' the Blues" is more than just a novelty listing of recent hit tunes; it represents a response to anxiety different from moaning or weeping. When the woman itemizes her troubles (inverting the traditional "count your blessings"), her pain is expressed, becoming more bearable than when it was inarticulate. In addition, counting the blues means counting specific blues songs, other expressions of sorrows; to anyone familiar with Ma Rainey's work, this series of allusions would be shorthand for the sentiments of the other songs.

Instead of counting the blues, a woman may turn to drink to numb her misery. Released in drunkenness, her emotions often show more hostility than sorrow, and she begins to describe her fury about her man. Sometimes she is an alcoholic, tortured by a jail sentence of sixty days without a drink:

> Sixty days ain't long when you can spend them as you
>   choose, (2)
> But they seem like years in a cell where there ain't no booze.

"Booze and Blues"

She may get drunk for an entire week in Texas, partly from sorrow and partly from alcoholic need:

> I'm going to get drunk, just one more time, (2)
> 'Cause when I'm drunk, nothing's gonna worry my mind.

"Dead Drunk Blues"

Or else she may get so riotously and comically drunk that the police haul her off to jail, as in the dialogue of "Blues the World Forgot." But Ma Rainey's most powerful statement about drunkenness occurs in the composition she wrote herself and used to begin her stage performance: "Moonshine Blues," which combines blues verses and irregular, couplet-like stanzas (figure 12).

Figure 12. "Moonshine Blues" sheet music. (*The Paramount Book of Blues*, p. 10. Courtesy John Steiner.)

I been drinkin' all night, babe, and the night before,
But when I get sober, I ain't gonna drink no more,
'Cause my friend left me, standing in my door.

My head goes 'round and around, babe, since my daddy left
    town,
I don't know if the river runnin' up or down,
But there's one thing certain is Mama's going to leave town.

You'll find me reelin' and a-rockin', howling like a hound,
I'll catch the first train that's runnin' Southbound,

Oh stop, you hear me say, stop, right to my brain,
Oh stop that train, so I can ride back home again.

Here I'm upon my knees, play that again for me,
'Cause I'm about to be losin' my mind, boys,

I can't stand up, I can't sit down,
The man I love has done left town;

I feel like screamin', I feel like cryin', Lord,
I've been mistreated, folks, and don't mind dyin';

I'm goin' home, I'm going to settle down,
I'm goin' stop my running around;

Tell everybody that come my way,
I got the moonshine blues, I'll say,
I got the moonshine blues.

"Moonshine Blues"

In contrast to the songs previously discussed, "Moonshine Blues" describes violent, angry emotions: no longer does the singer cry about her daddy until her cheeks are cherry red; instead she is "reelin' and a-rockin', howling like a hound." The image of the baying hound is probably intentionally comic, since misery and humor are seldom distinct in Ma Rainey's work. In a similar fashion, the woman in "Mountain Jack Blues" expresses the traditional wish to bray like a jackass to call her lover back, as if human words were not enough:

If I could holler, just like a mountain jack, (2)

I'd go up on the mountain, call my good man back.

"Mountain Jack Blues"

Throughout "Moonshine Blues" the woman's misery is described violently and physically as loss of control and near-insanity: her head spins; she cannot tell which way the river runs; "I can't stand up, I can't sit down"; "I feel like screamin', I feel like cryin' "; and she fantasizes standing on the railroad tracks, begging the homebound train to stop for her. The song ends with a wish to calm down and lead a quieter life, but also to broadcast her blues, which include rage, sorrow, and self-hatred, as well as the more positive desire to return home, back to a place of refuge.

If "Moonshine Blues" sees anxiety as near-craziness, "Stormy Sea Blues" by Thomas Dorsey describes the singer's emotional upheaval as a terrible storm on the ocean. The song was quite popular with audiences and Ma Rainey often used it to begin her show, acting out the scene: "Well, she'd sing it and then do whatever you'd do in a storm. The storm start to raining, you try to run here and run there and get away, and you become excited. Oh yeah, she had a good act there. Yeah, that was one of the best numbers on the show for a long time."[13] Despite an uninspired accompaniment, complete with crashing thunder, whistling wind, and phrases from Wagner's *Die Valkyrie*, the lyrics convey a powerful metaphor for psychic turmoil:

Rainin' on the ocean, it's storming on the sea, (2)
The blues are in that shower, storming down on me.

I hear thunder, I'm caught out in the storm, (2)
Man I love done packed his grip and gone.

I hear the wind blowin', I'm left here all alone, (2)
That storm won't be over, till my daddy come back home.

I see the lightnin' flashin', I see the waves a-dashin', I'm tryin'
to spread the news,
I feel this boat a-crashin', I'm tryin' to spread the news,
My man has done with me, and left me with the stormy sea
blues.[14]

"Stormy Sea Blues"

The anguish of broken love is here symbolized by a raging storm. The lightning and thunder evoke the violence of the woman's fear and confusion, the pouring rain and watery waves are her tears, and the storm—her emotional state—will subside only if the man returns. His departure is flatly stated—he simply packs his suitcase and leaves, without explanation—and the song focuses on the woman's reaction. Both the lyrics and the intense vocal energy with which Ma Rainey sings "I see the lightnin' flashin' " (so that we see it flash as well) reveal great emotional upheaval, although the singer never actually screams or cries, allowing the storm to express her feelings.

"Yonder Come the Blues" stands between the most depressed and more active songs; the singer attempts to take action, but the blues are so inescapable that anything done to avoid them simply brings them on.

I worry all day, I worry all night,
Every time my man comes home he wants to fuss and fight;
When I pick up the paper to read the news,
Just when I'm satisfied, yonder come the blues.

I went down to the river each and every day,
Cryin' to keep from trying to do myself away;
I walked and walked till I wore out my shoes,
I can't walk no further, yonder come the blues.

Some folks never worry [phrase obscure] all right,
Poor me, lie down and suffer, weep and cry all night;
When I get a letter, it never bring good news,
Every time I see the mailman, yonder come the blues.

Go back blues, don't come this way,
Only give me something else besides the blues all day;
Every man I've loved, I've been misused,
And when I want some lovin', yonder come those blues.

People have different blues and think they're mighty sad,
But blues about a man the worst I've ever had;
I get disgusted and all confused,
Every time I look around, yonder come the blues.

"Yonder Come the Blues"

This song is dominated by worry and anxiety; the lover who fights with the woman in the first stanza is symptomatic of her problems. Since every stanza ends with the same refrain, the blues become expected and inevitable by the end of the song. Almost every final line begins with a temporal clause ("just when . . . ," or "every time . . . "), setting up an expectation and dashing it with the refrain, "yonder come the blues." The repetition of the refrain strengthens the sense of personification, an inheritance from folk blues: the blues become an entity that stalks the singer throughout the stanzas, and surrounds her by the end of the song.

Although the woman is clearly depressed, at least she articulates her feelings quite precisely and attempts a series of strategies to defeat the blues. She may give the traditional response by crying all night, but she also tries to escape the blues by reading, walking, or hoping for the mail, and her mood seems more frustrated, disgusted, and angry than self-pitying.

In contrast to the most depressed group of songs, in which the woman passively wails about her fate, gets drunk, or has hysterics, is a second group in which she takes physical action. She may leave town and wander aimlessly, go South to her family, seek a fortune-teller to reclaim her man, or directly follow him and attempt to get him back. All these songs are characterized by an emphasis on action rather than emotional excess. Less self-indulgent, the woman is in motion, on the streets instead of crying in her bed; she has left the house, moving away from solitary depression to activity in the world.

The aimless walking to escape depression in the second stanza of "Yonder Come the Blues" is repeated in several songs. The narrator of "Dream Blues"[15] dreams that her man is unkind; she packs her clothes and walks the streets all night—a common motif in folk blues. In "Traveling Blues" (untraced) she buys a train ticket, unsure of her destination but certain she must leave: "I'm dangerous and blue, can't stay here no more." In "Morning Hour Blues" (untraced) she visits the grave of her old lover because her new one is cruel, and in "Lucky Rock Blues"[16] she wanders to New Orleans, seeking the lucky rock—a voodoo charm—to help forget her man and to change her luck.

"Lucky Rock Blues" anticipates another and more positive response to the broken affair: return home, back to the South. Since many popular blues were composed during a period of extensive black migration from the rural South to Northern cities, they often assign both areas a double nature. The North—a land of great opportunity and liberation—is also full of chaotic uncertainty and disrupted emotional ties, while the South signals terrible repression but remains a central, maternal image of home, roots, and family—a refuge from confusion and disappointed love in the North (see figure 13).

"South Bound Blues" (which is not a blues) describes perhaps an all-too-common scene: a man travels North, seeking better opportunities and bringing his country woman with him, only to abandon her there.

> Yes, I'm mad, my heart's sad,
> The man I loved treated me so bad;
> He brought me out of my home town,
> Took me to New York and threw me down.

> Without a cent to pay my rent,
> I'm left alone, without a home;
> I told him I would leave him and my time ain't long,
> My folks done sent the money, and I'm Dixie bound.

> *Chorus:*
> You done me wrong, you throwed me down,
> You caused me to weep and to moan,
> I told him I'd see him, honey, some of these days,
> And I'm going to tell him 'bout his low down dirty ways.

> Done bought my ticket, Lord, and my trunk is packed,
> Goin' back to Georgia, folks, I sure ain't comin' back.
> My train's in the station, I done sent my folks the news,
> You can tell the world I've got those Southbound blues.

> "South Bound Blues"

Alone and penniless, the woman remains remarkably rational. She is clearly shaken and hurt, but not immobilized by grief, and writes her family for the train fare home. Although she vaguely threatens to confront her lover some day, the song is more a soliloquy or a monologue addressed to a sympathetic listener than a direct rebuke to the man.

Figure 13. Sentimentalized Yearning for the South. ("Slow Driving Moan," *Chicago Defender*, 22 October 1927, Part I, p. 7.)

In contrast to this almost casual assertion of independence, "Lawd, Send Me a Man Blues" (untraced) paints a grimmer picture. Abandoned by her man in a strange place, the destitute woman has no recourse but to find a man—any man—to pay her rent.

Who gonna pay my board bill now?
Had a good man, and he turned me down.
Landlord comin', knock on my door,
I told him my good man don't stay here no more.

.   .   .   .

Oh, Lord, send me a man,
I'm the loneliest woman in the land.
I work hard both night and day,
Tryin' to find a good man to come my way.

Send me a zulu, a voodoo, any old man,[17]
I'm not particular, boys, I'll take what I can.
I've been worried, almost insane,
Oh Lordy, send me a man,
Oh Lordy, send me a man.

Without funds, possibly without family, the woman appeals to God to save her from starvation, barely mentioning love or desire; a man is an economic necessity. Significantly, however, her reaction is pragmatic rather than suicidal; having analyzed the situation, her response is to pray for someone to help pay her bills. She is at least beginning to focus on possible solutions, rather than simply wailing about the problem.

In many blues, men mistreat women financially as well as emotionally. Several songs show the woman generously giving all her money to her shiftless lover, who promptly abandons her, or, even worse, spends her money on other women. The working woman in "Misery Blues" (untraced) is cheated out of her savings by a man who promises that she may stop working when they marry.

I love my brownskin 'deed I do,
Folks [phrase obscure] know you tell me a thing or two,
I'm going to tell you what I went and done,
I gave him all my money just to have some fun.

He told me that he loved me, loved me so,
If I would marry him, I wouldn't need to work no mo';
Now I'm grievin' all the time,
Just because I didn't know that he was lyin'.

.   .   .   .

I'm such a fool, down in my shoes,
I've got those misery blues;
I've got to go to work now, get another start,
Work is the thing that's breaking my heart;
I've got those mean old misery blues.

Moving beyond the songs of aimless wandering, anxious flight, or return to the South, are a group of songs in which the woman actively attempts to find her man. In the traditional blues stanza, she goes South, looking for her lover or for just any man, and not intending to return unless she finds him.

I'm goin' down South, won't be back till fall, (2)
If I don't find my easy rider, ain't comin' back at all.

"Weepin' Woman Blues"

"Easy rider," an image of a good lover, compares the motions of intercourse to the rocking movement of riding a mule. In the country blues and black folk traditions, "easy rider," "C. C. Rider," and "see, see rider" are often interchangeable phrases. The singer also searches for her lover in "Slow Driving Moan" (untraced):

I've rambled till I'm tired, I'm not satisfied, (2)
Don't find my man, gonna ramble till I die.

Often the singer resorts to superstition and magic to find her lover, for fortunetellers, both male and female, are found in Ma Rainey's blues:

I went to the gypsy, to have my fortune told, (2)
She said, "Doggone you, girlie, doggone your bad luck soul."

I turned around, went to the gypsy next door, (2)
She said, "You'll get a man anywhere you go."

"Southern Blues"

In " 'Fore Day Honry Scat," composed by Billie McOwens and Ma Rainey, the woman consults a fortuneteller after her man leaves her, but the gypsy has bad news:

He said, "Your man has caught that 'fore day scat,
And left here tipping like a Maltese cat;
Poor girl I know your man has done you wrong,
Hit high timber, now he's long, long gone."

" 'Fore Day Honry Scat"

"Honry" (spelled "honory" on the record label and pronounced "hawn-ree") is ornery, "tipping" meant sneaking away on tiptoes, and the " 'fore day scat" was a common expression for slipping out before daybreak.[18]

One woman actually finds her man, only to face rejection once again:

I'm leavin' this mornin' with my clothes in my hand, (2)
I won't stop movin' till I find my man.

I'm standin' here wonderin' will a matchbox hold my
     clothes? (2)
I got a trunk too big to be botherin' with on the road.

I went up on the mountain, turned my face to the sky, (2)
I heard a whisper, said, "Mama please don't die."

I turned around to give him my right han', (2)
When I looked in his face, I was talkin' to my man.

Lord, look it yonder people, my love has been refused, (2)
That's the reason why Mama's got the lost wandering blues.

"Lost Wandering Blues"[19]

The dramatically realized situation makes this song stand out from other blues, despite its conventional opening. The matchbox image has a long blues history (see chapter two), and the woman's search for her man almost ends in suicide (cf. "I feel like goin' on a mountain, jumpin' into the sea," in "Deep Moaning Blues" by Ma Rainey).

But the finest expression of the wandering woman theme is found in Ma Rainey's own composition, "Walking Blues."

Woke up this morning, up this morning, with my head bowed
down, hey, hey, hey,
Woke up this morning, with my head bowed down,
I had that mean old feelin', I was in the wrong man's town.

Mailman's been here, mailman's been here, but didn't leave no
news, hey, hey, hey,
Mailman's been here, but didn't leave no news,
That's the reason why, Mama's got the walkin' blues.

Walked and walked till I, walked and walked till I almost lost
my mind, hey, hey, hey,
Walked and walked till I almost lost my mind,
I'm afraid to stop walking, 'cause I might lose some time.

Got a short time to make it, short time to make it, and a long
ways to go, Lord, Lord, Lord,
Short time to make it, and a long ways to go,
Tryin' to find the town they call San Antonio.

Thought I'd rest me, thought I'd rest me, I couldn't hear no
news, Lord, Lord, Lord,
Thought I'd rest me, I couldn't hear no news,
I'll soon be there, 'cause I got the walkin' blues.

"Walking Blues"

Here the reason for the break and the man's departure is not even
mentioned, and the song describes the woman's monotonous, ex-
hausting days on the road and her fruitless requests for information.
Like "Bo-Weevil Blues," "Walking Blues" shows indomitable will
and strength rather than weepy self-pity; the singer states her
complaints in a matter-of-fact way, and ends the song hoping she
will soon reach San Antonio and her man.

Finally, songs of despair and songs of the woman in motion
give way to songs in which she gets angry at the general situation,
the other woman, or the man himself. While her rage was suppressed and transformed into self-hatred and frenzied tantrums in
the first group of songs and into anxious walking and searching in
the second, in this group it is articulated as the woman admits her
sexual jealousy, abuses the man verbally, leaves him, takes revenge
on the other woman, plans revenge on the man, or (most desper-

ately) murders him. Significantly, as the woman's awareness and fury increase, so do her feelings of independence and self-worth. Gone or diminished are self-hatred and thoughts of suicide; the woman instead boasts of her sexual attractiveness and skill, and increasingly acts rather than being acted upon.

Furthermore, the tough aggression of women in these songs is balanced by a corresponding weakness and passivity in their men. Miserable suicidal wishes, hysterical tantrums, and frenzied searches are transformed into warnings, insults, and guns turned against men, while the vaguely described but all-powerful male mistreaters of the more depressed songs become sinking ships, passive sex objects, and victims of murder.

In the mildest of the confrontation songs, the woman asserts her rights, refuses to take ill treatment, or actually makes demands on her lover. Several songs describe her anger as sexual insecurity and jealousy. In "Jealous Hearted Blues" the singer proclaims her rights and warns other women away from her man (figure 14).

You can have my money and everything I own,
But for God sakes leave my man alone;
Chorus:

'Cause I'm jealous, jealous, jealous hearted me,
Lord, I'm just jealous, jealous as I can be.

It takes a rocking chair to rock, rubber ball to roll,
Takes the man I love to satisfy my soul;
Chorus.

Got a range in my kitchen cooks nice and brown,
All I need is my man to turn my damper down;
Chorus.

Gonna buy me a bulldog to watch him while I sleep,
To keep my man from making his midnight creep;
Chorus.

"Jealous Hearted Blues"

Although the song is copyrighted in Lovie Austin's name, all stanzas but the first are traditional. The lyrics are dominated by sexual insecurity, expressed in the chorus with five repetitions of "jealous." The second stanza describes intercourse with a variant of

Figure 14. Sexual Jealousy. ("Jealous Hearted Blues," *Chicago Defender*, 14 February 1925, Part I, p. 7.)

the traditional expression "rock and roll," and the pleasure in "satisfy my soul" is sexual as well. The third stanza is also erotic, for when the blues talk about food, they generally mean sex. The kitchen range that "cooks nice and brown" is a genital image, comparing the heat of the stove to sexual passion, and "cooking" to intercourse (cf. many blues verses about baking, baking biscuits, and baking jelly roll). Her stove is ready, but needs the man to turn her damper down—to take care of her sexual needs, to quench the flame of love through intercourse.

The metaphor of turning down the damper for sexual stimulation is common in blues, appearing directly in songs such as Ma Rainey's own "Damper Down Blues" (untraced), and indirectly in songs such as Clara Smith's recording of "Kitchen Mechanic Blues," which celebrate the man's skills. While not declaring total sexual independence, this stanza does describe a sensuality apart from the man, which he completes, but does not create: her range may cook "nice and brown," but she still needs the man to finish cooking.

Despite the woman's sexual bragging, she still expects the man to slip away while she is asleep ("make his midnight creep"), and the watchdog symbolizes her fear. Thus "Jealous Hearted Blues" is based on a suspicious guarding of the good lover, who may leave if the woman relaxes her vigilance for a moment.

Of course such suspicion is not confined to women: the singer loses her man through jealousy in "Jealousy Blues," and in "Explaining the Blues," her lover abandons her for the same reason:

Whole world seems against me, if I could just explain, (2)
Man I love has left me, because I called another man's name.

Too sad to whistle, too broken-hearted to sing, (2)
Let me explain the trouble a jealous man will bring.

"Explaining the Blues"

The love seems so tenuous, and the man so sure of being betrayed, that a hint of wrongdoing, a name called in the night, is enough to send him packing.

In other songs the jealousy is transformed into argument, as the woman directly confronts her lover. "Memphis Bound Blues" concerns a woman who tries to keep her man from leaving by pointing out that someday he will need her.

> You got your grip to leave me, you're going to leave your home
> today, (2)
> But drop it for a minute, and listen to what I've got to say.

> You can fly up high, you can spread your feathers all
> around, (2)
> But when you get in trouble, you got to fall back to the ground.

"Memphis Bound Blues"

Her appeal is unsuccessful, however, and in the last verse he leaves, heading for Memphis.

If the singer was pleading in "Memphis Bound Blues," she is aggressively demanding in "Hear Me Talking To You," whose lyrics are credited to Ma Rainey:

> Ramblin' man makes no change in me,
> I'm gonna ramble back to my used-to-be—ah
> *Chorus:*

> Hear me talkin' to you—I don't bite my tongue,
> You want to be my man, you got to fetch it with you when you
> come.

> Eve and Adam, in the Garden takin' a chance,
> Adam didn't take time to get his pants, ah
> *Chorus.*

> Our old cat swallowed a ball of yarn,
> When the kittens was born, they had sweaters on;
> *Chorus.*

> Hello, Central, give me 609,
> What it takes to get it in these hips of mine;
> *Chorus.*

> Grandpa got, grandma told,
> He says her jelly roll was 'most too old;
> *Chorus.* [20]

"Hear Me Talking To You"

Her stance is bold and assertive as she confronts her man: "*Listen* to me; I'm not holding anything back ('don't bite my tongue'). If you want to be my lover, you have to be good, potent, and sexy with me ('fetch it with you when you come')." The song is a series of jokes and cynical observations about sex, all united by the demanding, aggressive chorus and accompanied by a leering jug band. Both the tune and some of the lyrics are derived from the "Hesitation Blues," a song performed by many country blues singers and popularized by W. C. Handy's 1915 "Hesitating Blues."

In the first stanza, the woman's lover leaves her, but she is indifferent, and will return to her former man. The second stanza jokes about original sin, Adam and Eve's nakedness, and their haste to make love, while the third ridicules the birth process. The final stanzas become cruder: the fourth is a proposition over the telephone (609 may be code for 69) and the last, one of Ma Rainey's few references to old age, mocks Grandma, whose genitals and sexual technique ("jelly roll") were too old to interest Grandpa.

In another group of songs the narrator stops coercing and starts either abusing or planning to abuse her man. The woman in "See, See Rider Blues" writes an angry, accusing letter to the man who trifled with her until his steady woman returned:

> See, see rider, see what you done done, Lord, Lord, Lord,
> Made me love you, now your gal done come,
> You made me love you, now your gal done come.[21]

"See, See Rider Blues"

Wounded by her lover's infidelity, the singer in "Don't Fish in My Sea" scornfully rejects him in explicit physical terms and resolves to give up men:

> If you don't like my ocean, don't fish in my sea, (2)
> Stay out of my valley, and let my mountain be.

> Ain't had no lovin' since God knows when, (2)
> That's the reason I'm through with these no good triflin' men.

But the last stanza undercuts her claims of independence by showing regret at losing him:

Never miss the sunshine, till the rains begin to fall, (2)
You never miss your ham, till another mule's in your stall.

"Don't Fish in My Sea"

The conventional sentiment, "You never miss the water till the well runs dry" is given a franker interpretation: "ham" could mean both the penis and someone inadequate as a lover, while sexual betrayal was traditionally expressed by the phrase, "I know there's another mule kicking in my stall."

The woman in "Toad Frog Blues" actually threatens to leave:

You're gonna look for me some morning, but baby I will be long
    gone, (2)
Then your low-down ways will bring those mean blues on.

.   .   .   .

I can't get no higher, sure can't get no lower down, (2)
I got the toad frog blues, and I'm sure Lordy Dixie bound.

"Toad Frog Blues"

Sometimes the threat is delayed: you may not want me now, but when you do I'll reject you and laugh in your face:

You made me love you, you made your mama care,
You demanded money, I didn't scold,
When you asked for lovin', I gave you my soul;
I'm cryin' now, but still I feel somehow,
I'll be laughin', dearie,
When you got the broken soul blues.

"Broken Soul Blues"

And the singer details her man's wrongs in "Oh Papa Blues," vowing that some day he will find her in bed with another man:

Oh papa—think when you away from home,
You just don't want me now, wait and see,
You'll find some other man makin' love to me, now,
Papa, papa, you ain't got no mama now.

"Oh Papa Blues"

But for sheer rage, nothing can top "Black Eye Blues."

> Down in Hogan's Alley lived Miss Nancy Ann,
> Always fussin', squabbling with her man;
> Then I heard Miss Nancy say,
> "Why do you treat your gal that way?"

> I went down the alley, other night,
> Nancy and her man had just had a fight;
> He beat Miss Nancy 'cross the head,
> When she rose to her feet, she said,

> "You low down alligator, just watch me sooner or later,
> Gonna catch you with your britches down.
> You 'buse me and mistreat me, you dog me around and beat
>   me,
> Still I'm gonna hang around.

> "Take all my money, blacken both of my eyes,
> Give it to another woman, come home and tell me lies;
> You low down alligator, just watch me sooner or later,
> Gonna catch you with your britches down, I mean it,
> Gonna catch you with your britches down."

> "Black Eye Blues"

In the chorus, Nancy Ann threatens to catch her lover when he is defenseless, presumably when he is making love to another woman ("Gonna catch you with your britches down"); the image implies a spanking or some other kind of discipline to follow. Although he treats her cruelly, she remains with him, apparently less from love or sexual satisfaction than to bide her time, luring him into false confidence in order to achieve a sweeter revenge.

The tone of "Black Eye Blues" is consistently comic, from the low-life setting in Hogan's Alley to the diction: "fussin', squabblin' with her man," which sounds like angry chickens; "low-down alligator"; and "gonna catch you with your britches down." In addition, the tune is not a blues; it is played up-tempo, and the mood is almost lighthearted. Although the physical pain is unquestionably real—he blackens her eyes and hits her so hard that she falls down—the violence is casual, almost humorous, described in the third person rather than first, like a vaudeville sketch.

At some point, however, even insults are not enough, and the woman decides to leave her man. In "Oh My Babe Blues," composed by Ma Rainey, the narrator wavers between leaving and reconciliation, and the break seems only temporary.

Tell my dad I won't be home tonight, oh my babe,
My heart aches and I'm not treated right,
My heart's down, it's a shame, and I just can't call his name,
Still I'll ask to let me come back home.

.   .   .   .

I'm feeling now I'm sorry we have to part, oh my babe,
'Cause you tried to break my achin' heart;
But someday you will say, "Come back home, baby and stay,"
Then I'll know my daddy wants me back home.

"Oh My Babe Blues"

"Bessemer Bound Blues" describes a more serious rupture: the singer returns home to Alabama because living with her man is impossible. In the past, she had been willing to compromise and make hyperbolic sacrifices, but her patience has limits:

Papa, sugar papa, how come you do me like you do? (2)
I'll do anything you ask me, tryin' to get along with you.

I'll wade in the water, walk through the ice and snow, (2)
But from now on papa, I won't be your dog no more.

"Bessemer Bound Blues"

The woman in "Farewell Daddy Blues"[22] asserts her love for her man, but demands fidelity:

I'm wild about my daddy, I want him all the time, (2)
But I don't want you, daddy, if I can't call you mine.

He has left her and returned several times, and the penultimate stanza describes her frustration at being a sexual commodity: the woman with a lover is attractive to other men, while the lonely woman seems to drive them away.

Since my man left me, others can't be found, (2)
But before he left me, the other men was hanging around.

In the last stanza she leaves him permanently:

So fare you well, daddy, someday you hear bad news, (2)
When you look for your mama, she gone with the farewell
blues.

"Titanic Man Blues," by Ma Rainey and J. Mayo Williams,
offers the ultimate insult: the singer abandons her lover and taunts
him with her new man.

Everybody fall in line, going to tell you about that man of mine,
It's your last time, Titanic, fare thee well;
Now you've always had a good time, drinking your high-priced
wine,
But it's the last time, Titanic, fare thee well.

Rigged you up like a ship at sea, but you certainly made a fool of
me,
It's the last time, Titanic, fare thee well;
It's a hard and a bitter pill, but I've got somebody else that will,
It's the last time, Titanic, fare thee well.

Now I won't worry when you're gone, another brown has got
your water on,
It's the last time, Titanic, fare thee well;
Now I'm leavin' you there's no doubt, yes, mama's gonna put
you out,
It's the last time, Titanic, fare thee well.

"Titanic Man Blues"

This is one of the few Ma Rainey songs in which the woman wrongs
her man, although even here she is motivated by his infidelity. The
governing metaphor is, of course, the sinking of the ocean liner
Titanic, which had already been celebrated in a ballad. Characteristically, Ma avoids explicating the topical reference, using it only to
imply that the lover's fortunes have literally sunk. In addition, the
public shock at the catastrophe of the "unsinkable ship" is analo-
gous to the overconfident man's numbed realization that he has
been supplanted. Many years later Leadbelly used a variant of Ma's
version in his own Titanic recording, which concentrates on the
historical events.

As in many popular blues, the song begins with a public statement of private woe: like a drill sergeant, Ma Rainey lines up her audience and lectures them about her former lover. Although she spent money on him, and bought him fancy clothes ("rigged you up like a ship at sea"), he was unfaithful ("you certainly made a fool of me"). But he will never betray her again, declares the chorus, because she is leaving him. In the second and third stanzas she tortures him with her new lover: " . . . I've got somebody else that will [please me more than you did]"; and "Another brown has got your water on" (another brownskin man is sailing in my ocean —making love to me).

At the end of the song she throws him out of the house, with apparently little heartbreak. In fact, throughout this song Ma Rainey sounds lively and cheerful, and the "fare thee well" at the end of each line must be sarcastic: after all this abuse, she emphatically does *not* wish him well. Here the woman is independent, confident, almost cocky, sure of her power over men: if one lover fails her, she simply puts him out and finds another.

But sometimes her fury is too powerful to be satisfied by merely abusing or leaving him, and must be directed against either the other woman or the man himself. In Ma Rainey's lyrics to "Louisiana Hoodoo Blues" the narrator's solution to infidelity is to hex the other women away, and charm her lover back to her.

Going to the Louisiana bottom to get me a hoodoo hand, (2)
Gotta stop these women from taking my man.

Down in Algiers where the hoodoos live in their den, (2)
Their chief occupation is separating women from men.

The hoodoo told me to get me a black cat bone, (2)
And shake it over their heads, they'll leave your man alone.

Twenty years in the bottom, that ain't long to stay, (2)
If I can keep these tush-hog women from taking my man away.

So I'm bound for New Orleans, down in goofer dust land, (2)
Down where the hoodoo folks can fix it for you with your man.

"Louisiana Hoodoo Blues"

"Hoodoo" is the original term for that body of magic and superstition popularly known as voodoo; for several centuries its known center of activity was Algiers, a town across the river from New Orleans. The hoodoo hand is a powerful love charm composed of the victim's personal effects (armpit or pubic hair, fingernail parings, and even pieces of skin or shreds of underwear) combined with parts of bats or toads and ashes and feathers from symbolic birds. Wrapped in a small conjure bag, the mixture is either carried personally (to affect the victim when in his presence), buried under his doorstep, or hidden in his bed or hearth. Likewise, the black cat bone is a potent charm to return a straying lover.[23]

The singer will spend twenty years in the Louisiana Delta if she can separate her man from "tush-hog" women, a term usually used to mean violent men, mean-tempered as wild boars.[24] In this song it means rough, angry women, and carries the connotation of voracious sexuality as well. The "goofer dust" in the final stanza is dirt taken from a grave, widely used in hoodoo spells. Similarly, in Ma Rainey's recording of "Black Dust Blues,"[25] the singer steals another woman's man, and the wronged woman threatens the singer, who then finds black dust spread around her doorstep and experiences bizarre sickness.

"Louisiana Hoodoo Blues" is especially striking for the passivity of the man; utterly manipulated, he is caught between the charms of the tush-hog women on one side and the singer, aided by the sorcery of the hoodoos, on the other. Like the man in "Titanic Man Blues," he seems to have little awareness of his actual situation.

Although hexing the other woman may keep a lover faithful, at times only murdering her will satisfy the singer's lust for revenge. In "Wringing and Twisting Blues" the woman learns of her man's infidelity from a fortuneteller.

I had my fortune told, and the gypsy took my hand,
And she made me understand that I had lost my man,
She said I had the wringin' and the twistin' blues.

I twisted my nervous hands and then I shook my head,
Went home and jumped in bed, and then I heard what she said,
And now I've got the wringin' and the twistin' blues.

He told me that he loved me, I found it wasn't true,
'Cause he's done gone and left me, I've nothing else to do.

But if I know that woman, that caused my heart to moan,
I'd cook a special dinner, invite her to my home.

I had some green cucumbers, some half-done tripe and greens,
Some buttermilk and cod-fish, some sour kidney beans.

If she eats what's on my table, she will be graveyard bound,
I'll be right there to tell her, when they put her in the ground,
"You're the cause of me having those wringin' and a-twistin'
blues."

Get a paper in the morn, and you will read the news,
Where a poor gal's dead and gone, with the wringin' and
twistin' blues,
Now I've got the wringin' and the twistin' blues.

"Wringing and Twisting Blues"

Less lyric and more narrative than a true blues, the song has a strong sense of drama and its scenes are graphically realized, from the fortuneteller's revelation to the singer's emotional reaction. Even the dinner the woman feeds her rival is minutely described, revealing her pleasure in the variety of sickening, rotten foods. "Wringin' and twistin'," the vivid image of her anger and agony of betrayal, has several connotations besides anxiety. In Ma's recording of "Sweet Rough Man," it expresses sexual passion:

My man, my man, Lord, everybody knows he's mean, (2)
But when he starts to lovin', I wring and twist and scream.

In other blues records, it means wild dancing and sexual carousing.[26]
In the bridge of the song, the woman indirectly castigates her man for his lies, although she significantly takes action against the other woman. Since we are not certain she knows who her rival is, the revenge should probably be taken as a strong wish and possibility rather than a firm reality. The high point of the vengeance, whether actual or only imagined, comes when the singer confronts the corpse of her rival as it is lowered into the grave. In the very next stanza a "poor gal" dies from the wringing and twisting blues, but

although this reference seems to indicate the rival, the lead sheet places this stanza before the bridge and thus before any mention of the revenge murder. In addition, we are never told that the rival has the wringing and twisting blues, but only that the singer has them. Finally, the possibility that the murder is only a fantasy implies that the "poor gal" probably refers to the singer herself, and thus the song combines an angry, aggressive revenge vision with a more depressed and self-hating wish for death.

In Ma Rainey's composition "Rough and Tumble Blues" (figure 15) the singer is a multiple murderess:

> I'm going to the Western Union, type the news all down the line, (2)
> 'Cause Mama's on the warpath this mornin', and I don't mind dyin'.

> My man's so good lookin' and his clothes fit him so cute, (2)
> I cut up his box-back and bought him a struttin' suit.

> Then every little devil got on my man's road, (2)
> Mama Tree Top Tall and Miss Shorty Toad.

> Tree Top Tall give a stomp as I stepped in the door, (2)
> Miss Shorty Toad and my man was shimmying down to the floor.

> I got rough and killed three women 'fore police got the news, (2)
> 'Cause Mama's on the warpath with the rough and tumblin' blues.

"Rough and Tumble Blues"

The thematic unity and narrative development of this song mark it as a composed blues. Its opening stanza announces the angry tone of the song, while in succeeding stanzas the woman indicates her control over the man by replacing his formal, dignified "box-back" suit with a "struttin' suit"—a more flashy garment with a long-tailed coat, often worn in minstrel shows. The man's relationship to the singer is clearly dependent, and his "struttin' suit" implies the peacock, self-conscious sexuality of a man whose woman provides the means to display him. But the gift has unwelcome results: all kinds of women pursue him—women tall and

Figure 15. Taking Revenge on the Other Woman. ("Rough and Tumble Blues," *Chicago Defender*, 31 October 1925, Part I, p. 7.)

slender as trees, and women short and squat as toads. When the narrator catches her man in a compromising position at a party, she goes berserk and murders her rivals until the police restrain her. Her fury spares the man, however; she apparently cannot bring herself to hurt him.

As in "Louisiana Hoodoo Blues," the man is described as passive, weak, fickle, childlike in his appeal ("his clothes fit him so cute"), and hardly responsible for his actions, attracting strong women who battle for him. By contrast, his woman is characterized by great aggression: "on the warpath" evokes rampaging Indians; "rough and tumblin' " describes her violence as she wrestles her rivals to the floor and kills them: her response to betrayal is murderous anger rather than sadness.

Finally there is a group of songs in which the woman focuses her rage directly on her lover. Sometimes she threatens murder, as in "See, See Rider Blues":

> I'm gonna buy me a pistol, just as long as I am tall, Lord, Lord, Lord,
> Gonna kill my man and catch the Cannonball, [27]
> If he don't have me, he won't have no gal at all.

At other times she attempts to win him back by threatening him or eliminating her competition:

> See me reelin' and rockin', drunk as I can be,
> Man I love tryin' to make a fool of me;
> I'm leavin' this mornin', I'm leavin' this mornin',
> I'm leavin', tryin' to find a man of my own.

> When I get through drinkin', gonna buy a Gatlin' gun,
> Find my man, he better hitch up and run;
> 'Cause I'm leavin' this mornin', I'm leavin' this mornin',
> I'm going to Kansas City, to bring Jim Jackson home.

> I give him all my money, treat him nice as I can,
> Got another woman, wait till I find my man;
> Lord, I'm leavin' this mornin', leavin' this mornin',
> I'm leavin', tryin' to find a man of my own.

> I went up Eighteenth Street, found out where the other woman stays,

Cure my man of his triflin' ways;
'Cause I'm leavin' this mornin', honey I'm leavin' this mornin',
I'm goin' to Kansas City, to bring Jim Jackson home.

I walked down the street, didn't have on no hat,
Asking everybody I see where my daddy's at;
I'm leavin' this mornin', honey I'm leavin' this mornin',
I'm leavin', tryin' to find a man of my own.

"Leaving This Morning"

"Jim Jackson's Kansas City Blues" Parts I and II was an immensely
popular song composed and recorded by Jim Jackson in 1927; the
initial recording sold so well that a sequel, Parts III and IV, was also
released. "Leaving This Morning" is an answer song, which takes
advantage of the earlier recording's popularity.

Again the singer is fierce and violent: armed with a machine
gun, she boasts about getting her man back, but it is not clear
whether she will "cure my man of his triflin' ways" by using the
Gatling on him or on the other woman. Once again, rage rather than
sorrow predominates, directed toward not only the other woman
but the lover as well.

If "Leaving This Morning" indirectly threatens murder, "Sleep
Talking Blues" demands death as the price of infidelity.

Do all your talkin' daddy, before you go to bed, (2)
If you speak out of turn, your friends will hear of you being
    dead.

When you talk in your sleep, be sure your Mama's not awake,
    (2)
You call another woman's name, you'll think you wake up in a
    earthquake.

.   .   .   .

I warned you, daddy, nice as a mama could do, (2)
You hear me talkin' to you, undertaker will be visiting you.

"Sleep Talking Blues"

As in many of these aggressive songs, the threat is directly
addressed to the man, rather than spoken by a lone woman. What

she demands is the appearance, not the act, of fidelity: she will take action if she hears him mention another woman, with the implication that what she doesn't know won't hurt her. Jealous, violent, and threatening, she describes her rage as an earthquake, and backs up her threat in the final stanza. Despite all the fury, the song expresses great tenderness, especially in the way Ma Rainey lingers over the line "I warned you, daddy, nice as a mama could do."

In the most violent songs the woman completely loses control, murdering her man in a fit of anger or in self-defense, but with at least a hint of revenge. In Ma Rainey's lyrics to "Broken Hearted Blues," the woman kills everyone in sight:

> Good morning, Judge, Mama Rainey's done raised sand, (2)
> She's killed everybody, Judge, she's even killed her man.

"Broken Hearted Blues"

In "Cell Bound Blues," another Rainey composition, the woman gradually realizes that she is a murderess.

> Hey, hey, jailer, tell me what have I done? (2)
> You've got me all bound in chains, did I kill that woman's son?
>
> All bound in prison, I'm bound in jail, (2)
> Cold iron bars all around me, no one to go my bail.
>
> I've got a mother and father, livin' in a cottage by the sea, (2)
> Got a sister and brother, wonder do they think of poor me?
>
> I walked in my room, the other night,
> My man walked in and begin to fight;
>
> I took my gun in my right hand, said,
> "Hold him, folks, I don't wanta kill my man."
>
> When I did that he hit me 'cross my head,
> First shot I fired, my man fell dead.
>
> The paper came out and told the news,
> That's why I said I got the cell bound blues;
> Hey, hey, jailer, I got the cell bound blues.

"Cell Bound Blues"

The third stanza seems archaic and outside the blues idiom in its reference to family and a cottage by the sea; it is more likely interpolated from a ballad, and its mention of family emphasizes the woman's isolation. Unlike the revenge of "Sleep Talking Blues," the murder in this song seems unpremeditated, and committed in self-defense. The lead sheet, however, reads "I'm going to kill my man" instead of "I don't wanta kill my man," which certainly alters the meaning of the song. Although the recording clearly says "I don't wanta kill my man," the alternate version may sometimes have been used in performance, giving the murder more volition.

In sharp relief to the entire range of songs previously discussed—concerning misery, drunkenness, hysterics, searching for the man, revenge, and murder—are four songs so distinctive for their outspoken and frank statements of female aggression or unconventional sexuality that they must be discussed separately. "Sweet Rough Man" describes a sado-masochistic relationship; "Hustlin' Blues," a prostitute's liberation from her pimp; "Sissy Blues," a bizarre triangle involving a man, a woman, and a homosexual named "Miss Kate"; and "Prove It on Me Blues," a proud declaration of lesbianism. Each takes a theme to which traditional responses may be expected and varies it, with striking results.

"Sweet Rough Man" may be Ma Rainey's most violent and most erotic blues.

I woke up this mornin', my head was sore as a boil, (2)
My man beat me last night with five feet of copper coil.

He keeps my lips split, my eyes as black as jet, (2)
But the way he love me, makes me soon forget.

Every night for five years, I've got a beatin' from my man, (2)
People says I'm crazy, I'll explain and you'll understand.

My man, my man, Lord, everybody knows he's mean, (2)
But when he starts to lovin', I wring and twist and scream.

Lord, it ain't no maybe 'bout my man bein' rough, (2)
But when it comes to lovin', he sure can strut his stuff.

"Sweet Rough Man"

In this classic expression of the "hit me, I love you" tradition of masochistic women's songs, the singer's lover is a bootlegger who beats her not with his hands or a switch, but with five feet of copper tubing he uses for distilling. This bizarrely exaggerated symbol of both phallus and whip indicates the magnitude of his brutality. The images of abuse are explicit and repellent: her head is sore as a boil (connoting infection as well as pain), her lips are cracked, her eyes blackened from perpetual beatings. In contrast to some accounts by abused women, there is no hint in this song that the victim believes she has somehow provoked or deserved her treatment; she even realizes that her behavior is unhealthy by normal standards. Yet she confidently asserts that we will understand when she explains: yes, he is mean, but his loving makes her "wring and twist and scream"—words which also describe reactions to a beating.

In this song, more than any other in Ma Rainey's material, making love is an expression of rage, and violence is an expression of love; metaphorically, brutality is the orgasm of love, and further love-making compensates for the beating. Here is the most extreme polarization between the sexes in all Ma Rainey's songs: in contrast to the female aggression and male passivity in the group of songs just discussed, "Sweet Rough Man" shows a cruel, virile man abusing a helpless, passive woman. Both black and white popular songs reveal many variations on this theme, in which the lover is embraced in spite of (or even because of) his cruelty, although the white versions were generally expurgated or watered down until recently. [28]

To dismiss this song as merely sensational, masochistic, and thus sick, is to miss the point entirely: the combination of eros and violence affects all levels of human society, regardless of race or class. We cannot know for certain how much freedom Ma Rainey exercised over the choice of her material, or to what extent she agreed with the sentiments of "Sweet Rough Man," but throughout the rest of her recorded repertoire, brutality is rejected and excoriated. In addition, the words were composed not by Ma Rainey herself but by a male songwriter, and the song was recorded in 1928, when increasingly suggestive and sensational material appeared in blues recordings.

Yet the graphic violence, the strong, repulsive images, and the woman's unshakable and unnerving conviction that she experiences overwhelming sexual passion all make "Sweet Rough Man" unforgettable. Of all Ma Rainey's songs, it is closest to a masturbatory fantasy, where the man's attractiveness lies equally in his power as a lover and his physical strength in beating the woman. It is as if she could not have one without the other: brutality and eros are here inseparably wed. The explosive sexual power and graphic, often sickening physical images of "Sweet Rough Man" lift it apart from more common and generalized refrains of "my man treats me mean"; it is the most explicit and powerful description of sexual brutality in Ma Rainey's repertoire.

In contrast, "Black Eye Blues" treats a similar theme broadly and comically, distancing us from the experience by placing the narrative in third rather than first person and by using comic diction and setting. Its violence is Punch-and-Judy, and its characters are funny: the man who is always "fussin', squabblin' " with Nancy Ann and who hits her " 'cross her head," blackening her eyes, is no match for the sadist who whipped his woman with five feet of copper tubing. In addition, Nancy Ann's response to the brutality is as active as the other woman's is passive: she yells at her lover, insults him, and vows revenge. Finally, the beating in "Black Eye Blues" is condemned and repudiated, rather than eroticized and craved by the woman.

To move from "Sweet Rough Man" to "Hustlin' Blues" is to leave a passive woman for a more aggressive figure: the black prostitute. Written by Thomas Dorsey and Malissa Nix, the song describes a streetwalker who surrenders her pimp to the police and quits her trade.

> It's rainin' out here and tricks ain't walkin' tonight, (2)
> I'm goin' home, I know I've got to fight.
>
> If you hit me tonight, let me tell you what I'm going to do, (2)
> I'm gonna take you to court and tell the judge on you.
>
> I ain't made no money, and he dared me to go home, (2)
> Judge, I told him he better leave me alone.
>
> He followed me up and he grabbed me for a fight, (2)
> He said, "Girl, do you know, you ain't made no money to-
> night."

Oh Judge, tell him I'm through, (2)
I'm tired of this life, that's why I brought him to you.

"Hustlin' Blues"

Although the lyrics of this song are composed rather than traditional, the scene changes abruptly several times—a stylistic device common in folk blues. The first stanza is the streetwalker's soliloquy in the rain, gearing up her courage to face her pimp. The second stanza shows her confronting and threatening him, perhaps for the first time, and in the remaining stanzas she testifies against him in court. We are not informed how or whether she escaped a beating and brought the pimp to justice, but most likely she simply informed on him, and her casual decision in the rain not to work this one time became a resolve to escape the pimp and her old life. "Hustlin' Blues" shows great courage and strength of will, contradicting the stereotype of the hustler who is chained to her pimp by love, dope, or weakness. The very ease with which she breaks free indicates that the song may be more fantasy than reality; nevertheless it strikes a blow for dignity. She has so much contempt for the pimp that she refuses to speak to him in the final scene, instead telling the judge to inform him that she is through with prostitution. If she loves the pimp, she does not indicate it in the song, and seems to have no regrets about her actions.

In contrast to the independent, assertive prostitute of "Hustlin' Blues," the woman in Ma Rainey's own composition "Sissy Blues" is bewildered and driven half-crazy when her man leaves her for a homosexual. The rough instrumental accompaniment for this song includes a whining, insinuating musical saw.

I shimmied last night, the night before,
I'm going home tonight, I won't shimmy no more, ah
Chorus:
Hello, Central, it's 'bout to run me wild,
Can I get that number, or will I have to wait awhile?

I dreamed last night I was far from harm,
Woke up and found my man in a sissy's arms;
Chorus.

Some are young, some are old,
My man says sissies got good jelly roll;
Chorus.

My man's got a sissy, his name is Miss Kate,
He shook that thing like jelly on a plate;
Chorus.

Now all the people ask me why I'm all alone,
A sissy shook that thing and took my man from home;
Chorus.

"Sissy Blues"

Songs of unconventional sexuality were not unusual in the blues and in live black entertainment. There were several recorded variants of the lesbian song "Bull Dyker's Dream" (sometimes disguised as "B. D.'s Dream" or "B. D. Women"), and "freak shows" and drag shows—evenings set aside for homosexuals, lesbians, and transvestites—were common in many Harlem and Chicago nightclubs.[29] In some ways "Sissy Blues" describes the traditional theme of sexual jealousy: a woman driven to distraction by her man's attentions to her rival. The twist, of course, is that the rival is a homosexual (possibly a transvestite), and Ma Rainey must have sung this with a certain amount of irony, considering that she sometimes preferred her own sex to men. In the chorus, the singer frantically attempts to telephone her man, but the line is always busy, and she moves from happiness (dancing the shimmy, dreaming freely) to the shocked realization that he has a male lover.

In the third stanza the man insists that "sissies got good jelly roll"—a recurring image with several meanings. In the blues, almost everything connected with sex may be symbolized by jelly, jelly roll, or baking jelly roll—from the male or female organs to sperm and the secretions of the vagina to the sensual sweetness of sex. In this case it also means "sissies are good lovers." When Miss Kate shakes "that thing like jelly on a plate" (an obvious reference to "I Wish I Could Shimmy Like My Sister Kate"), he moves provocatively (cf. "shake that thing" used in many blues to refer to both men and women). The last stanza finds the woman abandoned by her lover in favor of the sissy, who apparently has a sweeter jelly roll than she does. As in the more passive blues songs discussed earlier in this chapter, the woman contents herself with feelings of anxiety ("It's 'bout to run me wild"), making no attempt to seek revenge on the man or the sissy.

A woman also prefers her own sex in perhaps Ma Rainey's most assertive song, "Prove It on Me Blues," which is not a blues at all, and is accompanied by the raspy, flatulent Tub Jug Washboard Band.

Went out last night, had a great big fight,
Everything seemed to go on wrong;
I looked up, to my surprise,
The gal I was with was gone.

Where she went, I don't know,
I mean to follow everywhere she goes;
Folks said I'm crooked, I didn't know where she took it,
I want the whole world to know:

They say I do it, ain't nobody caught me,
Sure got to prove it on me;
Went out last night with a crowd of my friends,
They must've been women, 'cause I don't like no men.

It's true I wear a collar and a tie,
Make the wind blow all the while;[30]
They say I do it, ain't nobody caught me,
They sure got to prove it on me.

Say I do it, ain't nobody caught me,
Sure got to prove it on me;
I went out last night with a crowd of my friends,
They must've been women, 'cause I don't like no men.

Wear my clothes just like a fan,
Talk to the gals just like any old man;
'Cause they say I do it, ain't nobody caught me,
Sure got to prove it on me.

"Prove It On Me Blues"

Written by Ma Rainey, the song combines lesbianism with sexual bragging and the deserted lover theme; it is extraordinary for the singer's proud affirmation of her sexual preference and her contempt for the rest of the world. She graphically spells out her relationship: when her lover leaves she sings, "I didn't know where she took it," and "it" means sexuality, physical body, and skill at love-making (cf. "Fetch it with you when you come," in "Hear Me Talkin' to You"). Admitting that the world condemns her ("Folks said I'm crooked"), the singer does not care, boasting, "I want the whole world to know." She qualifies her assertion by saying that people will have to prove their suspicions, implying that at least until then she will do what she pleases: dress like a man in a collar and tie, talk to women aggressively and flirtatiously, and "do it"—sleep with women.

Her stance in this song is proud, tough, and swaggering, as she dares the world to find evidence, admitting just enough (hating men, while adopting mannish dress and actions) to entice the gossips. This is a powerful statement of lesbian defiance and self-worth, and since Ma Rainey was herself bisexual, it may reflect some of her own feelings: as noted in chapter one, we know that she had sexual relationships with women, possibly including Bessie Smith. Paramount's *Defender* ad for this record depicts a massive Ma Rainey, wearing a man's hat, vest, jacket, and tie, flirting aggressively with two slender, femininely dressed women, as a policeman looks on suspiciously (figure 16).

Moving beyond this statement of indifference to men is a song which comments cynically on life and love with a great distance and detachment. "Trust No Man" by Lillian Hardaway Henderson seems to be a lesson delivered by an experience-hardened teacher rather than a personal statement of private sorrow or rage, as Ma Rainey lectures other, more inexperienced women:

I want all you women to listen to me,
Don't trust your man no further'n your eyes can see;
I trusted mine with my best friend,
But that was the bad part in the end.

Chorus:
Trust no man, trust no man, no further than your eyes can see,

I said, trust no man, no further than your eyes can see;
He'll tell you that he loves you, and swear it is true,
The very next minute he's going to trifle on you;
Ah—trust no man, no further than your eyes can see.

Just feed your daddy with a long-handled spoon,
Be sure to love him morning, night and noon,
Sometimes your heart will ache and almost bust,
That's why there's no daddy good enough to trust.

.   .   .   .

"Trust No Man"

All men are shifty, declares this song, including the one you
love: they say one thing, mean another, and betray you with your
own best friend. The controlling image is of a hawk-eyed woman,
whose glance makes a circle of suspicion: within, a man may tenta-
tively be trusted, but once outside, he is capable of anything. In the
second stanza, women are advised to be affectionate to their men,
while remaining suspicious and cautious ("feed your daddy with a
long-handled spoon").

"Trust No Man" implies that it is naive to think that any action,
no matter how extreme, can hold a man, and Ma Rainey seems to tell
women: don't blame yourself when your man leaves you; that's
his nature. Thus she encourages women to stop castigating themselves, accept the realities of relations between the sexes, and shift
the blame and anger from themselves to the men who abandon
them. The woman who is suspicious, who understands men, will
not be as wounded as the unsophisticated girl who believes she can
keep her man through her actions. Beneath the surface of this
tough, cynical song smolders great resentment against fickle men,
but it is expressed with comic distance from the actual pain of
betrayal, as seen in Ma Rainey's spoken comments on the second
chorus: "Hey—take Ma Rainey's advice! Don't trust *no* man. I mean
not even your *own* man! All right now! You'll all been [word
obscure]. Don't trust nobody! See where it got me, don't you? He
sure will leave."

The song thus deals comically, rather than sadly, with the same
suspicion, disappointment, and heartache found in the more serious songs. But now the audience has changed, and the singer has

Figure 16. Lesbianism. ("Prove It on Me Blues," *Chicago Defender*, 22 September 1928, Part I, p. 7.)

moved from soliloquy, through seeing other women as rivals and confronting her man, to a state in which she finally addresses herself to women and attempts to advise them.

Ma Rainey's recorded songs thus display a range of choices for the woman wronged in love. She may submerge herself in grief, crying hysterically, longing for death, and getting drunk, or she may attempt some form of action: aimless walking, returning home to the South, searching for her man, or asking a fortuneteller's aid in finding him. Her depression may be transformed into anger, as she admits her sexual jealousy, argues with her lover, threatens to leave him, finally abandons him, and taunts him with a new man. She may take revenge on the other woman, physically threaten her man, and even kill him. Or else she may descend into a pathological state of masochism, assert her rights against a pimp, lose her man to a "sissy," or grow indifferent to men, either by becoming a lesbian or by adopting a comic objectivity about romantic love. The cynicism, humor, and detachment found in "Trust No Man" characterize the next group of Rainey recordings, which ignore love or treat it in a subordinate manner; they form the subject of the following chapter.

◢▙ That Same Pleasure,

That Same Pain: Comic Songs

and Songs of Cynicism

Yeah, my right hand's raised to the good Lord above, (2)

If they was throwin' away money, I'd have on boxing gloves.

"Tough Luck Blues" (1928)

◥**U**p to this point we have discussed Ma Rainey's love songs and examined the variety of possible responses a woman may make when her man does her wrong. Although such songs constitute roughly three-quarters of the Rainey recordings, the remaining compositions are striking as well. But in these songs, when love is mentioned at all it is secondary to attempts to describe and occasionally to judge the quality of life as a whole and the various experiences touched upon in the love songs. Ignoring love or subordinating it to other concerns, these songs are thematically less unified than the love songs, and are more difficult to fit into neat critical categories.

The love songs were dominated by a single compelling thesis—men mistreat the women who love them—and antithesis—women react with sorrow and anger to this mistreatment. But this second group of songs is thematically more heterogeneous, encompassing a variety of subjects and situations, from which no single persona of the woman emerges. Although they contain sexual elements, the songs are no more dominated by sex than by love, and they show a relationship between the woman and her environment different from that described in the love songs. While the woman in love was most directly concerned with her man and her rivals, struggling in a social vacuum, in these songs she is usually more involved in social and communal activities—music, dancing, drinking—and sometimes she is punished by society for her excesses. If the love songs were romantic in the sense of portraying an isolated female protagonist and her stormy love affairs, then the remaining songs are more realistic in showing a woman's interactions with her community, and in dealing with a broader range of human experience than love.

As noted in the preceding chapter, the love songs were filled with a strong sense of anger, either internalized and converted into depression or objectified and directed toward a rival or the man himself. The remaining songs, on the other hand, are less emotionally self-indulgent and more detached, either through humor or through cynicism. Although the mood of these songs ranges from lusty enjoyment to cynical endurance, the self seems more an observer, and less personally involved, manipulated, or crushed by experience.

The songs may be divided into two general categories, lighthearted and cynical. The first group includes songs containing a good deal of vaudeville comedy, and songs celebrating music and dancing. Often these compositions parody more serious themes from the love songs: the search for a man becomes a comic proposition ("Big Feeling Blues"); the terrors of bankruptcy become a trip to the poorhouse with a congenial friend ("Ma and Pa Poorhouse Blues"); and Papa's carousing and infidelity are finally matched by Mama's ("Barrel House Blues"). Midway between the two groups are several songs about drinking, which are sometimes comic, sometimes grim and resigned. The more serious songs are concerned with prison, fortune, luck, and the quality of life, displaying what we would now call an absurdist sense of frustration at trying to decipher an increasingly baffling world.

Ma Rainey's long experience as a minstrel and vaudeville performer had a profound influence on her comic material and style. As noted previously, some of her songs were considerably less tragic in performance than they may sound in isolated recordings. She whole-heartedly used her physical appearance to comic advantage: as a heavy, mature, and rather homely woman, she must have contrasted humorously with the slender young men in her band, and her comic flirtations and nimble dance steps with them rely on much good-natured self-mockery. Other comic devices included placing a sad song in a humorous context, comic dialogue, theatrical effects, and humorous antiphonal comments by the band during her blues singing. Although elements of comedy appeared in some of the love songs, several other songs either have comic subjects or treat serious subjects comically. The topic of "Those Dogs of Mine" is sore feet; "Big Feeling Blues," a proposition; "Ma and Pa Poorhouse Blues," bankruptcy; and "Blues the World Forgot," drunkenness and jail.

"Those Dogs of Mine" (also known as the "Famous Cornfield Blues") was first advertised in *The Chicago Defender* with a picture of a foot, sprouting cornstalks from the toes as a grinning sun looks on (figure 17). The caption reads:

> "Oh, Lawdy, those dogs of mine—they sure do worry me all the time!"

> "Ma" Rainey, Mother of the Blues, sings a blues that appeals to every man or woman who wears shoes. Corns—corns —corns—she had to keep out of the light of the sun—had to walk on the shady side of the street—well, hear all the details in the Corn Field Blues . . . .[1]

This slow-paced but lively song is not a blues, and although the copyright claims Ma Rainey composed it, Thomas Dorsey recalls that it was performed by minstrel groups in 1912.

> Look-a here people, listen to me,
> Believe me, I'm telling the truth;
> If your corns hurt you, just like mine,
> You'd say these same words too.

> Out for a walk, I stopped to talk,
> Oh how my corns did burn;
> I had to keep on the shady side of the street,
> To keep out the light of the sun.

> *Chorus:*
> Oh, Lordy, these dogs of mine,

Figure 17. "Those Dogs of Mine: 'Ma' Rainey's Famous Corn Field Blues."
(*Chicago Defender*, 9 August 1924, Part I, p. 8.)

They sure do worry me all the time;
The reason why—I don't know,
Sometimes I soak 'em in Sapolio.

Lord I beg to be excused,
I can't wear me no sharp-toed shoes;[2]
Oh, Lordy, how the sun do shine,
Down on these hounds of mine.

"Those Dogs of Mine"

Ma Rainey appeals for our sympathy with mock self-pity, beginning with a command to listen to her story. This is a common device in popular blues (cf. "Everybody fall in line, going to tell you 'bout that man of mine," in "Titanic Man Blues"), but she bewails the corns on her feet instead· of a lost lover. As the humor of the subject is enhanced by the conventional introduction, so the pain of love is subtly parodied by her aching, swollen feet. Even the chorus plays with a love-song theme—"Why does my man treat me so mean?"—as the singer wonders why her feet hurt and suggests soaking them in Sapolio, a then-popular household cleaner. The "sharp-toed shoes" which she cannot tolerate may be fancy dress pumps, suitable for church, and she begs the Lord's indulgence to wear something more comfortable.

Other songs more directly undermine the serious sentiments of the love songs. The anxiety and wry humor of "Lawd, Send Me a Man Blues"—in which a destitute woman prays to God for someone to pay her rent—are transformed into a broad, comic proposition in "Big Feeling Blues," the last song Ma Rainey ever recorded. It features a vocal duet with Papa Charlie Jackson, a seasoned medicine show entertainer and popularizer of the famous "Salty Dog Blues." Accompanied by Jackson's simple but rhythmic banjo, the collaboration is excellent, and with their only other duet, "Ma and Pa Poorhouse Blues," makes one wish they had recorded together more frequently. The song is a four-line, twelve-bar blues that includes musical dialogue between a man-hungry woman and an interested man.

Ma Rainey (speaks):
All these many years I been pleadin' for a man. How come I can't get me a real monkey-man? I'm not no trifling woman.

(sings):
I been lookin' for a man I can call my own,
Been married many times but they left my home;

Chorus:
Ah—big feeling blues, worst I ever had,
I got the big feeling blues, I mean I've got 'em bad.

Charlie (sings):
If you looking for a brown, come get this chocolate cream;
I'm a big kid man, just out of my teens;

Ma: Chorus.

Ma:
Unlucky with my yellow, unlucky with my brown,
The blacks they just keep on throwing me down;
Chorus.

Charlie:
If you need a good man, why don't you try me?
I sure can put you out of your misery;

Ma: Chorus.

Ma:
There's a whole lot left, what's left is good,
Give me a chance, honey, I'll make you change your neighbor-
    hood;
Chorus.

"Big Feeling Blues"

This is a song of direct proposition rather than courtship, in
which a woman complains to a man that she has been unlucky in
love, at first ignoring him when he offers himself, but finally being
persuaded by his arguments. The song has the sense of a ritual or
game as she flaunts her loneliness to an eligible, interested man,
only pretending to disregard his advances; the audience knows
exactly what the result will be.

In the spoken introduction, Ma Rainey describes herself
with exaggerated self-pity as a faithful woman who deserves a
"monkey-man," a slang term for a West Indian or someone naive
and easily misled, who believes anything his woman or his friends

tell him. Thus she immediately qualifies our sympathy for her by asking for someone she can fool, and her familiar theme of searching for a good man is further undermined by the humorous "Been married many times but they left my home": perhaps she seeks a monkey-man because her former husbands were too shrewd to be deceived!

Papa Charlie Jackson makes his first offer in the next stanza: his image of the "chocolate cream" implies delicious, mouth-watering sexuality, and in view of Ma Rainey's weakness for youths, a "big kid man, just out of my teens" would be especially attractive. But she pretends to ignore him, giving the traditional complaint that all men, whether light-skinned, brown-skinned, or black, have abused her. When Charlie finally stops boasting about his sexuality and declares that he will treat her well, she overcomes her feigned objections and accepts him. Obviously much of the humor in this song was visual: the contrast between Ma Rainey's age, size, and her sophistication (embodied by her gradually shifting expressions and states of feeling) and the young man's honest offer must have been hilarious onstage.

In "Ma and Pa Poorhouse Blues" the subject moves from love to poverty, but the treatment is no less comic. With the same performers as "Big Feeling Blues," the song begins with humorous dialogue which introduces a twelve-bar blues.

> (spoken)
> *Ma:* Hello there, Charlie.
> *Charlie:* Hello, Ma.
> *Ma:* Charlie, where's that big banjo you had?
> *Charlie:* Ma, that big banjo's been pawned.
> *Ma:* Been pawned?
> *Charlie:* Yes, Ma'am.
> *Ma:* Too bad, Jim.
> *Charlie:* Hello, Ma.
> *Ma:* All right, Charlie.
> *Charlie:* What's become of that great big bus *you* had?
> *Ma:* Ah—somebody *stole* that bus.
> *Charlie:* Stole it?
> *Ma:* Yeah!
> *Charlie:* Mmmmmm!
> *Ma:* Charlie, you know I'm broke?

Charlie: Ma, don't you know I'm broke too?
Ma: I tell you what let's do.
Charlie: What we gonna do?
Ma: Let's both go to the poorhouse together.
Charlie: All right, let's go together.

(*sung*)
Ma: Too bad, too bad, too bad, too bad, too bad, (2)
   I lost all my money, lost everything I had.

Charlie: Ma, being broke's all right, when you know you got
       some more money comin' in, (2)
       But when you lose your money, that's where friend-
       ship ends.

Ma: Oh——here I'm on my knees, (2)
   Charlie (speaks): Don't worry Ma, I'll soon be down on my
                   knees with you.
Ma: I want the whole world to know, Mama's broke and can't
   be pleased.
Charlie (sings): When you have lots of money, you have plenty
                friends,
Ma: Lord—lost all my money, that was my end,
   Oh—ain't got no money now.
Both: We better go to the poorhouse, and try to live anyhow.

Ma: Oh——, *Charlie (speaks):* Ah, moan it, Ma!
   Oh——, *Charlie (speaks):* Hear me talking to you, dog-
   gone you!
Both: We better go to the poorhouse, and try to live anyhow.

"Ma and Pa Poorhouse Blues"

Both the melody and some of the lyrics are derived from Victoria Spivey's popular 1927 recording "T. B. Blues." The opening
dialogue establishes that both singers are destitute: Charlie's banjo
has been pawned and Ma's elaborate touring bus has been stolen.
(Jackson's early publicity photographs show him posed with a
banjo-guitar, a six-stringed instrument with the body of a banjo and
the neck of a guitar.) Neither was actually gone (Ma still had her bus
in 1928), but the mock-biographical details help to involve the audience personally—like them, Ma and Charlie are feeling hard times.

Their attitude to poverty is cheerful and irreverent: both freely admit they are bankrupt, and when Ma suggests a trip to the poorhouse, Charlie readily agrees.

In the second stanza Charlie humorously asserts that temporary poverty is bearable, but permanent poverty means losing friends as well—a conventional sentiment which would be repeated with far more force during the Depression in Bessie Smith's classic recording of "Nobody Knows You When You're Down and Out." In the third stanza Ma prays—obviously for comic effect, since the sight of the short, squat, thoroughly secular blues singer on her knees must have been funny. In the final stanza, the words are moaned and the tone is more than half-serious: both recognize that they must go to the poorhouse, but at least they have each other for company and commiseration.

Often humor is provided by the context rather than the content of a song, as in the previously cited "Gone Daddy Blues," which places a standard blues of losing a man in a funny scene about an unfaithful wife attempting to regain her husband's love. But Ma Rainey's talents as a comedienne are most clearly shown in the two-part sequence "Blues the World Forgot" (both untraced; see figure 18). Part I is entirely dialogue, while Part II has a few blues stanzas.[3] Portions of the conversations in both parts are unclear, and no lead sheets have been found, but enough can be understood for a general interpretation. Both recordings feature extensive dialogue between Ma and an unidentified man (labeled as X in the transcript) who tries to restrain her drinking; he provides a running commentary on some offstage action in Part I.[4]

"Blues the World Forgot" Part I finds the two characters at home. As Ma begins to drink heavily, her companion comments on the scene outside the window. The recording consists solely of spoken dialogue, with an instrumental twelve-bar blues accompaniment; most likely it came from a popular skit in Ma Rainey's touring show.

Ma: Lord, Lord, Lord, I got the blues this mornin' and don't care who know it. I want all you boys to lock your doors, and don't let nobody in but the police.
X: Lookit here, Ma.
Ma: What is it?

X: What's the matter with you?

Ma: I got the blues.

X: What kinda blues?

Ma: The blues that the world forgot.

X: Woman, I believe you is drunk.

Ma: Drunk? Don't gimme no *hambone!* Mm, mm, mm, mm, mm, Lord have mercy! The way I feel this morning, I don't mind going to jail!

X: Ma, don't talk so loud—don't you see the sergeant standing out there on the corner?

Ma: Tell the sergeant I said come on in, and bring all the corn mash he have with him! Lord have mercy! Now, that does it!

X: Lookit here, Ma.

Ma: What is it?

X: They done turn all them black cats loose there in that alley.

Ma: Turn all the cats loose? What do I care if they turn them cats loose? Let them bring all the drunken cats! Where is the bootlegger? Tell him I'm going to drink all the whiskey he made this week! I feel like going to jail!

X: Uh oh!

Ma: What is it?

X: Uh oh!

Ma: What's the matter?

X: Old Tack Annie's done cut her old man's head again.

Ma: Cut her old man's head? Tell Tack Annie t' come on down here! I ain't scared of her! Bring all the Tack Annies! The way I feel this morning, I'll tackle any Tack Annie! I wouldn't mind *seein' Tack Annie!*

X: Well, it won't be long now.

Ma: I know'd it, I know'd it, I know'd it; we'll all end up in jail. I'm going to tell the judge I don't know a thing about it!

X: Well, it wasn't me!

Perhaps in live performance, the police came onstage, arresting Ma and her companion, as well as the assailant and her victim; Ma's last words may be a refusal to testify against Tack Annie.

The humor in "Blues the World Forgot" Part I, as in many of Ma's records, derives from the contrast between the irrepressible Ma and her more anxious companion. She becomes increasingly drunk and effusive as he vainly attempts to restrain her behavior. The more violent and outrageous things he reports from the window, the more willing she is to invite everybody up for a drink or a brawl. Similarly, in "Georgia Cakewalk" and in "Ma Rainey's Black Bottom" her high spirits and suggestive dancing overwhelm and threaten her companions.

Part II of "Blues the World Forgot" finds both characters in jail.

(spoken):
Ma: I told that judge I didn't know a thing about it.
X: Yeah, but you're doin' time right here with me, sister. Huh!
Ma: All right, but I done my time for nothin'.
X: Yeah, I heard that before.
Ma: Everybody said I wasn't a little old drunk.
X: No, you don't get drunk.
Ma: How I feel this week brother, I'm gonna tell you right now.
X: Until Thursday. You go to jail every Friday mornin'.
Ma: That's all right.
X: Biggest whiskey head in town!

(Ma sings a blues, interspersed with the man's spoken comments:)
Ma (sings): Everybody cries mercy, tell me what mercy means,
    X: Now, ain't that one evil woman?
Ma: Everybody cries mercy, tell me what mercy means.
    X: Mm, mm, mm, mm!
Ma: If it means feelin' good, Lord have mercy on me.
    X: Aw—that's what I thought.

Ma: When your man start to quit you, you know there's somethin' goin' on wrong,
    X: That's it! That's it! Got one of them things in the bag.
Ma: When your man start to quit you, somethin' goin' on wrong,
    X: Ought to take that graveyard dust out of your pocket!
Ma: Lay down in your bed, can't sleep all night long.

(spoken):
Ma: Well, I'm drunk all right now, but I know just what I'm doin'!
X: Yeah, yeah, woman, yeah! Stop shaking that mess in here!
Ma: Yeah—well, look like the time ain't gonna be long now!

Figure 18. "Blues the World Forgot." (*Chicago Defender*, 28 July 1928, Part I, p. 7.)

X: You goin' back to jail again if you don't stop shakin' that
    thing here. Don't allow that in here!
Ma: Can anybody come help poor little bitty old me? Lawd, Lawd.
X: 'Round here carryin' a groundhog in your pocket.
Ma: Oh, how I feel this evening!
X: Aw! Somebody come here! Ma! Have you—have you com-
    pletely lost your head?
Ma: I'm drunk!

Like "Gone Daddy Blues," this recording places a mournful
song in a humorous setting. Sent to jail for drunkenness, Ma self-
righteously proclaims her innocence to her cellmate, even as she
takes drink after drink from a bottle smuggled into her cell. The
"graveyard dust" Ma keeps in a bag in her pocket is dirt from a
grave, widely used in voodoo spells for making charms and fetishes;
the "groundhog" may be another name for her charm, and perhaps
Ma is attempting to conjure with it when her companion tells her to
"stop shaking that mess." The final dialogue seems to indicate that
she falls to the floor; as in "Big Feeling Blues" and "Ma and Pa
Poorhouse Blues," the skit must be performed to be fully appreciated, and we can only imagine Ma Rainey and her companion
acting it out.

Less deliberately comic, but still in a light vein, are several
songs which celebrate the pleasures of music and dancing, describing the appeal of lusty, "low-down" music, often in contrast to more
pallid if more aesthetic songs. In this category falls "Countin' the
Blues" (see chapter three), an index to some of Ma Rainey's more
famous recordings. "Ya-Da-Do" is the scat title of a non-blues
composition about a pleasant, nameless tune.

Every evenin' 'bout half-past four,
Sweet piano playin' near my door,
And turn to raggin', you never heard such blues before.

There's a pretty little thing they play,
It's very short, but folks all say,
"Oh it's so pretty," then they start to want to cry for more.

I don't know the name,
But it's a pretty little thing, goes

Chorus:
Ya da da do,
Ya da da do,
Fill you with harmonizing, minor refrain,
It's the no-name blues, but I [words unclear].[5]

Ya da da do,
Ya da da do,
Everybody loves it,
Ya da do do do.

"Ya-Da-Do"

Although insubstantial thematically, this song provides a fine opportunity for Ma Rainey to display her scat singing. When the piano players "turn to raggin'" they begin playing in ragtime syncopation, although the word also has sexual connotations. (In a similar fashion, "jazzing" originally meant intercourse, but also came to mean playing jazz music, as in such expressions as "jazzing the classics." For "ragging" as sexual, cf. "If she beats me raggin', she's got to rag it some," in "Southern Blues," discussed later in this chapter.) Although Ma mentions a "minor refrain," the song is written in a major key, and reflects good-natured high spirits.

"Ma Rainey's Black Bottom" (see figure 19) and "Down in the Basement" show her singing and dancing to "low-down" music. She puns throughout the first song, as an unidentified male speaker makes clear:

Man (speaks):
Now, you heard the rest. Ah, boys, I'm gonna show you the best. Ma Rainey's gonna show you *her* black bottom!
Ma (sings):
'Way down South in Alabamy,
I got a friend they call dancin' Sammy,
Who's crazy about all the latest dances,
Black bottom stomps and the Jew baby prances;[6]

The other night at a swell affair,
Soon as the boys found out that I was there,
They said, "Come on, Ma, let's go to the cabaret,
Where that band, you ought to hear me say,"

Figure 19. "Ma Rainey's Black Bottom." (*Chicago Defender*, 18 February 1928, Part I, p. 7.)

Chorus:
I wanta see that dance you call the black bottom,
I wanna learn that dance,
Don't you see the dance you call your big black bottom,
That'll put you in a trance;

All the boys in the neighborhood,
They say your black bottom is really good,
Come on and show me your black bottom,
I want to learn that dance.

I want to see the dance you call the black bottom,
I want to learn that dance,
Come on and show that dance you call your big black bottom,
It puts you in a trance;

Early last morning 'bout the break of day,
Grandpa told my grandma, I heard him say,
"Get up and show your old man your black bottom,
I want to learn that dance."

Now I'm gon' to show y'all my black bottom,
They stay to see that dance,
Wait until you see me do my big black bottom,
It'll put you in a trance;

(Instrumental break, during which the man speaks):
Ah, do it Ma, do it honey. Lookit now Ma, you gettin' kinda
rough there! You got to be yourself, now, careful now, not too
strong, not too strong, Ma!

Ma (sings):
I done showed y'all my black bottom,
You ought to learn that dance.

"Ma Rainey's Black Bottom"

The term "black bottom" referred both to a black person's
backside and to the black sections of many Southern cities and
towns. Ma Rainey wrote these song lyrics, but the black bottom had
been a popular dance with Southern blacks even before Perry Bradford published "The Original Black Bottom Dance" in 1919. It may

have originated in Atlanta, and seasoned vaudeville teams like Butterbeans and Susie, and Bradford and Jeannette had performed it in tent shows and over the T.O.B.A. since the early teens.[7]

Bradford's lyrics, which describe the professional black bottom step, suggest provocative movements, although he substitutes the break-a-leg (a hobbling step) for the more obvious slapping of the backside:

> Hop down front and then you Doodle back,
> Mooch to your left and then you Mooch to the right,
> Hands on your hips and do the Mess Around,
> Break a Leg until you're near the ground,
> Now that's the Old Black Bottom Dance.[8]

The song became a nationwide hit in an expurgated version by three white composers (DeSylva, Brown, and Henderson); it was introduced by Ann Pennington in George White's Scandals of 1926. It eventually became refined for mass consumption, until all that remained of the original dance was a discreet slapping of the backside and a few hops forward and backward.[9]

Despite an uneven performance by the band, Ma Rainey's hearty good humor shines through the recording, whose meaning ranges from lively to ribald. It may be a rollicking description of the singer's skill at a popular dance, but the reference to showing "my black bottom" is too sexual to be dismissed. When the neighborhood males attest that "Your black bottom is really good," they must at least be hinting about her ability in bed. Unlike the depressed, solitary singer in the most passive love songs, she makes a sexual boast (more in line with the "damper down" sentiments of "Jealousy Blues") and is seen enjoying herself at a local bar, surrounded by grinning and eager neighborhood men.

The lyrics further suggest that the narrator may initiate boys into sex, since the implication of "I want to learn that dance" is sexual, and generally, any double meaning that may be read into the blues is already there. The Grandma-Grandpa verse implies intercourse as well (cf. Grandpa's mockery of Grandma's old jelly roll in "Hear Me Talking to You"). During the instrumental break, Ma Rainey dances, perhaps doing the ribald, tent show black bottom, judging from the man's alarmed comments.

Finally, in a song which may be said to summarize her approach
to music, Ma Rainey celebrates earthy, sensual songs as opposed to
refined music in "Down in the Basement." The song is not a blues.

I've gotta man, piano hound,
Plays anything that's goin' around,
When he plays that highbrow stuff,
I shout, "Brother, that's enough!"

So take me to the basement, that's as low as I can go,
I want something low-down, Daddy, want it nice and slow,
I will shimmy from A to Z, if you'll play that thing for me,
So take me to the basement, that's as low as I can go.

"Down in the Basement"

The term "low-down" may mean depressed, earthy, or sensual,
with an implication of lewdness, vulgarity, or bad living (cf. "low-
down ways" in many blues songs). As the lowest part of a house,
the basement is literally "as low as I can go," and both Clara Smith
and Rosa Henderson had recorded "Basement Blues" in 1924.
Low-down carries a connotation of literal earthiness: being close
to the ground, and thus to physical life; it may also mean "severely
depressed," as in "I got the toad low blues and I can't get no lower
down," in "Toad Frog Blues." Finally, "gully-low" (low as a ditch or
gully) and low-down derive from descriptions of the locations of
barrel houses and honky-tonks, and many speakeasies of the twenties were located in the basement.[10]

The "highbrow stuff" disdained by the singer is classical and
sentimental popular music, according to the lead sheet, which adds
a stanza insulting the classics:

Grand opera and parlor junk,
I'll tell the world it's all the bunk,
That's the kind of stuff I shun,
Let's get dirty and have some fun.

This stanza does not appear on the recording, but Ma Rainey may
well have performed it live, and the song shows that she was equally
at home with popular music and blues.

In her craving for something low-down, the woman promises
to do the alphabet of shimmy, to shake everything from A to Z if

the music is right. Like "jazz" and "rag," "shimmy" had both musical and sexual significance. The dance was introduced around the end of World War I, and was popularized in 1919 by the song "I Wish I Could Shimmy Like My Sister Kate." Although white vaudeville singer Gilda Gray claimed to have invented it, the shimmy had a long history in the black South, and may be traced back to the Shika of Nigeria. In the South, chemise (slip) was often pronounced "shimmy," and the term came to mean a woman's dance step that made her breasts and her "shimmy" shake.[11] Regardless of its origin, the shimmy meant provocative movements; the singer in "Rough and Tumble Blues" went on a murder spree when she found her man and "Miss Shorty Toad" shimmying "on down to the floor."

Thus in her songs of music and dancing, Ma Rainey emphasizes an earthy and frankly sexual enjoyment of life, whether she listens to piano players "raggin'," shows her black bottom to the neighborhood boys, or shimmies from A to Z. She often turns to liquor for amusement or escape, and the drunkenness in both parts of "Blues the World Forgot" is echoed by other songs about the joys and pains of whiskey. She celebrates its lighter side in "Barrel House Blues" (figure 20), which includes a comic clarinet solo on "How Dry I Am."

Got the barrel house blues, feelin' awfully dry, (2)
I can't drink moonshine, 'cause I'm afraid I'd die.[12]

Papa likes his sherry, Mama likes her port, (2)
Papa likes to shimmy, Mama likes to sport.

Papa likes his bourbon, Mama likes her gin, (2)
Papa likes his outside women, Mama likes her outside men.

"Barrel House Blues"

As early as 1883, a barrel house was defined as a cheap saloon; it became a particularly Southern term for a small beer-joint or tavern,[13] and the Paramount advertisement for the recording shows two elegant women drinking together at a table. The first stanza reveals that the singer wants a drink, but fears moonshine (with good reason, given the composition of many home-brewed concoctions). The remaining stanzas leave the singer and her problems to generalize about men and women, asserting that anything Papa

Figure 20. "Barrel House Blues" sheet music. (*The Paramount Book of Blues,*
p. 11. Courtesy John Steiner.)

can do, Mama can do as well: if he drinks sherry, she drinks port; if he shimmies, she "sports"—a term probably relating to sex (cf. "sporting-house" for brothel). In the final stanza the couple move on to harder liquor and more sophisticated sex: bourbon for him, gin for her, and outside lovers for both. In describing life's pleasures, "Barrel House Blues" cynically puts Papa and Mama on equal footing as drinkers and lovers.

As we have seen in the previous chapter, "Moonshine Blues" shows a woman going on a drunken binge to relieve her depression after her man has left her. Despite a rollicking scene in the *Defender* advertisement,[14] "Dead Drunk Blues" (figure 3) describes an alcoholic in the throes of her disease. The cause of her blues is never defined, and her drinking seems more habitual than temporary.

Ma (speaks):
My Man is _____ drunk this morning, daddy, be yourself!

(sings):
Oh give me Houston, that's the place I crave, (2)
So when I'm dry, I'll drink whiskey that's just made.[15]

Oh whiskey, whiskey, is some folks' downfall, (2)
But if I don't get whiskey, I ain't no good at all.

When I was in Houston, drunk most every day, (2)
     (speaks):
     Lord! [Where?] the police?
I drank so much whiskey, I thought I'd pass away.

Have you ever been drunk, slept in all your clothes? (2)
And when you wake up, feel like you want a dose.[16]

Daddy, I'm going to get drunk, just one more time,
     (speaks):
     Where's the whiskey bottle?
Honey, I'm going to get drunk, Papa, just one more time,
'Cause when I'm drunk, nothing's gonna worry my mind.

"Dead Drunk Blues"

"Dead Drunk Blues" was recorded by Margaret Johnson and by Sippie Wallace in early 1927, by Ma in the middle of the year, and by Lillian Miller in 1928.

The situation which drives the woman to drink is never fully explained, although she is surely trying to forget something, and her need for drink is a craving, not a pleasurable habit, in contrast to "Mama" in "Barrel House Blues." The song is most effective in showing the woman's helpless addiction to the bottle, her empty promises to stop after just one more time, and her drunken delirium, when she passes out with her clothes on. "Dead Drunk Blues" focuses on her alcoholism in itself, rather than as a response to external circumstances or disappointments in love.

Not quite as desperate but equally unfortunate is the woman in "Booze and Blues," whose drinking sends her to prison. The situation is reminiscent of "Blues the World Forgot," but treated far more seriously.

Went to bed last night, and folks, I was in my tea,
Went to bed last night, and I was in my tea,[17]
Woke up this morning, the police was shakin' me.

I went to the jailhouse, drunk and blue as I could be, (2)
But the cruel old judge[18] sent my man away from me.

They carried me to the courthouse, Lordy how I was cryin', (2)
They gave me sixty days in jail, and money couldn't pay my
    fine.

Sixty days ain't long when you can spend them as you
    choose, (2)
But they seem like years in a cell where there ain't no booze.

My life is all a misery when I cannot get my booze, (2)
I can't live without my liquor, got to have the booze to cure
    these blues.

"Booze and Blues"

The lead sheet interpolates a stanza directly after the first, explaining why the woman was sent to jail:

They raided my flat, caught my Daddy sellin' moon, (2)
And said, "We'll send you to a place where you won't see liquor
    soon."

Although the song is not copyrighted in Ma Rainey's name, and thus we cannot be sure that she was the original performer, the lead sheet and my transcription are in almost perfect agreement; thus in all probability she sang the additional lead sheet stanza in live performance. Without it, we do not know why the woman has been arrested, unless it is for drunkenness. With it, we discover that her man is a bootlegger, and the police have arrested them both, separating them in prison, and sentencing her without bail. Like many popular twelve-bar blues, "Booze and Blues" is more narrative than lyric, telling its story through brief, dramatic scenes. The action is vividly recounted from the moment the woman falls asleep drunk, and the lead sheet even supplies sarcastic arresting officers.

Apparently the woman's only crime is being drunk and associating with a bootlegger; nonetheless she is punished for her man's offenses. Her philosophical consideration of the long sentence reminds us of more comic observations: "Sixty days ain't long when you can spend them as you choose" carries the same humorous irony as Papa Charlie Jackson's "Bein' broke's all right, when you know you got some more money comin' in," in "Ma and Pa Poorhouse Blues." As in many blues, the theme of "Booze and Blues" is separation, but it is caused by the law rather than an unfaithful lover. The singer's last line suggests that she needs liquor not only to cope with a temporary, harsh situation, but also because, like the narrator of "Dead Drunk Blues," she cannot live without a drink.

Songs about women in prison were not uncommon in the blues, and often the singer is arrested for murdering her man or her rival. Compared with Bessie Smith's raucous "Send Me to the 'Lectric Chair," Ma Rainey's "Cell Bound Blues" is tamer, although by the end of the song the narrator does realize that she is a murderess. (See discussion in chapter three.) But Ma Rainey's repertoire also included a harsher song of women on the chain gang.

In *Blues Fell This Morning: The Meaning of the Blues*, Paul Oliver documented some of the appalling conditions on the work gangs:

By leasing gangs of convicts chained, and under armed guard, and by using them on state projects, the prisons were relieved whilst railroads were built, the gravel quarries worked, swamps drained and roads constructed. In 1902 there were 2,221 convicts employed in the chain gangs of Georgia alone, and of these, 2,113 were Negroes—amongst them 103 Negro

152152Mother of the Blues*

women. Children of twelve years of age were to be found
working in chains with old and embittered men in the very
streets of Atlanta, and men and women were shackled together
under inhuman conditions. . . .

The convicts rose with the sun and were bedded down
with the sun. When they lay down for their rest on the hard
earth their ankles were shackled to a long logging chain that ran
the length of their miserable quarters . . . . When not working,
the convicts—men and women—were heavily manacled, but
when employed on their tasks their hands had to be free, and
except when engaged in work requiring close order—ditch
digging for example—it was found expedient to free them from
the long chain. Instead, a step-chain, allowing a pace of only
eight inches, was used, or a twenty-pound ball chained to the
ankle. . . .

Boys and girls scarcely in their teens were worked side-
by-side for sixteen or more hours a day and slept chained in line
in the ditches. In the early part of the century as many as 250
prisoners, many of them first offenders, were shackled together on the "long chain" to work on the railroads, the wheat
farms and in the dreaded phosphate mines. When prisoners
were punished they were brutalized with clubs and compelled
to wear needle-sharp points affixed to their ankles which lacer-
ated their legs as they walked. . . . Women suffered privations
and humiliations, . . . being flogged naked before the eyes of
men prisoners. The campus of Georgia State College was dug
by aged Negro women working under the supervision of armed
guards whilst young girls carried their picks to the road
camps.[19]

"Chain Gang Blues" implies these horrors in an understated
but grim style.

The judge found me guilty, the clerk he wrote it down, (2)
Just a poor gal in trouble, I know I'm county road bound.

Many days of sorrow, many nights of woe, (2)
And a ball and chain, everywhere I go.

Chains on my feet, padlock on my hand, (2)
It's all on account of stealing a woman's man.

It was early this mornin' that I had my trial, (2)
Ninety days on the county road and the judge didn't even
smile.

"Chain Gang Blues"

The lead sheet includes another stanza before the final one:

Ain't robbed no train, ain't done no hanging crime, (2)
But the judge said I'd be on the county road a long, long time.

If Ma Rainey sang the additional stanza given on the lead sheet,
the woman's crime was clearly minor. What are we to make of "It's
all on account of stealing a woman's man"? We may only conjecture
that the jealous woman turned the singer in for a real or fabricated
crime. In any case, the privations of the chain gang are tangible, if
baldly stated: manacles on her hands and feet, a heavy ball and
chain, and grueling work building the county road. Like many other
blues, the song delivers a large amount of information in very few
words; to a black audience, the simple statement of the chains
would evoke the terrible conditions which Oliver has more fully
explicated.

One response to such horror and suffering is to embrace superstition as a way of explaining the world, warding off its ills, or
changing some of its conditions. As mentioned in the previous
chapter, Ma Rainey's blues include fortunetellers of both sexes,
whom women consult to look for straying men or to win them back.
Charms, hexes, and signs proliferate as well: the lucky rock which
the singer seeks to help forget her unfaithful man ("Lucky Rock
Blues"), the black cat bone and hoodoo hand to retrieve a lost lover
or keep a rival away ("Louisiana Hoodoo Blues"). In several songs,
however, superstition is more the subject than an adjunct, and
disappointed love relationships are secondary, if mentioned at all.
"Black Cat Hoot Owl Blues" (figure 21) invokes several powerful
symbols from black folklore.

Ma (speaks): Meow————Scat!
(sings):
Black cat on my doorstep, black cat on my window-sill, (2)
If one black cat don't cross me, another black cat will.

It's bad luck if I'm jolly, bad luck if I cry, (2)

It's bad luck if I stay here, it's still more bad luck if I die.

Last night a hootin' owl come and sit right over my door, (2)
A feelin' seems to tell me, I'll never see my man no more.

I feel my left eye jumpin', my heart a-bumpin',
    I'm on my P's and Q's,
I feel my brain a-thumpin', I got no time to lose,
Mama's superstitious, tryin' to overcome these blues.

"Black Cat, Hoot Owl Blues"

In general, the lead sheet agrees with my transcription, although it differs in specific phrasing. Related thematically to "Yonder Come the Blues" (cited in the previous chapter), the song shows
the blues as an omnipresent, inescapable reality. Bad luck is inevitable, no matter whether the singer laughs, weeps, endures, or dies.
In the opening stanza she is surrounded by black cats, and even if
she escapes one, another will surely find her.

The image yields several meanings; in addition to the animal
which brings bad luck when it crosses one's path, the black cat is
also a pun on "black man." In "Blues the World Forgot" Part I, the
singer tells her friend to bring in "all the drunken cats" from the
alley, and the use of "cat" to mean "man" evolved through blues
and jazz idioms, possibly originating in the black slang expression
"tom-cat" for a promiscuous man.[20] The archaic fear of black cats as
witches' familiars predated by centuries the appearance of black
culture in America, but the use of the black cat symbol in this song
and others may reveal the ambivalence of black folk culture toward
its color.

In Afro-American folklore black articles were frequently feared;
dreams of black butterflies or black water portended evil, and the
word "black" could signify "the worst," as in the expression "too
black bad."[21] Yet despite such negative connotations, the black cat
bone was a powerful charm to return a straying lover or to ward off
the attentions of a love rival (see "Louisiana Hoodoo Blues," discussed in chapter three). In any case, the combined implications of
the black cat image in this song condemn the singer to specific
man-trouble as well as to general misfortune.

The hooting owl, another omen of bad luck and death, also
warns the narrator that her man will leave her. The final stanza

Figure 21. "Black Cat Hoot Owl Blues." (*Chicago Defender*, 10 November 1928, Part I, p. 7.)

includes two more signs of impending evil: both the spasms in her brain and heart, and the twitching of her left eye (the "jumping" of the *right* eye, on the other hand, was supposed to signify good luck).[22] "On my P's and Q's" means "on guard and not likely to be fooled."[23]

Similarly, "Screech Owl Blues" uses an owl to portend misfortune, although this song barely mentions love.

When a hog makes a bed, you know the storm is due, (2)
When a screech owl hollers, mean bad luck for you.

Screech owl hollered this mornin', twice in front of my back door, (2)
I knew when he hollered, bad luck comin' back once more.

I got a taxi, begged the driver, "Show me some speed," (2)
Screech owl brought me bad luck, money's what my baby needs.

I called all over town, tryin' to find that good brown of mine, (2)
He called me from the station, said, "Fifty dollars was my fine."

When I got to the station, bad luck was waitin' there too, (2)
They said, "You need more money, and we've got a warrant for you."

"Screech Owl Blues"

While "Black Cat, Hoot Owl Blues" ended with only an expectation of bad luck, "Screech Owl Blues" fulfills the prophecy, expressing a similar sense of the futility of human action to change fortune. In this song, bad luck is a tangible entity which can be carried (the owl brings it to the singer), a personification which waits quietly at the police station and meets the woman when she arrives.

Like the superstitious songs, several compositions of marked cynicism and absurdity spring from an attempt to deal with a baffling world. These songs convey a sense of confusion through their abrupt shifts of subject or mood from stanza to stanza and in their lack of narrative coherence. In this respect they closely resemble folk blues, and except for "Blame It on the Blues," most of their lyrics are traditional. Thematically, they are closely linked to the suspicion of "Trust No Man," the skepticism of "Barrel House Blues," and the frustration of "Yonder Come the Blues."

"Blame It on the Blues" is filled with the sense that everything is going wrong. The song includes four antiphonal blues stanzas, while in the final stanza Ma Rainey sings both halves of the line. (For a further discussion of this doubling technique, see chapter two.)

> I'm so sad and worried, got no time to spread the news, (2)
> Won't blame it on my trouble, can't blame it on the blues.

> Lord, Lord; Lord, Lordy Lord,
> Lord, Lord; Lordy Lordy Lord,
> Lord, Lord; Lord, Lord, Lord, Lord.

> *(Ma Speaks):* Lord, who'm I gonna blame it on then?
> *(sings):*
> I can't blame my daddy, he treats me nice and kind, (2)
> Shall I blame it on my nephew, blame it on that trouble of
> mine?[24]

> This house is like a graveyard, when I'm left here by myself, (2)
> Shall I blame it on my lover, blame it on somebody else?

> Can't blame my mother, can't blame my dad,
> can't blame my brother for the trouble I've had,
> Can't blame my lover, that held my hand,
> can't blame my husband, can't blame my man,
> Can't blame nobody, guess I'll have to blame it on the blues.

"Blame It on the Blues"

The song appears to defy analysis on strictly logical grounds: the woman's depression cannot be grounded in any specific trouble, yet the blues remain, and her free-floating sadness seems inexplicable. In contrast to many popular blues whose singers broadcast their sorrow, "Blame It on the Blues" implies that she is too depressed to tell anyone. She mentions but never locates or defines a vague "trouble"; in the second stanza she moans her sorrow and questions its cause. The rest of the song vainly attempts to fix the blame, to find an objective reason for her depression.

Although the doubling technique in the final stanza, the reference to "spreading the news," and the mention of the song's title in the last line all stamp this as a composed blues, its mixture of incongruent and mutually exclusive events and moods shows the influence of folk blues as well. In the first stanza the woman cannot "blame it on the blues," while in the final stanza she does just that. She seems at the same time surrounded by family (mother, father, brother, husband, nephew, and possibly one or more lovers), yet utterly alone in a tomb-like house. Either her "daddy" refers to a husband or lover(s), or else she may have only one man and the terms are merely poetic repetitions. It is tempting, but probably wrong, to interpret the song as the complaint of a woman involved with too many men at the same time; such a situation would be more directly spelled out if it were the subject. Nor do her blues stem from the conventional mistreating man: her daddy treats her well; her lover held her hand. After assessing all her acquaintances, the woman finally realizes that she cannot blame anyone (significantly she does not list herself), and fixes her depression on "the blues."

In "Tough Luck Blues" the mood of self-defeat is extended beyond love, and could be called absurdist in the contemporary sense.

When a black cat crosses you, bad luck I heard it said, (2)
One must've started 'cross me, got half-way and then fell dead.

Things sure breakin' hard, worse than ever before, (2)
My sugar told me, speak to him no more.

Yeah, my right hand's raised to the good Lord above, (2)
If they was throwin' away money, I'd have on boxing gloves.

If it was rainin' down soup, thick as number one sand, (2)
I'd have a fork in my pocket and a sifter in my hand.

My friend committed suicide, while I was away at sea, (2)
They want to lock me up for murder in first degree.

"Tough Luck Blues"

The apparently nonsensical lyrics actually reveal a pattern of sardonic frustration and confusion. If a black cat crossing one's path is an image of bad luck, then a cat which dies halfway across the singer's path must indicate even worse fortune, or else the woman's luck was already so bad that it killed the cat. In the second stanza, she bewails both the general hard times and the rift with her man, while the third probably means, "I swear to God, if they were throwing away money I'd have on boxing gloves [and couldn't pick it up]."

Her sense of being thwarted becomes even more grotesque in the fourth stanza: even if thick, heavy soup rained down from the heavens, she would have only a fork and a sifter—both useless, because they would let the soup flow through without catching it. Beyond this literal reference, the sifter (which also means "sieve") was supposed to be able to catch a witch, who must stop and count all the holes before she may pass through. In black folklore from Maryland, people would put a sieve over their faces with a three-pronged fork under it, to trap a witch if she managed to get through the holes.[25] Thus the lines may also be read as, "If soup were raining down, I'd be trying to catch witches," a nightmare juxtaposition of incongruities. The final stanza continues the surreal mood, as the innocent narrator is accused of murder.

Repeatedly, the woman attempts to deal with a hallucinatory life that refuses to make sense; she is denied love, money, food, and physical freedom. Like the less bizarre but equally dissatisfied "Yonder Come the Blues," "Tough Luck Blues" expresses the confusing and almost comically perverse conditions of her existence.

This disorder, frustration, and sense of self-defeat are transformed in several songs into cynicism, both comic and grim. The traditional "Southern Blues" sums up a fatalistic approach to experience:

House catch on fire, and ain't no water 'round,
If your house catch on fire, and ain't no water 'round,
Throw your trunk out the window, buildin' burn on down.

I went to the gypsy, to have my fortune told, (2)
She said, "Doggone you, girlie, doggone your bad luck soul."

I turned around, went to the gypsy next door, (2)
She said, "You'll get a man, anywhere you go."

Let me be your rag doll, until your Chinee come, (2)
If she beats me raggin', she's got to rag it some.

"Southern Blues"

Interpreting this song is difficult: its four conventional stanzas have little in common according to any strict narrative sense, but are unified instead by a perceptive analysis of things as they are, combined with a healthy distrust of the way they appear. To Paul Oliver, the first stanza expresses "despairing fatalism" about the flimsy homes of poor Southern blacks.[26] Although I do not see despair in these lines, I do see a realistic assessment of the situation: put out the fire if you can, but if you have no water, grab your possessions and let it burn. Cursed by the first gypsy ("doggone" being a euphemism for "Goddamn"), the singer is assured of men aplenty by the second. The juxtaposition of two contradictory prophecies tends to make us dismiss them both; this suspicion is continued in the final stanza, which has a long and independent folk history, often appearing as

Let me be yo' rag doll, till yo' tidy come,
If he can beat me raggin', he's got to rag it some.

A "tidy" was a woman's well-dressed, steady man,[27] and the verse was a sexual boast sung by a man to a woman: let me be your lover, until your steady man returns; if he can make love better than I can, he will have to work at it. Ma's version transforms the "tidy" into a "Chinee," and the lead sheet, which places this stanza at the beginning of the song, gives yet another variation:

Let me be your rag doll, until your China comes, (2)
If she beats me raggin', girls she's got to rag it some.

"Rag doll" was idiomatic for someone with torn, ragged clothes, while "China doll" meant an attractive, charming, and beautifully dressed woman.[28] Thus the Rainey version offers the man illicit sex until his fine lady returns, and repeats the sexual boast.

The cynicism, compromise, and distrust of appearances in this song are even more exaggerated in "Shave 'Em Dry Blues," which increases the subject range to many areas of human interaction. The tune is an eight-bar blues whose stanzas have three independent lines with an *aab* rhyme-scheme; it is one of the fastest-paced songs Ma Rainey ever recorded, and she composed it with William Jackson.

There's one thing I don't understand,
Why a good lookin' woman likes a workin' man,

Chorus:
Hey hey hey—daddy let me shave 'em dry.[29]

Goin' away to wear you off my mind,
You keep me hot and broke, daddy, all the time,
Chorus.

Don't see how you hungry women can sleep,
She shimmies all day without a bite to eat,[30]
Chorus.

Going downtown to spread the news,
State Street women wearing brogan shoes,
Chorus.

If it wasn't for their powder and their store-bought hair,
State Street gals couldn't go nowhere,[31]
Chorus.

There's one thing I can't understand,
Some women [word unclear] State Street [?] like a man,[32]
Chorus.

Went to the show the other night,
Everybody on State Street was tryin' to fight,
Chorus.

Ain't crazy 'bout my yellow, I ain't wild about my brown,
You can't tell the difference when the sun goes down,
Chorus.

When you see two women running hand to hand,
Bet your life one's got the other's man,
Chorus.

Come here daddy, lay in my arms,
When your wife comes, tell her I don't mean no harm,
Chorus.

"Shave 'Em Dry Blues"

The title most directly refers to shaving a beard without using lather—which would be painful and bloody, but it also connotes brutal intercourse without foreplay, and both meanings are suggested by the sexual and violent aspects of the lyrics. "Shave 'Em

Dry" had a long blues history; it was widely performed, and was recorded by both men and women, Ma's version being the first on record. Her lyrics sound innocuous compared to Lucille Bogan's unissued version in 1935, which is blatantly pornographic.[33]

Like "Southern Blues," "Shave 'Em Dry Blues" tells no direct story; it is instead a grab-bag of violent and sexual imagery. Although Ma Rainey's first stanza seems innocent, Papa Charlie Jackson's 1925 recording of the song contains a more direct image of intercourse:

Now here's one thing I can't understand,
Why a bow-legged woman likes a knock-kneed man,
Mama can I holler, daddy let me shave 'em dry.[34]

Jackson may have learned the song from Ma Rainey, or may even have taught it to her.[35]

In the second stanza, a woman leaves her man because he keeps her sexually excited but penniless—a variation on the "you took all my money" theme common to the love songs. The "hungry women" in the third stanza are too busy carousing to eat or sleep; sex dominates their lives.

The fourth stanza probably describes the prostitutes on State Street, who wear work shoes, and the fifth disparages their looks: without heavy powder to lighten their skin, and wigs to disguise their hair, they could not attract men. During the era of race records, the prevailing standard of beauty for urban, sophisticated black people was clearly Caucasian: the pages of the *Chicago Defender* and similar black newspapers were filled with advertisements for skin bleaching lotions and preparations designed to produce "good" hair—wavy and silky rather than coarse and frizzy. A typical ad showed two little girls, one with light skin, refined features and wavy ringlets, carrying a white doll; the other, a dark-skinned pickaninny in tattered clothes. Ringlets: "My mother uses Arroway on my hair"; Pickaninny: "I wish my mother did" (figure 22).[36] The sixth stanza may hint at lesbianism.[37]

Remaining stanzas of "Shave 'Em Dry Blues" emphasize violence and cynicism, whether the crowd riots at a show, or all lovers are presumed to be the same. The latter sentiment is a convention, appearing in many blues songs about women sung by men. It reinforces the contemptuous mood of the song by insisting that in

Figure 22. "If it wasn't for their powder and their store-bought hair. . . ." (Arroway Hair Products, *Chicago Defender*, 2 August 1924, Part II, p. 4.)

bed, in the dark, all men are reduced to sex partners, and the woman who dislikes yellow- or brown-skinned men will not know the difference. In the next stanza, the singer admonishes us not to trust two women together: when you see them running hand in hand, one is actually chasing the other who betrayed her. In the final stanza a woman aggressively propositions a man; she sarcastically suggests that he tell his wife she is harmless.

More than almost any other song of Ma Rainey's, "Shave 'Em Dry Blues" expresses profound suspicion about life. The singer's lover arouses her sexually but steals her money; promiscuous women do not take time to eat or sleep; some prostitutes may be lesbians, others are phoney artifice with powder and wigs; all men are the same in bed; two women apparently united in friendship are actually united in jealousy and rage; adultery masquerades as innocence. Nothing is as it seems and all appearances are distrusted: almost every line sets up a situation which is undermined or reinterpreted by the following line. Uniting them all is the ribald refrain to "shave 'em dry."

Thus the remaining songs of Ma Rainey extend the range of subject material beyond individual struggles in love to a broader consideration of life. Sight gags, self-mockery, parody, and vaudeville comedy are reflected in the humorous songs, and to a lesser extent in the lusty and frankly sexual enjoyment of music and dancing. Liquor may be an amusement or a torment, and often sends the singer to jail. She may be arrested on a flimsy excuse or for murder, briefly sentenced without bail or put to work under inhumane conditions on the chain gang. The suffering and oppression which characterize the harsher side of her world may lead her to superstitious fear and suspicion, or to more philosophical attempts to understand a confusing and frustrating existence. But even at their most cynical, these songs express a tough, realistic appraisal, an ability to see through pretense, combined with a shrewd analysis of life as it is.

Conclusion

Ma Rainey's life symbolizes the confrontation between the black rural South and the changes wrought by industrialization, urban migration, and the development of modern mass communications. She represents a collision between the unchanging aphorisms of folk poetry and the nervous rhythms of modern life; she is both timeless and in time, both mythic and historical. As the first female blues star, already active by 1902, she serves as the prime link between country blues and black show business, at once folk artist and star performer, both "Ma" and Madame Rainey.

Like any professional entertainer's, her life was governed by tensions between art and the marketplace. She appeared at a crucial node of change in modern history, and her career was both made possible by and reflective of a number of complex events: the development of blues from folk art to national craze, the growth and decline of traveling black entertainment, the birth and expansion of the recording industry, the power of the black press, the influx of black migrants from the South to urban areas, and the general dislocation of American society after World War I. These forces lock in a net of causality, supporting a figure who became a powerful symbol of black womanhood.

In a more direct way than the minstrelsy that preceded it, the blues boom of the twenties was an explosion of black culture into the American mainstream, indelibly recreating a world of black experience, and making visible the lives and aspirations of millions of black Americans. Women were the first to record the blues, and while working within the partially composed and admittedly popularized form of the Classic Blues, Ma Rainey retained a high degree of folk blues consciousness, which dominates the structure of her recordings and is obvious in her style. Most of her recorded songs are linked to the blues in their twelve-bar melodies, three conventional chords, three-line repetitive stanzas, frequent rural diction and images from folk poetry, and traditional themes of love, violence, and loss. In performance, Ma Rainey revealed the folk influence in her rough voice, garbled diction, moans, blue notes, and slurs, as well as in her choice of accompanists and in their antiphonal instrumentals.

Physically and stylistically Ma Rainey was, in Sterling Brown's phrase, "a person of the folk." Short, heavy, dark-skinned, Georgia-born, she understood the deep South. As the folk artist "Ma," she had much in common with the early country blues singers: she wrote a great many of her own songs, drew on her personal life for their lyrics, and recounted events shared with her audience. In her finest performances, she was not a remote star, but as one with her listeners, and her extraordinary hold over people grew from the mutual identification between performer and audience: her life and theirs were similar, and she expressed their feelings better than they could themselves.

The pattern of her recording career reflects an artist's evolution from a popular style toward her true audience. If in 1923 she recorded a variety of song forms with jazz band accompaniments, by 1928 she followed the trend of recorded blues in the later twenties, moving back toward their roots in the country blues. While retaining the more narrative, coherent, and thematically unified structure of popular twelve-bar blues, she wrote an increasing number of her songs by the end of her recording career, and her accompaniments became more and more down-home. Given the high sales of country blues recordings in the late twenties, and given Ma Rainey's development toward this style, her dismissal from Paramount because "her down-home blues had gone out of fashion" was a foolish mistake. For even when she performed songs with no apparent elements of blues, the blues were manifest in her voice, delivery, and accompaniment, and her recording base in Chicago assured continuing links with the deep South, in both her musicians and her audience.

Unlike some other Classic Blues singers, she made all her recordings for a single company, and working for Paramount Records in Chicago had both drawbacks and advantages for her career. Cut off from New York, she never attracted the adulation of a Carl Van Vechten, and could not benefit from the more sophisticated recording techniques of some larger and wealthier New York companies. But Paramount was one of the most important companies making race records, its smaller scale and more countrified audience insured far less tampering with her style, and it promoted her vigorously. Working in Chicago also put her close to the *Chicago Defender*, making publicity easy, and it gave her a choice among some of the finest blues musicians in the country, including Thomas Dorsey, who served her well as band director, accompanist, composer, and arranger for much of her career.

Her style was grounded in blues, but Ma Rainey's recording career was bracketed at its opening and close by experience in minstrelsy, which influenced her repertoire and performance in important ways. However low its wages, minstrelsy gave black performers invaluable experience perfecting their acts in a variety of changing situations, and for a few black women, it offered an escape from domestic drudgery to a world of glamour, travel, and geographical freedom. Arising from Southern experience, and treating with irony the racist stereotypes inherited from its white progenitors, black minstrelsy contributed to Ma Rainey's style the music of ragtime and popular song, as well as a sense of hokum, comedy, parody, variety, and confidence gleaned from hundreds of one-night stands.

The roughness of country blues was reinforced by the often primitive conditions of minstrel performances under canvas: tents could collapse, vendors and circus acts competed with blues singers, Coleman lanterns and portable folding stages created a crude illusion of theater. But while most folk blues singers were farmers or laborers who played music on the side, paid by tips from the crowd at a dance in the neighborhood juke-joint, Madame Gertrude Rainey was a professional entertainer, performing amid chorus lines and comedians, and drawing her pay from the night's receipts. Such a setting emphasized a sense of dramatic distance from the audience, both in the physical gap between stage and seats, and in the masking devices of makeup, props, elaborate costumes, and lights. Her songs thus shared a double aspect: both the personal confessions of experience by the folk artist "Ma," and the dramatic performances and impersonations-of-character by Madame Gertrude Rainey. Country blues singers accompanied themselves; Madame Gertrude did not: her minstrel bands were composed of professional musicians, she sang ragtime and popular songs as well as blues, and her accompaniments could as easily be imitative or hokum as antiphonal.

The T.O.B.A. extended the basically Southern rural form of black minstrelsy to an urban and national scale, ranging throughout the Midwest and South, and spreading its influence as far as New York and the West Coast. By the time Ma Rainey toured this circuit, she was an established Paramount recording star, and the move from minstrelsy to Toby time was a step upward in prestige and power. For all its sham, poor management, and exploitation, Toby time demanded more polished, professional performances. Shows were presented in theaters rather than tents, in black urban areas rather than cotton fields, and by touring this circuit, Ma Rainey won new audiences in major cities of the North and Midwest.

If the blues formed Ma Rainey's voice, and black show business trained it, its sound was amplified and spread by the development of modern mass communications. Without the recording industry, Ma Rainey might have remained a Southern minstrel star, but through the rapid growth and distribution of race records, she could "perform" simultaneously nationwide, in scores of distant places. Even the poorest black bottom of the most remote Southern town could boast at least one portable record player, and Ma Rainey's tours and recordings were interdependent, each generating greater demand for the other.

Within the black community, the press—and particularly the *Chicago Defender*—played a crucial role in creating and reflecting Ma Rainey's personality. While most of the black press usually advertised blues records, the *Defender* was the most important black newspaper of its day; its national edition presented a broad range of information about the black community at large, and also served as a force for education, progress, and social change. To sponsor the blues may have been good business, but it was also consistent with the *Defender's* policy of uplifting the race and glorifying its achievements. Appealing to a broad spectrum of people, the *Defender* printed serious political analysis, editorials, society and religious news, and reviews of books and classical music, as well as sensational crime stories, sports coverage, and three pages about the entertainment business, thus exposing even more genteel and middle-class readers to Ma Rainey's records.

If, without the recording industry, Ma Rainey might have remained merely a Southern celebrity, it is equally valid to state that without the black press and especially the *Chicago Defender*, her recordings could never have achieved the same widespread publicity and distribution, for Paramount's aggressive promotional campaigns and frequent advertisements in the *Defender* for her records and tours reinforced her stature as a major recording artist. Since much of Paramount's business was mail-order, the *Defender's* large circulation brought Ma Rainey into remote rural areas as well as to new urban environments.

In addition, Ma Rainey's itinerant life and the development of her career in many ways paralleled the growth of an important segment of black consciousness, from roughly 1900 to 1930—from rural folk culture to modern urban metropolis; from privation in the South to opportunity and cultural chaos in the North.

For her audience, Ma Rainey was a folk figure who reached her greatest popularity at the same time that black writers like Jean Toomer, Zora Neale Hurston, Langston Hughes, and Sterling Brown were all celebrating the Southern folk experience in novels, poems, essays, and plays. The span of her career witnessed the uprooting of thousands of black people from their homes in the South and their movement to alien environments in major cities of the North and Midwest, and her lyrics frequently reflect this dislocation: the sentimentalized yearning for the South; the attraction to, yet fear of, the North; the man who takes his country woman to the city, only to abandon her there; the working woman whose sweetman cheats her of her savings; the young girl who heads South to her parents when her Northern love affair goes sour.

It is no mere coincidence that the blues flourished and achieved their greatest national popularity as the culture they sprang from was rent by departures and migrations. For the rural audience, listening to Ma Rainey's blues was an act of identification and communion, but for its displaced urban counterpart in the North and Midwest, the same music symbolized a quickly vanishing world, which lived faintly through letters and an occasional visit. Even for those with no wish to return South, attending a concert or listening to Ma Rainey's records was a way of witnessing, testifying to the strength of black cultural roots and shared communal experiences, recapturing the past and the values of a lost culture, while in a strange land.

Ma Rainey's success had implications as well for the white world of the twenties, for the extensive popularity of blues on a national scale was yet another symptom of the dominant culture's interest and receptiveness toward other, more exotic and nonrational forms of expression. Thousands of white people who would never hear of Ma Rainey were excited or disturbed by the "jungle rhythms" of jazz, the popular interpretations of Freud, and the violent changes in social mores after World War I. The twenties witnessed women's suffrage, women blues singers, and a new tolerance for more open expressions of female sexuality; the national celebrity of the vamp and the flapper as white female images mirrors, if faintly, the franker and more aggressive female eroticism found in the blues.

While expressing such sexual boldness in her lyrics and performance, Ma Rainey also represented a new kind of female symbol in black popular entertainment, different from minstrel stereotypes of suffering mammies, tragic mulattoes, "sepia lovelies," and hot-blooded sexpots: she was a *mama*, an authority generative, nurturant, yet sexual, who combined eros and homeliness, sex appeal and self-mockery, pathos and humor; the mythopoeic establisher of tradition, a black culture-heroine. Regardless of who in fact originated the blues (and evidence points increasingly to a collective, anonymous flowering in East Texas and the Mississippi Delta), Ma Rainey's professional debut is coeval with the birth of the blues, and the *myth* of Ma Rainey as Mother of the Blues, the one who taught other performers to sing the blues, is of lasting significance.

Her historical primacy, the unconscious birth imagery of her stage performance (as she issued from the doors of a giant Victrola cabinet), the rumors of her advanced age, her noted generosity, warmth, and encouragement toward younger performers—all reinforce the image of a creative and creating, nurturant and caring, yet authoritative and powerful figure. While white culture frequently views heavy women as ugly, and mothers as asexual, Ma Rainey could be both big and sexy, both maternal and erotic. She was fully alive to the varieties of sexual experience and expression; bisexual herself, she sang publicly of lesbians and homosexuals, joked about her motherly/incestuous attractions to younger men, and reaffirmed in her songs the centrality of passion in human affairs.

She was short and fat, and her features were plain—yet her personal success defied the myth that youth, light skin, "good" hair, and a tall slender figure were all that mattered. Denied all these "attributes," Ma Rainey proved that a strong black woman could travel the country, manage a minstrel troupe or a theater, earn a high salary, record almost one hundred songs, and command great personal devotion from thousands of fans. Her appeal was based not on glamour, but on warmth, talent, personality, and sheer stylistic power that ranged from comedy to pathos, cynicism to melodrama; in live performance, her hold on an audience defied easy description: "She jes' catch hold of us, somekindaway."

Musically, she established the classic performances of "Bo-Weevil Blues" and "Moonshine Blues" and made the first recordings of such standards as "See, See Rider" and "Hear Me Talking to You," and she was equally skilled in transforming a popular tune into a blues, as seen in her fine reinterpretation of "Oh Daddy." Her great professional resourcefulness was an ability to exploit whatever avenue of employment lay open to her, without seriously compromising her style. She reached a peak in minstrelsy, then recorded prolifically for five years, ranging from various types of songs with jazz band accompaniments to down-home blues; she toured the country on the T.O.B.A., but was able to return to minstrelsy when the Depression destroyed both Toby time and Paramount Records, and even after retirement she managed two theaters.

As a figure in black music, she is both representative of and distinctive among the early women blues singers. Bessie Smith had a greater voice; Sara Martin, too, recorded with jug bands; Ida Cox also sang a good proportion of pure blues; Mamie Smith actually began the blues boom; singers like Memphis Minnie were more purely country—but of them all, Ma Rainey was the first to perform professionally, retained the clearest blues influence of any first-ranked Classic Blues star, and remains the strongest single link between folk blues and black show business.

By clearly examining what she sang, we may see a representative of the messages blues women were addressing to their audiences. She undoubtedly performed the biggest hits of the day, but she also made songs hits by her own treatment, and her recorded lyrics combine powerful folk poetry with the more conventional versifying of popular song. Devoid of topical references, Ma Rainey's recorded lyrics are timeless in a way that more contemporary songs of the twenties are not; her love songs pare the emotional landscape down to a woman, her man, and her rival, while her other songs attempt to analyze experience and give the listener strategies for coping with it. In her most striking recordings Ma Rainey deals with prostitution, homosexuality, lesbianism, and sadomasochism. She defies easy stereotypes, singing of women who do not fall to pieces when love is gone, of a prostitute who leaves her pimp, of a lesbian who flaunts her preference; with only a single

exception her songs strongly condemn cruelty, brutality, and violence against women.

A few of her female characters despair about their situations,
but more attempt to change them, and she offers to women alterna-
tives, choices. The response to a lost love may be sorrow; more often
it is action, motion, and anger, as a woman tries a reconciliation,
gets rid of a rival, confronts the mean mistreater, or finally kills him.
While some songs see the lover as a necessity, most offer women
other means of emotional or financial satisfaction—going back to
work, searching for the man, returning to the South, finding
another "papa," or seeking revenge. Some songs profess indifference to men, and others analyze life situations beyond the range of
individual passion, commenting comically or cynically about sex,
music, drinking, dancing, prison, superstition, and more philosophical issues of luck and fortune. If many songs view women as
rivals and natural enemies, men as omnipotent mean mistreaters,
Ma Rainey does give advice to women in "Trust No Man," female
sexuality is frequently assertive and positive, and men are just as
often helpless pawns attracting powerful, combative women.

How to live when love is gone, how to enjoy life's pleasures,
how to face a world that makes no sense: by understanding the
message of Ma Rainey's blues, we may begin to recognize the black
folk themes that captivated the country during the twenties, and
that perennially re-emerge in American popular music. Whether
singing of wronged love, comic distress, or sardonic frustration,
Ma Rainey gives us an attitude, an indomitable approach to the
world that balances misery with humor, sorrow with anger, outer
chaos with inner will. As a singer, she had few equals; as a pioneer performer, she had none in her day. Her dual traditions of
minstrelsy and country blues—of show business and folk culture
—made her a particularly appropriate medium for her material:
in her we see most clearly the intermingling of these two great
traditions, expressed in their most classic form. It is for the diversity
of her talents and themes that she will be most remembered. Even
confining this study to her recordings, we have seen substantial
evidence of the range of her abilities—of her songwriting, dancing,
comedy, and acting as well as her singing. A star in blues, minstrelsy, and vaudeville, she was equally impressive performing
traditional blues, composed blues, or popular songs.

Her significance and achievement continue to touch later performers. Recorded by Memphis Minnie in 1940, one year after Ma Rainey's death, "Ma Rainey Blues" contains a tribute she would have appreciated:

She was born in Georgia, traveled all over this world, (2)
And she's the best blues singer, people, that I ever heard.

Through her recordings, Ma Rainey has traveled the world in fact, and the Mother of the Blues has passed into the blues herself.

Discography

Abbreviations[1]

Instruments

as	alto saxophone	p	piano
bb	brass bass	ss	soprano saxophone
bj	banjo	sw	slide-whistle
bsx	bass saxophone	tb	trombone
c	cornet	v	vocal
cl	clarinet	vn	violin
d	drums		
g	guitar		
j	jug		
k	kazoo		

Record Labels. The following abbreviations have been used for record labels, all other labels being shown in full. Unless otherwise noted, all labels are of American origin. Recordings pressed from dubbed stampers are indicated by italics.[2]

AFCDJ	Association Française des Collectionneurs de Disques du Jazz (French)
AFG	Association de Gramophilie (French)
AM	American Music
Amp	Ampersand (Australian)
Bwy	Broadway
Hg	Harmograph
Jazz	Jazz (English)
JC	Jazz Collector (English)
JD	Jazz Document (French)
JI	Jazz Information
JRS	Jazz Record Society (French)
Pm	Paramount
Ri	Ristic (English)
Sig	Signature
Stv	Storyville (Danish)
UHCA	United Hot Clubs of America
XX	XX (Australian)

Ma Rainey

This artist's real name is Gertrude Rainey. The first four couplings are all labeled *Madame "Ma" Rainey*, and Pm 12098 is labeled *"Ma" Rainey*. On most of the others, the quotation marks are omitted.

Ma Rainey, v; acc. Lovie Austin and Her Blues Serenaders: Tommy Ladnier, c; Jimmy O'Bryant, cl; Lovie Austin, p.   Chicago, December 1923.

1596–2	Bad Luck Blues	Pm 12081
1597–2	Bo-Weavil Blues [*sic*]	Pm 12080, *Ri 13, Stv J50*
1598–2	Barrel House Blues	Pm 12082, *JC L48; AFCDJ A047*
1599–1,–2	Those All Night Long Blues	Pm 12081
1608–1,–2	Moonshine Blues	Pm 12083, *Hg 896, JC L66*
1609–2	Last Minute Blues	Pm 12080, *Ri 13, Stv J50*
1612–2	Southern Blues	Pm 12083, *Hg 896, JC L66*
1613–2	Walking Blues	Pm 12082, *JC L48, AFCDJ A047*

Hg 896 as by Anne Smith acc. by Goldie Hall and Her Blues Serenaders, using matrix 1608–2. It is not known which take of 1608 is used on JC L66. Matrices 1610 and 1611 are untraced.[3] Ri 13 and Stv J50 are ten-inch standard-groove 45 rpm pressings.

Acc. The Pruitt Twins: Miles Pruitt, bj; Milas Pruitt, g.   Chicago, c. March 1924.

1698–2	Lost Wandering Blues	Pm 12098
1699–1	Dream Blues	Pm 12098

Acc. Lovie Austin's Blues Serenaders (Her Georgia Band on Pm 12227 and 12257): Tommy Ladnier, c; Jimmy O'Bryant, cl; Charles Harris, as; Lovie Austin, p. Chicago, c. March 1924.

1701–2	Honey Where You Been So Long	Pm 12200, *JC L82*
1702–2,–3	Ya-Da-Do	Pm 12257
1703–1	Those Dogs Of Mine (Famous Cornfield Blues)	Pm 12215, *AM 6, JC L78*
1704–2	Lucky Rock Blues	Pm 12215, *AM 6, JC L78*

Chicago, c. April 1924.

1741–1[4]	South Bound Blues	Pm 12227, *JC L107, AFCDJ A010*

Chicago, c. May 1924.

| 1758-2 | Lawd Send Me A Man Blues | Pm 12227, *JC L107, AFCDJ A010* |
| 1759-2 | Ma Rainey's Mystery Record | Pm 12200, *JC L82* |

Acc. poss. Milas Pruitt, g; unknown, 2nd g-1.   Chicago, c. August 1924.

| 1824-2,-3 | Shave 'Em Dry Blues-1 | Pm 12222 |
| 1825-2 | Farewell Daddy Blues | Pm 12222 |

Acc. Her Georgia Jazz Band: Howard Scott, c; Charlie Green, tb; Don Redman, cl; Fletcher Henderson, p; Charlie Dixon, bj; unknown, percussion effects-1.   New York City, c. 15 October 1924.

1922-2	Booze And Blues-1	Pm 12242
1923-2	Toad Frog Blues-1	Pm 12242
1924-1,-2	Jealous Hearted Blues	Pm 12252, *UHCA 86, JI 9, JC L20, Amp R101, AFG 6*

It is not known which take of 1924 is used on JC or AFG; all other dubbed reissues use 1924-2.

Louis Armstrong, c; Buster Bailey, cl; replace Scott and Redman.   New York City, c. 16 October 1924.

1925-1,-2	See See Rider Blues-1	Pm 12252, *UHCA 85, JI 9, JC L20, Amp R101, AFG 6*
1926-2	Jelly Bean Blues-1	Pm 12238, *14016, UHCA 84, JI 8, JC L10, XX 9, AFCDJ A02*
1927-2,-3	Countin' The Blues	Pm 12238, *14016, UHCA 83, JI 8, JC L10, XX 9, AFCDJ A02*

It is not known which takes are used on AFCDJ, AFG, or JC; other dubbed reissues use 1925-1 or 1927-2. XX 9 as by Mama Can Can and Orphan Will (with The Elastic Band).

Acc. Her Georgia Jazz Band: Tommy Ladnier, c; Jimmy O'Bryant, cl; Lovie Austin, p.   Chicago, c. November 1924.

| 10001-2 | Cell Bound Blues | Pm 12257 |

Acc. Her Georgia Band: Hooks Tilford, as; unknown, k/sw-1; poss. Lil Henderson, p; poss. Happy Bolton, d. No drums on 2139 and only one crash on 2138. Chicago, May 1925.

2136-1,-2	Army Camp Harmony Blues	Pm 12284, *Ri 13, Stv J50*
2137-1,-2	Explaining The Blues	Pm 12284, *Ri 13, Stv J50*
2138-1	Louisiana Hoodoo Blues	Pm 12290
2139-1	Goodbye Daddy Blues-1	Pm 12290

Ri 13 and Stv J50 are ten-inch standard-groove 45 rpm pressings; takes used are not known.

Acc. Her Georgia Band. Probable personnel: Kid Henderson, c; Lucien Brown, cl–1/as; Lil Henderson, p; George Williams, bj; Happy Bolton, d/chimes. Chicago, c. August 1925.

2209–1,–2	Stormy Sea Blues–1	Pm 12295
2210–2	Rough And Tumble Blues	Pm 12311
2211–1,–2	Night Time Blues	Pm 12303
2212–2	Levee Camp Moan–1	Pm 12295
2213–1,–2	Four Day Honory Scat [sic]	Pm 12303
2214–2	Memphis Bound Blues	Pm 12311

Acc. Her Georgia Band: Joe Smith, c; Charlie Green, tb; Buster Bailey, cl; Coleman Hawkins, bsx; Fletcher Henderson, p; Charlie Dixon, bj. New York City, c. December 1925.

2369–2	Slave To The Blues	Pm 12332, JC L87
2370–1,–2	Yonder Come The Blues	Pm 12357, Sig 908, JC L73, Jazz 5001
2371–1,–2	Titanic Man Blues	Pm 12374
2372–2	Chain Gang Blues	Pm 12338
2373–1,–2	Bessemer Bound Blues	Pm 12374
2374–1	Oh My Babe Blues	Pm 12332, JC L87
2375–2	Wringing And Twisting Blues	Pm 12338
2376–2	Stack O'Lee Blues	Pm 12357, Sig 908, JC L73, Jazz 5001

It is not known which take of 2370 is used on JC L73; Sig 908 and Jazz 5001 use 2370–1.

Acc. Her Georgia Band: prob. Bernie Young or Dave C. Nelson, c; poss. Albert Wynn, tb; poss. Stump Johnson or Barney Bigard, ss/as; prob. Lil Henderson, p; unknown, bj. Chicago, c. March 1926.

2448–1,–2	Broken Hearted Blues	Pm 12364
2451–3,–4	Jealousy Blues	Pm 12364
2452–1,–2	Seeking Blues	Pm 12352

Matrices 2449 and 2450 are untraced.[5]

Acc. Jimmy Blythe, p. Chicago, c. March 1926.

2466–1,–3	Mountain Jack Blues	Pm 12352

Acc. Her Georgia Band: Homer Hobson, c; Albert Wynn, tb; Tom Brown, cl/as; Doc Cheatham, ss; unknown, musical saw; Lil Henderson, p; Rip Bassett, bj; Ben Thigpen, d. Chicago, c. June 1926.

2627–1	Down In The Basement	Pm 12395
2628–1	Sissy Blues	Pm 12384
2629–2	Broken Soul Blues	Pm 12384

Acc. Lil Henderson, p.   Chicago, c. June 1926.

2631–1   Trust No Man   Pm 12395

Acc. Blind Blake, g; poss. Leroy Pickett, vn.   Chicago, c. December 1926.

4019–2   Little Low Mama Blues   Pm 12419, Bwy 5005
4020–1   Grievin' Hearted Blues   Pm 12419
4020–2   Grievin' Hearted Blues   Pm 12419, Bwy 5005

Bwy 5005 as by Lila Patterson.

Acc. Jimmy Blythe, p.   Chicago, c. December 1926.

4021–2   Don't Fish In My Sea   Pm 12438, Bwy 5010, AM 5, JC L16,
                                             JRS AA121

Bwy 5010 as by Lila Patterson.

Acc. prob. Jimmy Blythe, p; Blind Blake, g.   Chicago, c. February 1927.

405   Morning Hour Blues   Pm 12455, JC L57, AFCDJ A11

It is not clear whether this is a true matrix number or a control number.

Acc. prob. B.T. Wingfield, c; Johnny Dodds or unknown, cl; prob. Jimmy Blythe or
Tiny Parham, p.   Chicago, c. February 1927.

407–2   Weepin' Woman Blues   Pm 12455, JC L57, AFCDJ A11
408–2   Soon This Morning   Pm 12438, Bwy 5010, AM 5,
                                            JC L16, JRS AA121

Bwy 5010 as by Lila Patterson. Pm 12438 as by Ma Rainey and Her Georgia Band. It is
not clear whether these are true matrix numbers or control numbers.

Acc. Her Georgia Band: Shirley Clay, c; Kid Ory, tb; Claude 'Hop' Hopkins, p;
unknown, bj; unknown, bb.   Chicago, c. August 1927.

4682–2   Big Boy Blues   Pm 12548, JD 015
4683–2   Blues Oh Blues   Pm 12566, 4, JC L98, JRS AA108

Ma Rainey and male voice, talking–1.   Chicago, c. August 1927.

4690–3   Damper Down Blues   Pm 12548, JD 015
4691–2   Gone Daddy Blues–1   Pm 12526, 3, JC L120
4692–1   Oh Papa Blues   Pm 12566, 4, JC L98, JRS AA108

Hopkins only–2; Ory, Hopkins, and bb only –3.   Chicago, c. August 1927.

4707–1   Misery Blues   Pm 12508, Bwy 5018, JC L52
4708–2   Dead Drunk Blues–2   Pm 12508, Bwy 5018, JC L52
4709–1   Slow Driving Moan–3   Pm 12526, 3, JC L120

Bwy 5018 as by Lila Patterson. Pm 12508 label states "piano acc. Hop Hopkins."

Acc. Her Georgia Band: prob. Shirley Clay, c; prob. Al Wynn, tb; poss. Artie Starks, cl; unknown, p; unknown, d; male voice talking–1; Ma Rainey also speaks–2.   Chicago, c. December 1927.

20228–3	Blues The World Forgot— Part 1–1,–2	Pm 12647, *P1*, *JC L35*
20229–2	"Ma" Rainey's Black Bottom–1	Pm 12590, *JD 014*
20230–2	Blues The World Forgot— Part 2–1,–2	Pm 12647, *P1*, *JC L35*
20231–2	Hellish Rag	Pm 12612
20232–1	Georgia Cake Walk–1,–2	Pm 12590, *JD 014*
20233–1	New Bo-Weavil Blues [*sic*]	Pm 12603, *P2*, *JC L42*
20234–2	Moonshine Blues	Pm 12603, *P2*, *JC L42*
20235–3	Ice Bag Papa	Pm 12612

Matrices 20231 and 20235 feature an unknown male vocalist in place of Ma Rainey, and are jazz rather than blues performances, but are listed for completeness. The Paramount label lists Prof. C.M. Russell, director.

Acc. Her Tub Jug Washboard Band: poss. Tampa Red, k; poss. a second k; Georgia Tom Dorsey, p; unknown, bj; unknown, j; moaning by the band–1.   Chicago, c. June 1928.

20661–1	Black Cat Hoot Owl Blues	Pm 12687
20662–3	Log Camp Blues	Pm 12804
20663–2	Hear Me Talking To You	Pm 12668, *Ri 6*
20664–2	Hustlin' Blues	Pm 12804
20665–2	Prove It On Me Blues	Pm 12668, *Ri 6*
20666–1	Victim Of The Blues	Pm 12687
20667–1,–2	Traveling Blues	Pm 12706, *14011*, *JC L1*
20668–1,–2	Deep Moaning Blues–1	Pm 12706, *14011*, *JC L1*

It is not known which takes are used on 14011 or *JC L1*.

Acc. Georgia Tom Dorsey, p; Tampa Red, g.   Chicago, c. September 1928.

20878–1	Daddy Goodbye Blues	Pm 12963
20879–2	Sleep Talking Blues	Pm 12760
20880–2	Tough Luck Blues	Pm 12735
20881–1	Blame It On The Blues	Pm 12760
20882–2	Sweet Rough Man	Pm 12926
20883–3	Runaway Blues	Pm 12902

Acc. poss. Eddie Miller, p.   Chicago, c. September 1928.

20885–2	Screech Owl Blues	Pm 12735
20886–1	Black Dust Blues	Pm 12926

Matrix 20884 is by Blind Blake.

Acc. Georgia Tom Dorsey, p; Tampa Red, g.   Chicago, c. September 1928.

20897–1	Leaving This Morning	Pm 12902
20898–1	Black Eye Blues	Pm unissued; *Yazoo L–1039 (mg)*
20898–2	Black Eye Blues	Pm 12963

Ma Rainey and Papa Charlie Jackson: vocal duet; acc. Papa Charlie Jackson, bj. Chicago, c. October 1928.

| 20921–4 | Ma And Pa Poorhouse Blues | Pm 12718, *JD 013, Ri 5* |

Chicago, c. December 1928.

| 21044–1 | Big Feeling Blues | Pm 12718, *JD 013, Ri 5* |

Microgroove Issues[6]

LPs are listed first, followed by EPs and finally odd titles from miscellaneous issues. Those odd titles which are also to be found on "collection" LPS (LPS featuring more than two artists) will be designated thus*. The speed shown for the microgroove issues distinguishes the LP from the EP: LPS are normally recorded at 33-1/3 rpm, while EPS are recorded at 45 rpm. Where matrix numbers are not available, the titles are listed in their place. The letters in the column preceding the matrix numbers are abbreviations for the following: C, Continental issue; E, English issue; D, Deleted. American microgroove issues show no letter abbreviation after the catalogue number.[7]

Riverside RLP 12–108		1598–2	4020	20663–2
12" 33-1/3	D	1613–2	4683–2	20665–2
		2370[8]	4692–1	20666–1
		2376–2	20661–1	21044–1

Riverside RM 8807	C	1596–2	1612–2	1702–3
12" 33-1/3	D	1597–2	1613–2	1703–1
		1598–2	1698–2	1704–2
		1599–2	1699–1	1741–1
		1608–2	1701–2	1758–2
		1609–2		

Riverside RLP 12–137		1612–2	1758	2452
12" 33-1/3	D	1701–2	1759–2	2466
		1703–1	2448	4021–2
		1704–2	2451	Soon This Morning

Riverside 1016, London AL 3538	1701–2	2448	2466
	1758–2	2451	20229–2
	1759–2	2452	

Riverside 1045, London AL 3558	2372–2	4708–2	2628–1
10" 33-1/3	D	2375–2	20233–1	2629–2
	4707–1	20234–2	

Riverside 1003, London AL 3502	20667	20879–1	20897–1
10" 33-1/3	D 20668	20881–1	20898–2
	20878–1	20883–3	

Biograph BLP 12001		1922–2	2212–2	20667–1
12″ 33-1/3		1923–2	2371–1	2629–2
		2138–1	20228–3	4707–1
		2209–1	20230–2	Weepin' Woman Blues

Ristic 19	E	1597–2	2137	20921–4
10″ 33-1/3	D	1609–2	20663–2	21044–1
		2136	20665–2	

Milestone 2001		1924–2	2210–2	2369–2
10″ 33-1/3		10001–2	2211–1	2373–2
		2136–1	2213–1	4691–2
		2137–1	2214–2	4709–1

Biograph BLP 12011		1824–3	2451–4	20664–2
12″ 33-1/3		1825–2	2628–1	20921–4
		1927–3	4021–2	21044–1
		2374–1	20662–3	Soon This Morning

| Biograph BLP 12032 | (same as Riverside RM 8807) |
| 12″ 33-1/3 | |

Milestone MLP 2008	2372–2	20233–2	20880–2
12″ 33-1/3	2375–2	20234–2	20881–1
	4708–2	20668	20882–2
	20229–2	20878–1	20898

Milestone MLP 2017	2448	4683–2	20665–2	20897–1
12″ 33-1/3	2466	4692–1	20666–1	Morning Hour Blues
	2627–1	20661–1	20879–2	
	2631–1	20663–2	20883–3	

Milestone M 47021	1924–2	2466	20233–2	20879–2
12″ 33-1/3	1925–1	2631–1	20234–2	20880–2
(two-record set)	1926–2	4683–2	20661–1	20881–1
	1927–2	4691–2	20663–2	20882–2
	2369–2	4692–1	20665–2	20883–3
	2372–2	4708–2	20666–1	20897–1
	2373–2	4709–1	20668	20898–2
	2375–2	20229–2	20878–1	Morning Hour Blues

Rarities RAL 9	E	20878	20882
10″ 33-1/3		20879	20883
		20880	20885

| Riverside EP 107 | 4692–1 | 1598–2 | 21044–1 |
| 7″ 45 rpm | D 4683–2 | | |

Jazz Collector JEL 12 7″ 45 rpm Reverse by Ida Cox	E 4019–2 D	4020	
Jazz Collector JEL 22 7″ 45 rpm Reverse by Trixie Smith	E 20667 D	20668	
Riverside RLP 12–131 Riverside RLP 12–101	D 1925 D 1926–2	1927	
Folkways FP 75/FJ 2811	20663–2		
*Riverside RLP 12–113	D 2371		
*Riverside RLP 12–121	D 2374–1	2627–1	2631–1
*Riverside RLP 12–134	D 2375–2		
*Riverside 1001, London AL 3501	D 1925	1926–2	1927
*Riverside 1032, London AL 3530	D 4021–1	Soon This Morning	
*Folkways FP 55/FJ 2802	4707–1		
*Folkways FP 59/FJ 2804	20667		
*Audubon AAC *Audubon AAM	Weepin' Woman Blues; Soon This Morning 20921–4	21044–1	
*Southern Preservation Records NRC 656	20662–3	20664–2	

Appendices

Appendix A

Classification of Ma Rainey's Recordings

Matrix #	Title	Issue #
Twelve-Bar Blues (51):		
1596	"Bad Luck Blues"	Pm 12081
1598	"Barrel House Blues"	Pm 12082
1609	"Last Minute Blues"	Pm 12080
1612	"Southern Blues"*	Pm 12083
1613	"Walking Blues"	Pm 12082
1698	"Lost Wandering Blues"	Pm 12098
1699	"Dream Blues"	Pm 12098
1759	"Ma Rainey's Mystery Record"	Pm 12200
1825	"Farewell Daddy Blues"	Pm 12222
1922	"Booze and Blues"	Pm 12242
1923	"Toad Frog Blues"	Pm 12242
1924	"Jealous Hearted Blues"	Pm 12252
1927	"Countin' the Blues"	Pm 12238
2136	"Army Camp Harmony Blues"*	Pm 12284
2137	"Explaining the Blues"	Pm 12284
2138	"Louisiana Hoodoo Blues"	Pm 12290
2209	"Stormy Sea Blues"	Pm 12295
2210	"Rough and Tumble Blues"	Pm 12311
2211	"Night Time Blues"	Pm 12303
2214	"Memphis Bound Blues"	Pm 12311
2369	"Slave to the Blues"	Pm 12332
2372	"Chain Gang Blues"	Pm 12338
2373	"Bessemer Bound Blues"	Pm 12374
2448	"Broken Hearted Blues"	Pm 12364
2466	"Mountain Jack Blues"*	Pm 12352
2628	"Sissy Blues"	Pm 12384
4019	"Little Low Mama Blues"*	Pm 12419
4021	"Don't Fish in My Sea"	Pm 12438

*Indicates completely traditional lyrics. Other blues range from completely composed to mixtures of composed and traditional lyrics.

Matrix #	Title	Issue #
405	"Morning Hour Blues"*	Pm 12455
407-2	"Weepin' Woman Blues"*	Pm 12455
408	"Soon This Morning"*	Pm 12438
4682	"Big Boy Blues"*	Pm 12548
4690	"Damper Down Blues"*	Pm 12548
4708	"Dead Drunk Blues"	Pm 12508
20661	"Black Cat Hoot Owl Blues"	Pm 12687
20662	"Log Camp Blues"	Pm 12804
20663	"Hear Me Talking to You"	Pm 12668
20664	"Hustlin' Blues"	Pm 12804
20666	"Victim of the Blues"	Pm 12687
20667	"Traveling Blues"	Pm 12706
20668	"Deep Moaning Blues"*	Pm 12706
20879	"Sleep Talking Blues"	Pm 12760
20880	"Tough Luck Blues"	Pm 12735
20881	"Blame It on the Blues"	Pm 12760
20882	"Sweet Rough Man"	Pm 12926
20883	"Runaway Blues"*	Pm 12902
20885	"Screech Owl Blues"	Pm 12735
20886	"Black Dust Blues"	Pm 12926
20897	"Leaving This Morning"	Pm 12902
20921	"Ma and Pa Poorhouse Blues"	Pm 12718
21044	"Big Feeling Blues"	Pm 12718

Eight-Bar Blues (2):

1824	"Shave 'Em Dry Blues"	Pm 12222
20878	"Daddy Goodbye Blues"*	Pm 12963

Mixtures of Blues and Popular Song Forms (14):

1597	"Bo-Weevil Blues"	Pm 12080
1608	"Moonshine Blues"	Pm 12083
1704	"Lucky Rock Blues"	Pm 12215
1925	"See, See Rider Blues"	Pm 12252
1926	"Jelly Bean Blues"	Pm 12238
10001	"Cell Bound Blues"	Pm 12257
2139	"Goodbye Daddy Blues"[1]	Pm 12290
2371	"Titanic Man Blues"[2]	Pm 12374
2452	"Seeking Blues"	Pm 12352
4020	"Grievin' Hearted Blues"	Pm 12419
4691	"Gone Daddy Blues"	Pm 12526
4709	"Slow Driving Moan"	Pm 12526
20233	"New Bo-Weevil Blues"	Pm 12603
20234	"Moonshine Blues"	Pm 12603

Matrix #	Title	Issue #
Ballad (1):		
2376	"Stack O' Lee Blues"	Pm 12357
Comedy (3):		
20228	"Blues the World Forgot" Part I	Pm 12647
20230	"Blues the World Forgot" Part II[3]	Pm 12647
20232	"Georgia Cake Walk"	Pm 12590
Non-blues (21):		
1599	"Those All Night Long Blues"	Pm 12081
1701	"Honey, Where You Been So Long?"	Pm 12200
1702	"Ya-Da-Do"	Pm 12257
1703	"Those Dogs of Mine"	Pm 12215
1741	"South Bound Blues"	Pm 12227
1758	"Lawd, Send Me a Man Blues"	Pm 12227
2212	"Levee Camp Moan"	Pm 12295
2213	" 'Fore Day Honry Scat"	Pm 12303
2370	"Yonder Come the Blues"	Pm 12357
2374	"Oh My Babe Blues"	Pm 12332
2375	"Wringing and Twisting Blues"	Pm 12338
2451	"Jealousy Blues"	Pm 12364
2627	"Down in the Basement"	Pm 12395
2629	"Broken Soul Blues"	Pm 12384
2631	"Trust No Man"	Pm 12395
4683	"Blues Oh Blues"	Pm 12566
4692	"Oh Papa Blues"	Pm 12566
4707	"Misery Blues"	Pm 12508
20229	"Ma Rainey's Black Bottom"	Pm 12590
20665	"Prove It on Me Blues"	Pm 12668
20898	"Black Eye Blues"	Pm 12963

Appendix B

"Goodbye Mama Forever Blues"

I have discovered at the Library of Congress the copyright deposit and lead sheet for one song which does not appear in Ma Rainey's discography—"Goodbye Mama Forever Blues," written by Ma Rainey. I believe that this is either matrix 2449 or 2450, both listed as "untraced" in Godrich and Dixon. This seems plausible because the lead sheet is dated June 21, 1928, the day it was received at the Library of Congress; on that same date the following matrices were also received: 2448 ("Broken Hearted Blues"), 2451 ("Jealousy Blues"), 2628 ("Sissy Blues"), 2631 ("Trust No Man"), 4019 ("Little Low Mama Blues"), 4020 ("Grievin' Hearted Blues"), 4021 ("Don't Fish in My Sea") and 407 ("Weepin' Woman Blues"). It is likely that 2449 and 2450 were recorded during the same session as 2448, 2451 and 2452: around March 1926. Except in a few instances, Ma Rainey's songs were usually sent in for copyright in groups, after one or more recording sessions. Since "Goodbye Mama Forever Blues" fits sequentially with 2448, 2451, and 2452, and since its lyrics were received for copyright on the same day as the others, it is probably either 2449 or 2450.[1]

The following is a copy of the lead sheet for "Goodbye Mama Forever Blues" (by Ma Rainey, © 1928 by Chicago Music Publishing Company, renewed 1956 by John Steiner). The text has been edited to normalize spelling and punctuation.

> Here comes that train to take my man away, (2)
> I'm gonna stay right here, he might come back some day.
>
> Mr. Conductor, why do you treat me so bad? (2)
> You've got the man I love, the only man I've ever had.
>
> My heart's on fire, I'm going round and round, (2)
> It's the man I love, he leaves 'em burning down.

Appendix C
Recordings Cited

Recordings by Ma Rainey:

Issue number	Title	Author(s)	Publisher and date
Pm 12081	"Bad Luck Blues"	Lovie Austin	CMPC,[1] 1924
Pm 12082	"Barrel House Blues"	Lovie Austin	CMPC, 1924
Pm 12374	"Bessemer Bound Blues"	Everett Murphy	CMPC, 1926
Pm 12718	"Big Feeling Blues"	"Selma Davis" (w)[2] Ma Rainey (m)[3]	CMPC, 1929
Pm 12687	"Black Cat Hoot Owl Blues"	Thomas Dorsey	CMPC, 1928
Pm 12926	"Black Dust Blues"	Selma Davis (w) Ma Rainey (m)	CMPC, 1928
Pm 12963	"Black Eye Blues" (© as "Gonna Catch You with Your Breeches [sic] Down")	Thomas Dorsey	CMPC, 1928
Pm 12760	"Blame It on the Blues"	Thomas Dorsey	CMPC, 1928
Pm 12566	"Blues Oh Blues"	Ma Rainey	CMPC, 1928
Pm 12647	"Blues the World Forgot," Parts I & II	(untraced)[4]	
Pm 12242	"Booze and Blues"	J. Guy Suddoth	CMPC, 1924
Pm 12080	"Bo-Weevil Blues"	Ma Rainey	CMPC, 1924
Pm 12364	"Broken Hearted Blues"	Ma Rainey	CMPC, 1928
Pm 12384	"Broken Soul Blues"	H. Strathedene Parham	CMPC, 1926
Pm 12257	"Cell Bound Blues"	Ma Rainey	CMPC, 1925
Pm 12338	"Chain Gang Blues"	Charles J. Parker (w) Thomas Dorsey (m)	CMPC, 1926
Pm 12238	"Countin' the Blues"	Ma Rainey	CMPC, 1924
Pm 12963	"Daddy Goodbye Blues"	Ma Rainey	CMPC, 1928
Pm 12548	"Damper Down Blues"	(untraced)	
Pm 12508	"Dead Drunk Blues"	George W. Thomas	George W. Thomas, 1927

Issue number	Title	Author(s)	Publisher & date
Pm 12706	"Deep Moaning Blues"	Ma Rainey	CMPC, 1928
Pm 12438	"Don't Fish in My Sea"	Bessie Smith (w) Ma Rainey (m)	CMPC, 1928
Pm 12395	"Down in the Basement" (© as "Take Me to the Basement")	H. Strathedene Parham	CMPC, 1926
Pm 12098	"Dream Blues"		(notice of use filed by CMPC, 1924)[5]
Pm 12284	"Explaining the Blues"	Thomas Dorsey	CMPC, 1925
Pm 12222	"Farewell Daddy Blues"		(notice of use filed by CMPC, 1924)
Pm 12303	" 'Fore Day Honry Scat"	Billie McOwens & Ma Rainey	CMPC, 1925
Pm 12590	"Georgia Cakewalk"	(untraced)	
Pm 12526	"Gone Daddy Blues"	(untraced)	
(unknown)[6]	"Goodbye Mama Forever Blues"	Ma Rainey	CMPC, 1928
Pm 12668	"Hear Me Talking to You"	Ma Rainey	CMPC, 1928
Pm 12200	"Honey, Where You Been So Long?"	Tom Delaney	Tom Delaney, 1921
Pm 12804	"Hustlin' Blues"	Malissa Nix & Thomas Dorsey	CMPC, 1928
Pm 12252	"Jealous Hearted Blues"	Lovie Austin	CMPC, 1924
Pm 12364	"Jealousy Blues"	Glasco & Glasco	CMPC, 1928
Pm 12238	"Jelly Bean Blues"	Lena Arrant	CMPC, 1924
Pm 12080	"Last Minute Blues"	Thomas Dorsey	Thomas Dorsey, 1924
Pm 12227	"Lawd, Send Me a Man Blues"	(untraced)	
Pm 12902	"Leaving This Morning"	Selma Davis (w) Ma Rainey (m)	CMPC, 1928
Pm 12295	"Levee Camp Moan"	(untraced)	
Pm 12419	"Little Low Mama Blues"	Ma Rainey	CMPC, 1928
Pm 12098	"Lost Wandering Blues"		(notice of use filed by CMPC, 1924)
Pm 12290	"Louisiana Hoodoo Blues"	Ma Rainey	CMPC, 1925
Pm 12215	"Lucky Rock Blues"	Katie Winters (w) Lovie Austin (m)	Katie Winters, 1924

Issue number	Title	Author(s)	Publisher and date
Pm 12718	"Ma and Pa Poorhouse Blues"	Selma Davis (w) Ma Rainey (m)	CMPC, 1929
Pm 12590	"Ma Rainey's Black Bottom"	Ma Rainey	CMPC, 1928
Pm 12200	"Ma Rainey's Mystery Record"	Guy Early & Thomas Dorsey	CMPC, 1924
Pm 12311	"Memphis Bound Blues"	Thomas Dorsey	CMPC, 1925
Pm 12508	"Misery Blues"	(untraced)	
Pm 12083	"Moonshine Blues"	Ma Rainey	CMPC, 1924
Pm 12352	"Mountain Jack Blues"	Sid Harris	E. E. Forbes & Harry Charles, 1926
Pm 12455	"Morning Hour Blues"	(untraced)	
Pm 12603	"New Bo-Weevil Blues" (see "Bo-Weevil Blues")		
Pm 12303	"Night Time Blues"	Ma Rainey (w) Thomas Dorsey (m)	CMPC, 1925
Pm 12566	"Oh, Daddy, You Won't Have No Mama at All"	Edward Herbert (w) W. L. Russell (m)	W. L. Russell, 1921
Pm 12332	"Oh My Babe Blues"	Ma Rainey	CMPC, 1926
Pm 12566	"Oh Papa Blues" (see "Oh Daddy. . . .")		
Pm 12668	"Prove It on Me Blues"	Ma Rainey	CMPC, 1928
Pm 12311	"Rough and Tumble Blues"	Ma Rainey	CMPC, 1925
Pm 12902	"Runaway Blues"	Ma Rainey	CMPC, 1928
Pm 12735	"Screech Owl Blues"	J. Sammy Randall (w) Ma Rainey (m)	CMPC, 1928
Pm 12252	"See See Rider Blues"	Lena Arrant	CMPC, 1924
Pm 12222	"Shave 'Em Dry Blues"	Ma Rainey & William Jackson	CMPC, 1925
Pm 12384	"Sissy Blues"	Ma Rainey	CMPC, 1928
Pm 12332	"Slave to the Blues"	Thomas Dorsey	CMPC, 1926
Pm 12760	"Sleep Talking Blues"	J. Sammy Randall (w) Ma Rainey (m)	CMPC, 1928
Pm 12526	"Slow Driving Moan"	(untraced)	
Pm 12227	"South Bound Blues"	Tom Delaney	Tom Delaney, 1923
Pm 12083	"Southern Blues"	Ma Rainey	CMPC, 1924
Pm 12357	"Stack O' Lee Blues"	Jasper Taylor	CMPC, 1926
Pm 12295	"Stormy Sea Blues"	Thomas Dorsey	CMPC, 1925
Pm 12926	"Sweet Rough Man"	J. Sammy Randall (w) Ma Rainey (m)	CMPC, 1928

Issue number	Title	Author(s)	Publisher and date
Pm 12081	"Those All Night Long Blues"	J. Guy Suddoth	CMPC, 1923
Pm 12215	"Those Dogs of Mine"	Ma Rainey	CMPC, 1924
Pm 12374	"Titanic Man Blues"	Ma Rainey & J. Mayo Williams	CMPC, 1926
Pm 12242	"Toad Frog Blues"	J. Guy Suddoth	CMPC, 1924
Pm 12735	"Tough Luck Blues"	J. Sammy Randall (w) Ma Rainey (m)	CMPC, 1928
Pm 12706	"Traveling Blues"	(untraced)	
Pm 12395	"Trust No Man"	Lillian Hardaway Henderson	CMPC, 1928
Pm 12082	"Walking Blues"	Ma Rainey (w) Lovie Austin (m)	CMPC, 1924
Pm 12455	"Weepin' Woman Blues"	Bessie Smith (w) Ma Rainey (m)	CMPC, 1928
Pm 12338	"Wringing and Twisting Blues"	Paul Carter	CMPC, 1926
Pm 12687	"Victim of the Blues"	Thomas Dorsey	CMPC, 1928
Pm 12257	"Ya-Da-Do"	L.A.[7]	Lovie Austin, 1924
Pm 12357	"Yonder Come the Blues"		(notice of use filed by CMPC, 1926)

Recordings by other blues artists:

Artist	Title	Issue number
Thomas Dorsey (with Tampa Red)	"It's Tight Like That"	Vocalion 1216
Rosa Henderson	"Basement Blues"	Banner 1437
Alberta Hunter	"Downhearted Blues"	Pm 12005
Papa Charlie Jackson	"Shave 'Em Dry"	Pm 12264
Jim Jackson	"Jim Jackson's Kansas City Blues"	Vocalion 1144
Blind Lemon Jefferson	"Match-box Blues"	Okeh 8455; Pm 12474
Margaret Johnson	"Dead Drunk Blues"	Victor 20982
Lillian Miller	"Dead Drunk Blues"	Gennett 6518
Memphis Minnie	"Ma Rainey Blues"	Okeh 05811 Conqueror 9763
Monette Moore	"Gulf Coast Blues"	Pm 12030
Bessie Smith	"Back Water Blues"	Columbia 14195-D

Artist	Title	Issue number
	"Bo-Weevil Blues"	Col 14018-D
	"Empty Bed Blues"	Col 14312-D
	"Florida Bound Blues"	Col 14109-D
	"Jailhouse Blues"	Col A-4001
	"Midnight Blues"	Col A-3936
	"Moonshine Blues"	Col 14018-D
	"Nobody Knows You When You're Down and Out"	Col 14451-D
	"Oh Daddy Blues"	Col A-3888
	"Rocking Chair Blues"	Col 14020-D
	"Send Me to the 'Lectric Chair"	Col 14209-D
	"Yes Indeed He Do!"	Col 14354-D
Clara Smith	"Basement Blues"	Col 14039-D
	"Kitchen Mechanic Blues"	Col 14097-D
Mamie Smith	"Crazy Blues"	Okeh 4169
	"That Thing Called Love"	Okeh 4113
	"You Can't Keep a Good Man Down"	Okeh 4113
Victoria Spivey	"T. B. Blues"	Okeh 8494
Tampa Red (see Thomas Dorsey)		
Sippie Wallace	"Dead Drunk Blues"	Okeh 8499
Ethel Waters	"Oh Daddy"	Pm 12169
Peetie Wheatstraw	"C. and A. Blues"	Vocalion 04592

Notes

Introduction

1. Al Young, *Dancing; poems* (New York: Corinth Books, 1969), pp. 14–15.
2. Sterling A. Brown, "Ma Rainey," *The Collected Poems of Sterling A. Brown* (New York: Harper and Row, 1980), pp. 62–63. Sketchy accounts exist of obscure women singers who predate Ma Rainey. John Jacob Niles mentions Ophelia Simpson, a "shouter and moaner in Dr. Parker's Medicine Show," who performed "Black Alfalfa's Jail-house Shouting Blues" in 1898, and Jelly Roll Morton recalls prostitutes and a woman named Mamie Desdoumes singing the blues in New Orleans around 1902. (See John J. Niles, "Shout, Coon, Shout!" *The Musical Quarterly* 16 [October 1930]: 519–21; and Alan Lomax, *Mister Jelly Roll: The Fortunes of Jelly Roll Morton, New Orleans Creole and "Inventor of Jazz"* [New York: Duell, Sloan and Pearce, 1950], pp. 21–25.)
3. Derrick Stewart-Baxter, *Ma Rainey and the Classic Blues Singers* (New York: Stein and Day, 1970), p. 7.
4. Stewart-Baxter, pp. 35–44. Hettie Jones' *Big Star Fallin' Mama: Five Women in Black Music* (New York: Viking, 1974) is a children's book which generally repeats previously published information about Ma Rainey (pp. 25–39).
5. A fine reissue of Ma Rainey's work is the double album *Ma Rainey* Milestone M4701, which contains thirty-two of her best songs; for other reissues, see the discography. As of this writing (1980), Vintage Jazz Music has announced a monaural series of her complete works, beginning with *Ma Rainey, Volume 1* VLP 81.
6. Recent books on Bessie Smith are Chris Albertson, *Bessie* (New York: Stein and Day, 1972); and Carman Moore, *Somebody's Angel Child: The Story of Bessie Smith* (New York: T. Y. Crowell, 1969). Paul Oliver's earlier biography was published in 1959 (Paul Oliver, *Bessie Smith*, Kings of Jazz Series [New York: A. S. Barnes, 1959]). Linda Hopkins' *Me and Bessie* recently had a successful run, both in New York and on tour.
7. For an excellent survey of black and white minstrelsy in the nineteenth century see Robert C. Toll, *Blacking Up: The Minstrel Show in Nineteenth Century America* (New York: Oxford University Press, 1974).
8. See Paul Oliver, *Blues Fell This Morning: The Meaning of the Blues* (New York:

Horizon Press, 1961); Samuel Charters, *The Poetry of the Blues* (New York: Oak
Publications, 1963); and Harry Oster, *Living Country Blues* (Detroit: Folklore
Associates, 1969), chapters 3–4. Paul Garon, *Blues and the Poetic Spirit* (London:
Eddison Press, 1975) is an eclectic analysis of the blues from a surrealist perspec-
tive.

9. See Rudi Blesh, *Shining Trumpets: A History of Jazz* (New York: Alfred A. Knopf,
1958), chapter 5. Derrick Stewart-Baxter discusses the problems of defining the
Classic Blues on pp. 6–9 of his book.

Chapter 1. The Paramount Wildcat

1. Walter C. Allen, *Hendersonia: The Music of Fletcher Henderson and His Musicians.
A Bio-discography* (Highland Park, N.J.: Walter C. Allen, 1975), p. 580.
2. Reprinted in Vic Schuler and Claude Lipscombe, "Mystery of the Two Ma
Raineys," *Melody Maker* 25 (13 October 1951): 9.
3. In preparing this chapter, I have drawn freely on research of the late Charles
Edward Smith, including: his unpublished notes at the Rutgers Institute of Jazz
Studies, Newark, New Jersey; Charles Edward Smith, "Ma Rainey," in *Notable
American Women, 1607–1950, A Biographical Dictionary*, ed. Edward T. James
(Cambridge, Mass.: The Belknap Press of Harvard University Press, 1971), vol.
3, pp. 110–11; Charles Edward Smith, "Ma Rainey and the Minstrels," *Record
Changer* 14, no. 6 (1955): 5–6. Specific references will be identified in the notes
wherever appropriate.
4. Smith reports that Ma Rainey's death certificate (Georgia Department of Public
Health) incorrectly gives her birth date as 1892, which is actually Essie's birth
year (unpublished notes, Rutgers).
5. One of Ma Rainey's songs, "Hustlin' Blues," is copyrighted under the name of
"Malissa Nix." Either the composer was Ma Rainey's sister, or else someone
erred in transcribing the name. According to the *Chicago Defender*, Ma's sister
was a "Mrs. Dr. Taylor, of Columbus, Georgia." (*Chicago Defender*, national ed.,
13 September 1924, Part I, p. 6. All subsequent citations of the *Defender* refer to
the national edition.) Either Malissa was originally married to a Dr. Taylor, or
"Mrs. Dr. Taylor" could be the fifth Rainey child, whose name and sex Smith
did not discover.
6. Charles Edward Smith, liner notes to *Blame It on the Blues*, Milestone MLP 2008.
7. John W. Work, Jr., *American Negro Songs and Spirituals: A Comprehensive Collection of 230 Folk Songs, Religious and Secular* (New York: Bonanza Books, 1940), pp.
32–33.
8. For accounts of early blues, see David Huhn Evans, Jr., "Tradition and Creativity in the Folk Blues" (Ph.D. diss., University of California at Los Angeles,
1976), and Jeff Todd Titon, *Early Downhome Blues: A Musical and Cultural Analysis*
(Urbana: University of Illinois Press, 1977).
9. Gunther Schuller, *Early Jazz: Its Roots and Musical Development* (New York:
Oxford University Press, 1968), p. 37; Evans, "Tradition and Creativity," pp.
76–80. Folk blues are discussed more thoroughly in chapter 2.

10. Titon, pp. 27–28.

11. Paul Oliver, *The Story of the Blues*, 2nd ed. (Philadelphia: Chilton, 1969), p. 61.

12. Robert C. Toll, *Blacking Up: The Minstrel Show in Nineteenth Century America* (New York: Oxford University Press, 1974), chapters 1, 7, and 8.

13. Oliver, *Story of the Blues*, p. 58.

14. Derrick Stewart-Baxter, *MaRainey and the Classic Blues Singers* (New York: Stein and Day, 1970) p. 38.

15. George W. Kay, "William Christopher Handy, Father of the Blues: A History of Published Blues," *Jazz Journal* 24 (March 1971): 11.

16. Cited in Leonard Feather, *The Book of Jazz from Then till Now: A Guide to the Entire Field*, rev. ed. (New York: Horizon Press, 1957), pp. 147–48. Clarinetist Willie Humphries of Preservation Hall Jazz Band also recalls her singing this tune. She would step back and look at the floor while singing the last line. (Interview with author, hereinafter referred to as S.R.L., 4 July 1974, Stanford, California.)

17. Oliver, *Story of the Blues*, pp. 58–60. John Steiner attributes the management of the Rabbit Foot Minstrels to Fats Chapelle, a black entrepreneur ("Beyond the Impression," *Record Research* 67 [April 1965]: 11–12). For the introduction and development of variety acts and brass bands in minstrelsy, see Toll, pp. 55, 135, 147, 248–51.

18. Steiner, "Beyond the Impression," pp. 11–12; Smith, "Ma Rainey and the Minstrels," p. 5.

19. Musician Norman Mason, in Paul Oliver, *Conversation with the Blues* (New York: Horizon Press, 1965), p. 122.

20. Musicians Norman Mason and Al Wynn, in Oliver, *Conversation*, pp. 122, 132.

21. Oliver, *Conversation*, p. 130.

22. Smith, "Ma Rainey and the Minstrels," p. 6.

23. Clyde Bernhardt, taped interview with S.R.L., Newark, New Jersey, 31 December 1974.

24. Smith, "Ma Rainey and the Minstrels," p. 6.

25. Interview with S.R.L. Unless otherwise indicated, all quotations are Mr. Bernhardt's.

26. Sam Chatmon, taped interview with S.R.L., Santa Cruz, California, May 1975.

27. For Japanese and other ethnic caricatures in *white* minstrelsy, see Toll, pp. 168–70.

28. Sterling A. Brown, *The Collected Poems of Sterling A. Brown* (New York: Harper and Row, 1980), pp. 62–63.

29. Chris Albertson, *Bessie* (New York: Stein and Day, 1972), p. 27.

30. Albertson, *Bessie*, p. 26.

31. Ibid., p. 28; Oliver, *Story of the Blues*, pp. 63, 96.

32. Jim O'Neal and Amy O'Neal, "*Living Blues* Interview: Georgia Tom Dorsey," *Living Blues* 20 (March–April 1975), pp. 22, 28.

33. Clyde Bernhardt, Sam Chatmon, and Thomas Dorsey all characterize her this way. For Ma Rainey's generosity to her musicians, see p. 26.

34. Bernhardt, interview with S.R.L.

35. Stewart-Baxter, p. 42.

36. Albertson, *Bessie*, p. 104. While noting that Bessie was bisexual, and that Ma

was "similarly inclined," Albertson does not think that Ma initiated Bessie into lesbianism (p. 117). For Bessie's affairs with women, see Albertson, *Bessie*, pp. 116–22.

37. See chapter 3.
38. Taped interview with S.R.L.
39. Stewart-Baxter, p. 42.
40. Albertson, *Bessie*, p. 104.
41. For the Raineys' separation, see Oliver, *Story of the Blues*, p. 61; for Pa's death and Ma's remarriage, see Thomas Dorsey, taped interview with S.R.L., Chicago, 14 March 1976. The *Chicago Defender*, 13 September 1924, Part I, p. 7, mentioned that Ma's "hubby" drove down from Chicago to watch his wife perform in Alabama.
42. Dorsey, interview with S.R.L.; Bernhardt, interview with S.R.L.
43. Trombonist Al Wynn, in Oliver, *Conversation*, pp. 131–32.
44. Ronald Clifford Foreman, Jr., "Jazz and Race Records, 1920–1932: Their Origins and Their Significance for the Record Industry and Society" (Ph.D. diss., University of Illinois, 1968), pp. 15, 18, 44.
45. Foreman, pp. 24, 39, 50.
46. Foreman, pp. 24–25, 34; David Evans, "An Interview with H. C. Speir," *John Edwards Memorial Foundation Quarterly* 8 (1972): 118.
47. For a vivid but quite bitter and often confusing account of these events, see Perry Bradford, *Born with the Blues; Perry Bradford's Own Story. The True Story of the Pioneering Blues Singers and Musicians in the Early Days of Jazz* (New York: Oak Publications, 1965).
48. Bradford, p. 118.
49. Robert M. W. Dixon and John Godrich, *Recording the Blues* (New York: Stein and Day, 1970), pp. 13, 32, 44, 46.
50. *Chicago Defender*, 2 June 1923, p. 7.
51. Dixon and Godrich, pp. 19, 41–42.
52. Albertson, *Bessie*, p. 37; Dan Morgenstern, liner notes to *Ma Rainey* (Milestone M 47021).
53. John Steiner, "Chicago," in *Jazz: New Perspectives on the History of Jazz by Twelve of the World's Foremost Jazz Critics and Scholars*, ed. Nat Hentoff and Albert J. McCarthy (New York: Holt, Rinehart, and Winston, 1959), pp. 140–41.
54. Albertson, *Bessie*, p. 74. Today, Chicago remains a vital and exciting center for black music, especially the blues.
55. Stewart-Baxter, p. 35.
56. *Chicago Defender*, 2 February 1924, Part II, p. 10.
57. Albertson, *Bessie*, p. 36.
58. *Chicago Defender*, 31 May 1924, Part I, p. 7.
59. *Chicago Defender*, 13 September 1924, Part I, p. 8.
60. *Chicago Defender*, 7 June 1924, Part I, p. 8.
61. Albertson, *Bessie*, p. 75.
62. Ibid., pp. 75–76.
63. *Chicago Defender*, 14 February 1925, Part I, p. 8.
64. Oliver, *Story of the Blues*, pp. 67–71; *Chicago Defender*, 28 March 1925, Part I, p. 7.

65. Oliver, *Conversation*, p. 135.

66. *Chicago Defender*, 24 June 1924, Part I, p. 8.

67. O'Neal and O'Neal, pp. 18–19; excerpt from Thomas A. Dorsey's unpublished biography, cited in Hans R. Rookmaaker, liner notes to *Ma Rainey, Mother of the Blues*, Riverside RM 8807.

68. *Chicago Defender*, 12 April 1924, Part I, p. 6.

69. Rookmaaker.

70. O'Neal and O'Neal, pp. 22, 29. On the other hand, Bessie Smith left her companies stranded on several occasions. (See Albertson, *Bessie*, p. 126.)

71. O'Neal and O'Neal, p. 22.

72. Oliver, *Conversation*, pp. 132–33.

73. O'Neal and O'Neal, p. 22. Mary Lou Williams also recalled the hot jewelry story in *Hear Me Talkin' to Ya: The Story of Jazz by the Men Who Made It*, ed. Nat Shapiro and Nat Hentoff (New York: Rinehart, 1955), p. 248.

74. There are numerous references to Ma's appearances in Chicago, Pittsburgh, Detroit, Indianapolis, and various Ohio cities in the *Chicago Defender*, 1924–1928. For her shows in Philadelphia, Cincinnati, and Newark, see Bernhardt, interview with S.R.L., and Bernhardt, letter to S.R.L. (30 March 1975). For Ma Rainey's New York engagements, see *Chicago Defender*, 30 March 1926, Part I, p. 7; *New York Amsterdam News*, 31 March 1926, p. 5; Bernhardt, interview with S.R.L., and letter to S.R.L. (30 March 1975); Thomas Dorsey, interview with S.R.L.; Oran "Hot Lips" Page, in Shapiro and Hentoff, *Hear Me Talkin' to Ya*, p. 297.

75. *The Paramount Book of Blues* (Port Washington, Wisc.: The New York Recording Laboratories, n.d.), p. 9.

76. Albertson, *Bessie*, p. 65.

77. *New York Amsterdam News*, 30 December 1926, p. 5.

78. Schuler and Lipscombe, p.9.

79. Jim O'Neal, "Blues for the Tourists at Blues Alley in Memphis," *Living Blues* 41 (November–December 1978): 29; *Memphis Press-Scimitar*, 1 February 1975.

80. *Chicago Defender*, 21 February 1925, Part I, p. 6; 14 March 1925, Part I, p. 7; 28 March 1925, Part I, p. 6; 13 June 1925, Part I, p. 6; 18 July 1925, Part I, p. 6; 31 January 1925, Part I, p. 6; 8 August 1925, Part I, p. 7; 2 January 1925, Part I, p. 6; 23 May 1925, Part I, p. 6; 18 July 1925, Part I, p. 6.

81. Albertson, *Bessie*, pp. 101, 104.

82. *Chicago Defender*, 2 January 1926, Part I, p. 6; 23 January 1926, Part I, p. 7; 3 April 1926, Part I, p. 7; O'Neal and O'Neal, p. 22; Bob Rusch, "Georgia Tom Dorsey Interview," *Cadence* 4 (December 1978): 11.

83. *Chicago Defender*, 13 February 1926, Part I, p. 6; 30 March 1926, Part I, p. 7; *New York Amsterdam News*, 31 March 1926, p. 5.

84. *Chicago Defender*, 3 July 1926, Part I, p. 7.

85. Albertson, *Bessie*, p. 135.

86. Sam Chatmon, interview with S.R.L.; *Chicago Defender*, 25 June 1927, Part I, p. 7; 27 August 1927, Part I, p. 7; 3 September 1927, Part I, p. 7; 29 October 1927, Part I, p. 9; 31 December 1927, Part I, p. 6.

87. *Chicago Defender*, 24 December 1927, Part I, p. 7.

88. See Chadwick Hansen, "Social Influences on Jazz Style: Chicago, 1920–1930," *American Quarterly* 12 (1960):493–507; Neil Leonard, *Jazz and the White Americans: The Acceptance of a New Art Form* (Chicago: University of Chicago Press, 1962), pp. 106–07.

89. Hansen, pp. 505–07.

90. Albertson, *Bessie*, p. 164. Jeff Titon suggests that record companies promoted country blues singers over Classic Blues singers because they were more comfortable with a down-home image of black people. See Titon, pp. 208–09.

91. For Dorsey's recovery and employment, see *Chicago Defender*, 2 June 1928, Part I, p. 6; O'Neal and O'Neal, p. 23.

92. *Chicago Defender*, 14 January 1928, Part I, p. 7; 7 January 1928, Part I, p. 6; 21 January 1928, Part I, p. 7; 18 February 1928, Part I, p. 7.

93. *Chicago Defender*, 12 May 1928, Part I, p. 7; 21 July 1928, Part I, p. 7; 3 November 1928, Part I, p. 6; 6 October 1928, Part I, p. 7; 20 October 1928, Part I, p. 7.

94. *Chicago Defender*, 24 November 1928, Part I, p. 7; Morgenstern, liner notes to *Ma Rainey*. For a detailed discussion of Ma Rainey's style, see chapter 2.

95. *Chicago Defender*, 12 January 1929, Part I, p. 7; 19 January 1929, Part I, p. 7; 16 February 1929, Part I, p. 6; 2 March 1929, Part I, p. 7; 16 March 1929, Part I, p. 6; 6 April 1929, Part I, p. 6.

96. Salem Tutt Whitney, "Salem Tutt Whitney Blames Theater Owners and Managers for Decline in Show Business," *Chicago Defender*, 27 July 1929, Part I, p. 6.

97. *Chicago Defender*, 6 April 1929, Part I, p. 7; 13 April 1929, Part I, p. 6; 27 April 1929, Part I, p. 7; 18 May 1929, Part I, p. 6.

98. *Chicago Defender*, 3 August 1929, Part I, p. 6; 16 November 1929, p. 7; 14 December 1929, p. 7; 11 January 1930, p. 7; 15 March 1930, p. 7; 22 March 1930, p. 7; Albertson, *Bessie*, p. 177.

99. *Chicago Defender*, 25 January 1930, p. 7; Albertson, *Bessie*, p. 168; *Chicago Defender*, 21 June 1930, p. 5.

100. *Chicago Defender*, 21 June 1930, p. 5.

101. O'Neal and O'Neal, p. 28.

102. Dixon and Godrich, p. 64.

103. Thomas Fulbright, "Ma Rainey and I," *Jazz Journal* 9 (March 1956):1–2, 26. All the following quotations are from this article. Fulbright, a white actor, appeared in a dramatic stock company which was performing in the same town as Ma's group.

104. Sunnyland Slim, taped interview with S.R.L., Palo Alto, California, 17 September 1975.

105. Norman Turner-Rowles, "The Paramount Wildcat," *Jazz Journal* 7 (March 1954):3.

106. *Chicago Defender*, 1 April 1933, p. 5; 6 October 1934, p. 8; 24 November 1934, p. 8; 8 September 1934, p. 9; 18 May 1935, p. 17; 9 February 1935, p. 9.

107. Smith, liner notes to *Blame It on the Blues*.

Chapter 2. "Blame It on the Blues"

1. Of Ma Rainey's ninety-two extant recordings, fifty-one are twelve-bar blues, two are eight-bar blues, and fourteen mix twelve-bar blues stanzas with popu-

lar song stanzas (eight- or sixteen-bar melodies with lyrics in quatrains, couplets, or more irregular stanzas). Two songs were recorded twice because they
were so popular: "Bo-Weevil Blues" (Pm 12080 and 12603) and "Moonshine
Blues" (Pm 12083 and 12603).

2. Less than one-fourth of her songs (twenty-one) are not blues at all; an additional
song is a ballad ("Stack O' Lee Blues," Paramount 12357), and another three are
comedy accompanied by music ("Blues the World Forgot, Parts I and II," both
Pm 12647, and "Georgia Cake Walk," Pm 12590).

3. Composer credits on the original Paramounts may be found in Max Vreede,
Paramount 12000/13000 Series (London: Storyville Publications, 1971). According to the composer credits on the original Paramount 78s, Ma was sole composer of thirty-one songs and joint composer of fifteen. Copyright entries are
probably more trustworthy: in at least one case ("Oh Papa Blues," Pm 12566),
the record label lists Ma Rainey as the composer, when actually she had simply
rearranged, revised, and reinterpreted the song, "Oh Daddy, You Won't Have
No Mama at All," written by Edward Herbert and W. L. Russell, and widely
recorded by women blues singers in the early twenties, beginning with Ethel
Waters. Copyright information is obviously misleading for blues singers who
were cheated out of composer credits to their songs, but the high percentage of
songs that give composer credits to Ma Rainey makes copyright files valid in her
case. Composer credits on the record labels may sometimes be correct for songs
which were not copyrighted.

4. Of the twenty-five blues that Ma wrote, copyright credits show her responsible
for the music to ten, and the words to fifteen; of those fifteen, six contain
completely traditional lyrics: "Southern Blues" (Pm 12083), "Army Camp Harmony Blues" (Pm 12284), "Little Low Mama Blues" (Pm 12419), "Deep Moaning Blues" (Pm 12706), "Daddy Goodbye Blues" (Pm 12963), and "Runaway
Blues" (Pm 12902). The other nine songs are mostly dominated by composed
lyrics.

5. Jim O'Neal and Amy O'Neal, *"Living Blues* Interview: Georgia Tom Dorsey,"
Living Blues 20 (March–April 1975):24.

6. Sterling A. Brown, *The Collected Poems of Sterling A. Brown* (New York: Harper
and Row, 1980), p. 63; Clyde Bernhardt, interview with S.R.L., Newark, New
Jersey, 31 December 1974.

7. Paul Oliver, *Aspects of the Blues Tradition*, 2nd ed. (New York: Oak Publications,
1970), pp. 24, 165, 180.

8. Wayne Shirley (Music Division, Library of Congress, Washington, D.C.), letter
to S.R.L., 30 April 1975.

9. Thomas A. Dorsey, interview with S.R.L., Chicago, Illinois, 14 March 1976.

10. For accounts of early folk blues, see Jeff Todd Titon, *Early Downhome Blues: A
Musical and Cultural Analysis* (Urbana: University of Illinois Press, 1977); David
Huhn Evans, Jr., "Tradition and Creativity in the Folk Blues" (Ph.D. diss.,
University of California at Los Angeles, 1976); and William Ferris, *Blues from the
Delta* (New York: Doubleday, 1978).

11. David Evans, "Structure and Meaning in the Folk Blues," in *The Study of*

American Folklore, by Jan Harold Brunvand, 2nd ed. (New York: W. W. Norton, 1978), pp. 422–24.

12. Evans, "Structure and Meaning," pp. 425, 431–36, 439. For a more detailed explanation, see Evans, "Techniques of Blues Composition Among Black Folk-singers," *Journal of American Folklore* 87 (1974):240–49.

13. Paul Oliver, *Aspects of the Blues Tradition,* 2nd ed. (New York: Oak Publications, 1970), p. 18.

14. Titon, pp. xv–xvi.

15. Evans, "Structure and Meaning," p. 425.

16. Titon, p. xiv.

17. Similar blues stanzas appear in country blues singer Tommy Johnson's "Maggie Campbell Blues" (Victor 21409; reissued on *Really! The Country Blues,* Origin Jazz Library OJL 2). Transcriptions of Johnson's recording may be found in David Evans, *Tommy Johnson* (London: Studio Vista, 1971), pp. 52–53; and in Titon, pp. 98–99.

18. John Randolph, "Lucien Brown," *Storyville* 47 (June–July 1973):176. Clyde Bernhardt describes her speech as "thick-tongued" (interview with S.R.L.).

19. For a comparison between Ma's and Bessie's musicians, see Barry MacRae, "The Ma Rainey and Bessie Smith Accompaniments," *Jazz Journal* 14 (March 1961):6–8.

20. George Hoefer, "Lovie Austin Still Active as a Pianist in Chicago," *Down Beat* 17 (16 June 1950):11.

21. Robert C. Toll, *Blacking Up: The Minstrel Show in Nineteenth Century America* (New York: Oxford University Press, 1974), pp. 50, 93–96, 172, 248–51.

22. For some reissues of various Tampa Red recordings, see *Guitar Wizard,* American RCA AXM2 5501; and *Tampa Red: Bottleneck Guitar, 1928–1937,* Yazoo L 1039.

23. These singers may be heard on *The Country Girls,* Origin Jazz Library OJL 6.

Chapter 3. "Blues About a Man the Worst I've Ever Had"

1. Notice of use filed by the Chicago Music Publishing Company in 1926; no lead sheet exists.

2. Harry Oster, *Living Country Blues* (Detroit: Folklore Associates, 1969), p. 1.

3. Oster, pp. 113–14.

4. Oster, p. 24. For examples of women's reactions to trains, see *Sorry But I Can't Take You; Women's Railroad Blues,* Rosetta Records, RR 1301.

5. For discussion of the issue of protest in blues lyrics, see Paul Oliver, *Aspects of the Blues Tradition,* 2nd ed. (New York: Oak Publications, 1970), pp. 12, 254–58; Oliver, *Blues Fell This Morning: The Meaning of the Blues* (New York: Horizon Press, 1960), pp. 257–58, 320–26; Samuel Charters, *The Poetry of the Blues* (New York: Oak Publications, 1963), pp. 98–110; and Jeff Todd Titon, *Early Downhome Blues: A Musical and Cultural Analysis* (Urbana: University of Illinois Press, 1977), pp. 182, 190–92, 223–24.

6. Paul Oliver has suggested that the sorrow expressed by both sexes in the blues is in part a collective, suppressed, and internalized anger against their oppression by white people (see Oliver, *Aspects of the Blues Tradition*, pp. 257–59). But in the opinion of most blues singers themselves, the anger in early recorded blues is between the sexes (see Titon, pp. 190–93, 223–24).

7. Two comic treatments of love are discussed in chapter 4.

8. Cited by Oliver, *Blues Fell This Morning*, p. 346.

9. "Gone Daddy Blues," previously mentioned, and "Blues the World Forgot," Parts I and II (both Pm 12647), dominated by comic dialogue about getting drunk and going to jail.

10. Although this line does not seem to make sense, it is clearly sung on the recording.

11. "Bo-Weevil Blues" and "Moonshine Blues" were both quite successful for Ma Rainey: Bessie Smith recorded them both, and Ma recorded them again for Paramount after the company switched from acoustic to electric recording process.

12. Stanza 4, line 1: 'rested = arrested. The lead sheet gives this additional verse, placed between the second and third stanzas: "I'm now in Tishomingo, going to hear the Houston news, (2) / Far away Kansas City Man, give me those Hooking Cow Blues."

13. Jim O'Neal and Amy O'Neal, "*Living Blues* Interview: Georgia Tom Dorsey," *Living Blues* 20 (March–April 1975):23.

14. Lead sheet: "My man has gone and left me, that's why I've got the stormy sea blues."

15. Notice of use filed by Chicago Music Publishing Company in 1924; no lead sheet exists.

16. Words by Katie Winters, music by Lovie Austin, © 1924 by Katie Winters, Chicago.

17. Hans Rookmaaker transcribes this line as, "Give me a fool, a fool, any old man." (See liner notes to *Ma Rainey, Mother of the Blues*, Riverside RM 8807.)

18. Clyde Bernhardt, letter to S.R.L. 29 June 1975.

19. Notice of use filed by the Chicago Music Publishing Company in 1924; no lead sheet exists. Titon gives a slightly different transcription, p. 103.

20. The lead sheet continues the sexual boast with an additional stanza: "I'm a little mama, ain't got no fear, / I can climb a hill without shifting my gear; / *Chorus*."

21. This song also contains murder threats, discussed later in this chapter.

22. Notice of use filed by the Chicago Music Publishing Company in 1924; no lead sheet exists.

23. Oliver, *Blues Fell This Morning*, p. 164.

24. Zora Neale Hurston, *Mules and Men: Negro Folktales and Voodoo Practices in the South* (1935; rpt., New York: Harper and Row, 1970), p. 307.

25. Pm 12926, words by "Selma Davis" (Althea Dickerson) and music by Ma Rainey, © 1928, renewed 1956.

26. At the beginning of "House Rent Rag" by the Dixieland Jug Blowers (Victor 20420), a mock sermon is given. Later on, says the preacher, there will be "a house-rent ball upstairs," and he wants to be "the first one to shake a leg."

Trying to hold his listeners' attention, the preacher instructs: "Let me have your most kind and noble attention / If you don't mind, for a few minutes, if you will, / And don't start that wringin' and twistin'." (Chadwick Hansen, letter to S.R.L., 6 February 1977.)

27. The term could refer to any one of several trains: one was the famous Wabash Cannonball, another was an express on the L. and L. Railroad Line from Cincinnati to New Orleans. See Rudi Blesh, *Shining Trumpets: A History of Jazz*, 2nd ed. (New York: Alfred A. Knopf, 1958), p. 12.

28. Bessie Smith's "'Tain't Nobody's Biz-ness If I Do" (Col A 3898) and many of Billie Holiday's songs have masochistic subjects. Contemporary rock music is full of explicit sadistic and masochistic themes, particularly in the work of groups like the Rolling Stones.

29. Oliver, *Aspects of the Blues Tradition*, p. 206. For an interesting album of reissues on these themes, see *AC/DC Blues: Gay Jazz Reissues*, Stash ST 106.

30. The recording seems to say this. The lead sheet reads, "Like to watch while the women pass by," which makes more sense.

Chapter 4. That Same Pleasure, That Same Pain

1. *Chicago Defender*, 9 August 1924, Part I, p. 7.

2. Hans R. Rookmaaker, liner notes to *Mother of the Blues*, gives a slightly different transcription of these lines: "Lord I've begged to B.Q. / I can't wear me no sharpnosed shoes."

3. The Biograph reissue of these songs mislabels them, mixing up their order: what is called Part I on the reissue is actually Part II, and vice versa. The songs appear on *Blues the World Forgot: Ma Rainey and Her Georgia Jazz Band*, Biograph BLP 12001.

4. I am grateful to Michael Jones for assistance on the transcriptions of Parts I and II. In the transcript, unclear phrases will be indicated by italics.

5. Possibly: "Fill you with harmonizing sing, / But you know there's room for this little bitty thing." (See Rookmaaker, liner notes.) The lead sheet has been lost from the Library of Congress.

6. Apparently a popular Southern dance. Ida Archer, a performer with the Whitman Sisters, was nicknamed "Jew Baby."

7. Marshall Stearns and Jean Stearns, *Jazz Dance: The Story of American Vernacular Dance* (New York: Macmillan, 1968), pp. 110–11.

8. Ibid. "Doodle" means slide.

9. Ibid.

10. Frederick Ramsey, Jr., and Charles Edward Smith, eds., *Jazzmen* (New York: Harcourt, Brace, 1939), p. 12; cited in Robert S. Gold, *Jazz Lexicon: An A–Z Dictionary of Jazz Terms in the Vivid Idiom of America's Most Successful Nonconformist Minority* (New York: Alfred A. Knopf, 1964), p. 196.

11. Stearns and Stearns, p. 105; see also "A Note on 'Shake the Shimmy,'" *Journal of Abnormal and Social Psychology* (April–June 1927), 16n, cited in Gold, pp. 274–75.

12. Lead sheet: "I'd drink a little moonshine, but I'm afraid I'd die."

13. Gold, p. 13.

14. *Chicago Defender*, 13 August 1927, Part I, p. 7.

15. Eric Sackheim transcribes this line as, "So when I'm dry I can get whiskey some place," in *The Blues Line: A Collection of Blues Lyrics* (New York: Grossman, 1969), p. 39.

16. The lead sheet omits this stanza. In his transcription of Lillian Miller's version of this song, Titon gives this line as, "When you wake up, feel like you out of doors." (See Jeff Todd Titon, *Early Downhome Blues: A Musical and Cultural Analysis* [Urbana: University of Illinois Press, 1977], pp. 70–71.)

17. "In my tea" means "drunk."

18. The lead sheet says "jailer."

19. Paul Oliver, *Blues Fell This Morning: The Meaning of the Blues* (New York: Horizon Press, 1961), pp. 238–40. Oliver gives a partial transcription of the following song on p. 239.

20. Gold, p. 48.

21. Oliver, *Blues Fell This Morning*, pp. 101, 158.

22. Newbell Niles Puckett, *Folk Beliefs of the Southern Negro* (1926; rpt., Montclair, N.J.: Patterson Smith, 1968), pp. 448–49.

23. Clyde Bernhardt, letter to S.R.L., 30 July 1975.

24. Lead sheet: "Can't blame it on my daddy—he treats me nice and kind, (2) / Shall I blame it on my nephew—or blame my troublin' mind?"

25. "Number one sand means very heavy, thick sand." Bernhardt, letter, July 1975. The fork and sifter reference is explicated in Puckett, p. 163.

26. Oliver, *Blues Fell This Morning*, pp. 273–74.

27. Abbe Niles, introduction to *A Treasury of the Blues: Complete Words and Music of 67 Great Songs from Memphis Blues to the Present Day*, ed. W. C. Handy and Abbe Niles, 2nd ed. (New York: Charles Boni, 1949), p. 10.

28. Bernhardt, letter, July 1975.

29. Lead sheet: "This is one thing that I don't understand, why a / Good looking woman don't like a working man, / Hey, hey, I got to shave 'em dry."

30. Lead sheet: "I don't see how some hungry women sleep, / They run all day without a bite to eat."

31. Lead sheet: "Some of these good looking women couldn't go nowhere."

32. Lead sheet: "Some women got big feet like a man."

33. Oliver, *Aspects of the Blues Tradition*, 2nd ed. (New York: Oak Publications, 1970), pp. 225–31. Lucille Bogan's "Shave 'Em Dry" and other unexpurgated songs may be heard on the album *Copulatin' Blues*, Stash ST 101.

34. Cited by Oliver in *Aspects of the Blues Tradition*, pp. 226–27.

35. Ibid.

36. *Chicago Defender*, 2 August 1924, Part II, p. 4.

37. Paul Oliver finds hints of lesbianism in this song, transcribing a line in the sixth stanza as, "Some women walkin' State Street like a man," and citing another line in the fourth stanza, "State Street women wearing brogan shoes" (*Aspects of the Blues Tradition*, p. 227). Given Ma Rainey's own preferences, the inference is possible, but perhaps not as strong as Oliver states. My transcription of the sixth

stanza is not conclusive, and the lead sheet reads, "Some women got big feet like a man." While the fourth stanza is probably intended more to ridicule prostitutes than to accuse them of lesbianism, the sixth may indeed point in that direction, whether describing women with big feet or women walking mannishly.

Discography

1. The abbreviations and discography are reprinted by permission from John Godrich and R. M. W. Dixon, *Blues and Gospel Records, 1902–1943*, 3rd fully rev. ed., 1981. Published by Storyville Publications, 66 Fairview Road, Chigwell, Essex, IG7 6HS, U.K.
2. "Recordings pressed from dubbed stampers" are 78 rpm reissues.
3. Matrices 1610 and 1611 may possibly be by the same group; see "Paramount Serenaders, 1923–1926," *Storyville* 68 (December 1976–January 1977), p. 53.
4. Matrices 1743 through 1746 may be unissued titles by Ma or Ethel Waters; see "Paramount Serenaders," *Storyville* 69 (February–March 1977), p. 91.
5. See appendix B.
6. "Microgroove issues" means recordings reissued on extended play (EP, 45 rpm) or on long play (LP, 33-1/3 rpm).
7. This discussion is condensed from Godrich and Dixon, *Blues and Gospel Records, 1902–1942*, 2nd ed. (London: Storyville Publications, 1969), p. 830; the third edition does not include microgroove issues. The following discography is by no means comprehensive, since new reissues appear so frequently; it incorporates information from Godrich and Dixon, p. 865, and some of the more important reissues released after publication of the second edition of *Blues and Gospel Records*.
8. Where no take number appears, this information was missing from the reissue.

Appendix A

1. "Goodbye Daddy Blues" is neither precisely a blues nor a mixture of blues and non-blues stanzas. The song has a twelve-bar, three-line, AAB structure throughout, but the chords in the first two lines (IVI) are not blues, the rhythm is tango, and the melody (which employs anacrusis) sounds more like a popular song, particularly in the first two lines.
2. "Titanic Man Blues" is also difficult to classify. The song's sixteen-bar, six-line stanza divides into two three-line groups, each containing two lines of verse plus one line of chorus. The stanza may thus be considered a grouping of two eight-bar blues verses, but while the chords show blues influence, they are not precisely blues.
3. "Blues the World Forgot," Part II is accompanied by a twelve-bar instrumental blues, and features Ma singing two blues verses.

Appendix B

1. On the other hand, *Storyville* suggests that 2451 ("Jealousy Blues") is a remake session of the missing 2449 and 2450; see "Paramount Serenaders, 1923–1926," *Storyville* 73 (October–November 1977), pp. 29–30.

Appendix C

1. Chicago Music Publishing Company.
2. Words. "Selma Davis" is a pseudonym for Althea Dickerson, J. Mayo Williams' secretary.
3. Music.
4. "Untraced" means that no copyright information or notices of use could be found.
5. A notice of use lists only the publisher and date, and does not guarantee rights to the song.
6. See appendix B.
7. Probably Lovie Austin.

Bibliography

Albertson, Chris. *Bessie.* New York: Stein and Day, 1972.
_____. Liner notes, *Oh My Babe Blues: Ma Rainey, Volume 2.* Biograph BLP 12011.
Allen, Walter C. *Hendersonia: The Music of Fletcher Henderson and His Musicians. A Bio-discography.* Jazz Monographs No. 4. Highland Park, N.J.: Walter C. Allen, 1975.
_____, ed. *Studies in Jazz Discography: I.* New Brunswick, N.J.: Institute of Jazz Studies, University Extension Division, Rutgers University, 1971.
Balliett, Whitney. *Such Sweet Thunder: Forty-Nine Pieces on Jazz.* Indianapolis: Bobbs-Merrill, 1966.
Baraka, Imamu Amiri (LeRoi Jones). *Blues People: Negro Music in White America.* New York: William Morrow, 1963.
Bernhardt, Clyde E. B. Letters to S.R.L.: 8 December 1974; 30 March 1975; 29 June 1975; 30 July 1975.
_____. Taped interview with S.R.L. Newark, New Jersey, 31 December 1974.
Blesh, Rudi. *Shining Trumpets: A History of Jazz.* 2nd ed. New York: Alfred A. Knopf, 1958.
Bluestein, Gene. "The Blues as a Literary Theme." *Massachusetts Review* 8 (1967):593–617.
Bone, Robert A. *The Negro Novel in America.* Rev. ed. New Haven: Yale University Press, 1965.
Bradford, Perry. *Born with the Blues: Perry Bradford's Own Story. The True Story of the Pioneering Blues Singers and Musicians in the Early Days of Jazz.* New York: Oak Publications, 1965.
Brown, Sterling A. "Ma Rainey." In *The Collected Poems of Sterling A. Brown.* New York: Harper and Row, 1980.
Charters, Samuel. *The Poetry of the Blues.* New York: Oak Publications, 1963.
Chatmon, Sam. Taped interview with S.R.L. Santa Cruz, California, May 1975.
The Chicago Defender (national edition). 22 September 1923 to 3 November 1923; 5 January 1924 to 28 December 1935; 30 December 1939 to 10 February 1940.
Chilton, John, ed. *Who's Who of Jazz.* London: Peridon, 1970.
Cone, James H. *The Spirituals and the Blues: An Interpretation.* New York: The Seabury Press, 1972.
Cook, Bruce. *Listen to the Blues.* New York: Charles Scribner's Sons, 1973.
Davis, John P., ed. *The American Negro Reference Book.* Englewood Cliffs, N.J.: Prentice-Hall, 1966.

De Lerma, Dominique René, ed. *Reflections on Afro-American Music*. Kent, Ohio: Kent State University Press, 1973.

Dixon, Robert M. W., and Godrich, John. *Recording the Blues*. New York: Stein and Day, 1970.

Dorsey, Thomas. Taped interview with S.R.L. Chicago, Illinois, 14 March 1976.

Evans, David Huhn, Jr. "An Interview with H. C. Speir." *John Edwards Memorial Foundation Quarterly* 8 (1972):117–21.

———. "Structure and Meaning in the Folk Blues." In *The Study of American Folklore*, 2nd ed., by Jan Harold Brunvand. New York: W. W. Norton, 1978.

———. "Techniques of Blues Composition Among Black Folksingers." *Journal of American Folklore* 87 (1974):240–49.

———. *Tommy Johnson*. London: Studio Vista, 1971.

———. "Tradition and Creativity in the Folk Blues." Ph.D. dissertation, University of California at Los Angeles, 1976.

Feather, Leonard. *The Book of Jazz from Then till Now: A Guide to the Entire Field*. Rev. ed. New York: Horizon Press, 1957.

———. *The New Edition of the Encyclopedia of Jazz*. New York: Bonanza Books, 1960.

Ferris, William. *Blues from the Delta*. New York: Doubleday, 1978.

Foreman, Ronald Clifford, Jr. "Jazz and Race Records, 1920–1932: Their Origins and Their Significance for the Record Industry and Society." Ph.D. dissertation, University of Illinois, 1968.

Fulbright, Thomas. "Ma Rainey and I." *Jazz Journal* 9 (March 1956):1–2, 18.

Garon, Paul. *Blues and the Poetic Spirit*. London: Eddison Press, 1975.

Godrich, John, and Dixon, Robert M. W. *Blues and Gospel Records, 1902–1942*. 2nd ed. London: Storyville Publications, 1969.

Gold, Robert. *Jazz Lexicon: An A–Z Dictionary of Jazz Terms in the Vivid Idiom of America's Most Successful Nonconformist Minority*. New York: Alfred A. Knopf, 1964.

Groom, Bob. *The Blues Revival*. London: Studio Vista, 1971.

Handy, William C. *Father of the Blues: An Autobiography*. Edited by Arna Bontemps. New York: Macmillan, 1941.

Handy, William C., and Niles, Abbe, eds. *Blues: An Anthology*. New York: A. and C. Boni, 1926.

———. *A Treasury of the Blues: Complete Words and Music of 67 Great Songs from Memphis Blues to the Present Day*. 2nd ed. New York: Charles Boni, 1949.

Hansen, Chadwick. "Social Influences on Jazz Style: Chicago, 1920–1930." *American Quarterly* 12 (1960):493–507.

———. Letter to S.R.L., 6 February 1977.

Hentoff, Nat, and McCarthy, Albert J., eds. *Jazz: New Perspectives on the History of Jazz by Twelve of the World's Foremost Jazz Critics and Scholars*. New York: Holt, Rinehart, and Winston, 1959.

Hobson, Wilder. *American Jazz Music*. New York: W. W. Norton, 1939.

Hoefer, George "Lovie Austin Still Active as a Pianist in Chicago." *Down Beat* 17 (16 June 1950):11.

Hoffman, Frederick J. *The Twenties: American Writing in the Postwar Decade*. Rev. ed. New York: Collier Books, 1962.

Humphries, Willie. Taped interview with S.R.L. Stanford, California, 4 July 1974.

Hurston, Zora Neale. *Mules and Men: Negro Folktales and Voodoo Practices in the South.* 1935; rpt., New York: Harper and Row, 1970.

Jones, Hettie. *Big Star Fallin' Mama: Five Women in Black Music.* New York: Viking, 1974.

Jones, Max. "She Jest Catch Hold of Us." *Melody Maker* 25 (24 September 1949):5.

Kay, George W. "William C. Handy, Father of the Blues: A History of Published Blues." *Jazz Journal* 24 (March 1971):10–12.

Keepnews, Orrin. Liner notes, *Tommy Ladnier: Blues and Stomps.* Riverside RLP 154 Jazz Archives.

Keepnews, Orrin, and Grauer, Bill, Jr. *Pictorial History of Jazz: People and Places from New Orleans to Modern Jazz.* New York: Crown, 1955.

Kennington, Donald. *The Literature of Jazz.* 2nd ed. Chicago: American Library Association, 1971.

Leonard, Neil. *Jazz and the White Americans: The Acceptance of a New Art Form.* Chicago: University of Chicago Press, 1962.

Lomax, Alan. *Mister Jelly Roll: The Fortunes of Jelly Roll Morton, New Orleans Creole and "Inventor of Jazz."* New York: Duell, Sloan and Pearce, 1950.

Lomax, John A., and Lomax, Alan. *American Ballads and Folk Songs.* New York: Macmillan, 1934.

Love, William C. "Ma Rainey Discography." *Jazz Information* 2 (6 September 1940):9–14.

MacRae, Barry. "The Ma Rainey and Bessie Smith Accompaniments." *Jazz Journal* 14 (March 1961):6–8.

McCarthy, Albert J. *Jazz on Record: A Critical Guide to the First Fifty Years: 1917–1967.* London: Hanover Books, 1968.

The Memphis Press-Scimitar, 1 February 1975.

Merriam, Alan P. *A Bibliography of Jazz.* Publications of the American Folklore Society Bibliographical Series, Volume IV. Philadelphia, 1954.

Moore, Carman. *Somebody's Angel Child: The Story of Bessie Smith.* New York: T. Y. Crowell, 1969.

Morgenstern, Dan. Liner notes, *Ma Rainey.* Milestone M 47021.

The New York Amsterdam News. 29 November 1922 to 26 September 1923; 14 January 1925 to 31 October 1926.

Niles, John J. "Shout, Coon, Shout!" *The Musical Quarterly* 16 (October 1930):519–21.

Oliver, Paul. *Aspects of the Blues Tradition.* 2nd ed. New York: Oak Publications, 1970.

———. *Bessie Smith.* Kings of Jazz Series. New York: A. S. Barnes, 1959.

———. *Blues Fell This Morning: The Meaning of the Blues.* New York: Horizon Press, 1961.

———. *Conversation with the Blues.* New York: Horizon Press, 1965.

———. *The Story of the Blues.* 2nd ed. Philadelphia: Chilton, 1969.

O'Neal, Jim. "Blues for the Tourists at Blues Alley in Memphis." *Living Blues* 41 (November–December 1978):28–29.

O'Neal, Jim, and O'Neal, Amy. "*Living Blues* Interview: Georgia Tom Dorsey." *Living Blues* 20 (March–April 1975):16–34.

Oster, Harry. *Living Country Blues.* Detroit: Folklore Associates, 1969.

Panassié, Hugues. *Hot Jazz—The Guide to Swing Music.* Translated by Lyle and Eleanor Dowling. Rev. ed. London: Cassell, 1936.

――――. *The Real Jazz.* Translated by Anne Sorell Williams. Adapted for American Publication by Charles Edward Smith. New York: Smith and Durell, 1942.

The Paramount Book of Blues. Port Washington, Wisc.: The New York Recording Laboratories, n.d.

"Paramount Serenaders, 1923–1926." *Storyville* 68 (December 1976–January 1977): 52–54; 69 (February–March 1977):91–94; 70 (April–May 1977):149–50; 72 (August–September 1977):226–30; 73 (October–November 1977):29–30; 74 (December 1977–January 1978):67–69; 75 (February–March 1978):84–85.

Pridgett, Thomas. "The Life of Ma Rainey." *Jazz Information* 2 (6 September 1940):8.

Puckett, Newbell Niles. *Folk Beliefs of the Southern Negro.* 1926; rpt., Montclair, N.J.: Patterson Smith, 1968.

Ramsey, Frederic, Jr., and Smith, Charles Edward, eds. *Jazzmen.* New York: Harcourt, Brace, 1939.

Randolph, John. "Lucien Brown." *Storyville* 47 (June–July 1973):176–90.

Reisner, Robert G. *The Literature of Jazz, a Preliminary Bibliography.* New York: New York Public Library, 1954.

Rookmaaker, Hans R. Liner notes, *Ma Rainey, Mother of the Blues.* Riverside RM 8807.

Rusch, Bob. "Georgia Tom Dorsey Interview." *Cadence* 4 (December 1978):9–13.

Rust, Brian. *Jazz Records: 1897–1942.* 4th rev. ed. New Rochelle: Arlington House, 1978.

Sackheim, Eric. *The Blues Line: A Collection of Blues Lyrics.* New York: Grossman, 1969.

Schuler, Vic, and Lipscombe, Claude. "Mystery of the Two Ma Raineys." *Melody Maker* 25 (13 October 1951):9.

Schuller, Gunther. *Early Jazz: Its Roots and Musical Development.* The History of Jazz, vol. 1. New York: Oxford University Press, 1968.

Shapiro, Nat, ed. *Popular Music: An Annotated Index of American Popular Songs.* Vol. 5 (1920–1929). New York: Adrian Press, 1969.

Shapiro, Nat, and Hentoff, Nat, eds. *Hear Me Talkin' to Ya: The Story of Jazz by the Men Who Made It.* New York: Rinehart, 1955.

――――. *The Jazz Makers.* New York: Rinehart, 1957.

Shirley, Wayne. Letter to S.R.L., 30 April 1975.

Slim, Sunnyland. Taped interview with S.R.L. Palo Alto, California, 17 September 1975.

Smith, Charles Edward. Liner notes, *Blame It on the Blues.* Milestone MLP 2008.

――――. "The Making of a King." *Record Changer* 9 (July–August 1950):19–21.

――――. "Ma Rainey." In *Notable American Women, 1607–1950: A Biographical Dictionary*, edited by Edward T. James, vol. 3, pp. 110–11. Cambridge, Mass.: The Belknap Press of Harvard University Press, 1971.

――――. "Ma Rainey and the Minstrels." *Record Changer* 14, no. 6 (1955):5–6.

――――. Unpublished notes. Ma Rainey file, Rutgers Institute of Jazz Studies, Rutgers University, Newark, N.J.

Smith, Charles Edward, and Ramsey, Frederic, Jr. *The Jazz Record Book.* New York: Smith and Durrell, 1942.

Southern, Eileen. *The Music of Black Americans: A History.* New York: W. W. Norton, 1971.

Stearns, Marshall. *The Story of Jazz.* Oxford: Oxford University Press, 1956.

Stearns, Marshall, and Stearns, Jean. *Jazz Dance: The Story of American Vernacular Dance.* New York: Macmillan, 1968.

Steiner, John. "Beyond the Impression." *Record Research* 67 (April 1965):11–12.

———. "Chicago." In *Jazz: New Perspectives on the History of Jazz by Twelve of the World's Foremost Jazz Critics and Scholars,* edited by Nat Hentoff and Albert J. McCarthy. New York: Holt, Rinehart, and Winston, 1959.

Stewart-Baxter, Derrick. *Ma Rainey and the Classic Blues Singers.* New York: Stein and Day, 1970.

Titon, Jeff Todd. *Early Downhome Blues: A Musical and Cultural Analysis.* Urbana: University of Illinois Press, 1977.

Toll, Robert C. *Blacking Up: The Minstrel Show in Nineteenth Century America.* New York: Oxford University Press, 1974.

Traill, Sinclair. "Jazz on Brunswick 04516." *Melody Maker* 26 (15 July 1950):9.

Turner-Rowles, Norman. "The Paramount Wildcat." *Jazz Journal* 7 (March 1954):2–3.

Ulanov, Barry. *A History of Jazz in America.* New York: Viking, 1952.

United States Copyright Office. *Catalogue of Copyright Entries. Music. Third Series.* Washington, D.C.: Copyright Office, Library of Congress, 1921–1931.

Vreede, Max E. *Paramount 12000/13000 Series.* London: Storyville Publications, 1971.

Waters, Ethel, and Samuels, Charles. *His Eye Is on the Sparrow: An Autobiography.* Garden City, N.Y.: Doubleday, 1951.

Welding, Pete. Liner notes, *Women of the Blues.* RCA Victor Vintage Series LPV 534.

Williams, Ora. *American Black Women in the Arts and Social Sciences: A Bibliographic Survey.* Metuchen, N. J.: The Scarecrow Press, 1973.

Work, John W., Jr. *American Negro Songs and Spirituals: A Comprehensive Collection of 230 Folk Songs, Religious and Secular.* New York: Bonanza Books, 1940.

Wyler, Michael. *A Glimpse at the Past: An Illustrated History of Some Early Record Companies That Made Jazz History.* West Moors, Dorset: Jazz Publications, 1957.

Young, Al. "A Dance for Ma Rainey." In *Dancing; poems.* New York: Corinth Books, 1969.

General Index

Index of Song Titles

For copyright information about Ma Rainey's recordings, see Appendix C. All other references to song titles are indexed below, and transcriptions of two or more stanzas are indicated. When the same song was recorded by different artists, the singer is shown in parentheses.